"Karlgaard leaves his Silicon Valley lair and sets out to explore 'flyover country' from an up-close and personal perspective in his little Cessna Skyhawk. As he discovers the joy of controlling flight, he also discovers countless Americans taking control of their environment by moving to the hinterlands for higher-quality life with a sense of purpose."

—John and Martha King, King Schools

"Rich Karlgaard has crafted a delightful, and surprisingly moving, tale that will allay the greatest fear of many upwardly mobile Americans: Not death. Not even public speaking. But the terror of waking up, alive and well, a resident of Bismarck, North Dakota."

—Michael Lewis, bestselling author of
Moneyball, Liar's Poker, Next, and *The New New Thing*

"Aboard his sky cabin, Karlgaard flies in with a companion concept to David Brooks's *On Paradise Drive* and Joel Garreau's *Edge City.*"   —Tom Wolfe

"Rich Karlgaard's stories show that America offers an array of routes to personal fulfillment that, while counterintuitive to those on the conventional fast track, offers great promise to those who are open to personal innovation."

—Clayton Christensen, professor of business administration,
Harvard Business School; author of *The Innovator's Dilemma;*
and coauthor of *The Innovator's Solution*

"Written with literary flair and analyzed with rare social and financial insight, *Life 2.0* combines a gifted novelist's sense of personal drama and pace with a technology visionary's insight into the future. Take an epochal ride in Rich Karlgaard's aerobatic new book. Not only will it stretch your mind and widen the horizons of your life, it also could renew your health and wealth."

—George Gilder,
futurist and author

"Talk about timely! Rich Karlgaard takes a thoroughly original approach to examining the sustaining upheaval in the American white-collar professional labor market. As someone who gritted his teeth and jilted Palo Alto for Vermont a decade ago, I was entranced by Karlgaard's very human stories—and their very profound consequences. No one has a pat answer to the 'great jobs conundrum'—but this fascinating treatise will make you think deeply, and may just give you the impetus to uproot. And, hooray, our amateur pilot–tour guide lived to tell the tale!"

—Tom Peters,
management consultant
and bestselling author

"*Life 2.0* is an original and exhilarating look at options many Americans don't realize are now open to them. Rich Karlgaard's enthusiasm is contagious, based on the evidence he has found on his explorations from coast to coast. Anyone stuck in a traffic jam or beset by big-city woes will think long and longingly about the prospects this book lays out."

—James Fallows,
national correspondent,
Atlantic Monthly

LIFE 2.0

How People Across America Are

Transforming Their Lives by

Finding the *Where* of Their Happiness

Rich Karlgaard

Forbes Magazine's "Flying Publisher"

WWW.LIFE2WHERE.COM

CROWN
BUSINESS
NEW YORK

Published by Crown Business, New York, New York.
Member of the Crown Publishing Group, a division of Random House, Inc.
www.crownpublishing.com

CROWN BUSINESS is a trademark and the Rising Sun colophon is a registered trademark of Random House, Inc.

Printed in the United States of America

Design by Karen Minster

Library of Congress Cataloging-in-Publication Data

Karlgaard, Richard.
   Life 2.0 : how people across America are transforming their lives by finding the *where* of their happiness / Rich Karlgaard.—1st ed.
      p. cm.
   1. Cities and towns—United States.   2. Quality of life—United States.
3. United States—Economic conditions—2001.   4. United States—Social conditions—21st century.   I. Title: Life two point zero.   II. Title: How people across America are transforming their lives by finding the *where* of their happiness.   III. Title.
   HT123.K363 20004
      307.76—dc22   2004010507

ISBN 1-4000-4607-6

10 9 8 7 6 5 4 3 2 1

FIRST EDITION

FOR MARJI, KATIE,
AND PETER

I go back to look at our house,
555 Hudson Street [in New York City],
and I know that I could never afford it now.

—JANE JACOBS,
author of
The Death and Life of Great American Cities,
quoted in the May 17, 2004, issue of *The New Yorker*

CONTENTS

LIFE 2.0

Living Large in Smaller Places

Three years ago a *Forbes* magazine colleague living in San Francisco told me that all her thirty-something friends were leaving town.

"Where is everyone going?" I asked.

"You'd be surprised," she said. "Sacramento. Portland. Boise. Tucson. Smaller places than that, even."

On one level I wasn't surprised. Housing costs in San Francisco had gone to the moon during the 1990s. The dot-com bust that began in mid-2000 had done zippo to slow down house-price inflation. Tiny two-bedroom condos in San Francisco were fetching $600,000. Try paying the mortgage on that without a job. My colleague's friends simply had to leave town. They were running out of money.

Yet on another level I was surprised. People who had lived in a sophisticated city such as San Francisco, I was certain, would hold a snob's view of "boonyack" towns such as Boise. It would never occur to fancy urban dwellers to move *there*. Yet they have moved there—in droves.

After eighteen years with Morgan Stanley in Dallas I now hang my shingle out at Smith Barney in McKinney, Texas (pop. 50,000), the county seat of Collin County.

MY LIFE TODAY

COMMUTE: One minute, thirty seconds each way (old commute: two hours round-trip)

COUNTRY CLUB: Three blocks from the office and six blocks from the house

INTERNET: At the office, industrial strength; at home, always-on digital

HOUSING COST: $0.73 per square foot versus high-end Dallas cost of $1.50 per square foot

CULTURE: Local community college

DINING: With two small kids, who really needs another trendy restaurant?

SCHOOLS: Exemplary rankings—one kid at school three blocks from home, another in special-ed program, but only five minutes away

INCOME: Down a little with rough brokerage industry conditions, but expenses way down also

IMPROVED WORK ATTITUDE AND FAMILY RELATIONSHIPS: Priceless

RONALD JOHNSON
McKinney, Texas

Okay. Let's stop here for a reality check.

I realize that *droves* is an imprecise word and, moreover, that out-migration from a dot-com boomtown such as San Francisco was to be expected during an economic bust. Also, haven't we heard this song before? As I began to study U.S. internal migration patterns and regional economic development for *Life 2.0*, I learned that some carefully reasoned books had appeared during the last fifteen years that had predicted just such an out-migration from cities to smaller cities and towns. One of them,

Penturbia, was written in 1991 by a University of California professor named Jack Lessinger. *Penturbia* asserted that high costs and urban crowding would drive the middle class out of cities and suburbs.

But it didn't happen. In fact, the booming 1990s economy produced quite the opposite result. It sucked the professional middle class into cities and their suburbs. (Was Lessinger wrong or just fifteen years ahead of his time? Good question. I think he was ahead of his time.)

Then in 1998 a futurist named Harry Dent, in a book called *The Roaring 2000s,* took a similar tack. He said white-collar professionals in big cities and suburbs "lived with the daily stress of trying to handle two imperatives: being a success at work and creating a comfortable home. For many of us, this has meant buying a house in the suburbs where we could raise our families safely and affordably—and paying for it every day with an exhausting commute."

Ouch. Sound familiar?

Dent went on to say: "We are about to see the next great population migration in our country, which will be the force driving real-estate appreciation in the next decade. An enormous number of people will escape overcrowded, expensive suburbs and move to a variety of small towns, new-growth cities, exurban areas beyond the suburbs, and even back to trendy urban areas. Whether you're looking for a new home or a new investment, you can be among those to reap the huge profits."

My verdict on Harry Dent is that he got it mostly right. What Dent got wrong is the relationship between the stock market— *The Roaring 2000s* foresaw "a Dow that would reach at least 21,500 and possibly 35,000 by the year 2008"—and out-migration. Dent thought a boom and out-migration marched together. I believe the relationship is exactly the opposite. A sustained poor or flat stock market is what will trigger the professional middle-class flight out of cities and suburbs. The logic is easy to understand. We will suffer with a small house, a hefty mortgage, and a grinding commute *if* we think by these sacrifices we can retire by age fifty-five, thanks to our rapidly appreciating house and retirement portfolio. But take away double-digit annual appreciation of our two biggest assets and throw in worries about retirement, and we begin to feel like slaves.

Since Lessinger wrote *Penturbia* in 1991 and Dent wrote *The Roaring 2000s* in 1998, these developments have occurred.

In Economics

The stock market may have entered a fifteen-year period during which it will underperform relative to the historical average (the boomlet of 2003 notwithstanding). There goes your portfolio and retirement savings! As to your salary, well, China, India, and other low-cost nations have entered the scene. They are pouring scores of millions of hardworking, white-collar workers into the global labor force. This could dampen American salaries and bonuses for at least a generation to come.

In Technology

Broadband Internet and search tools such as Google have made it possible to perform sophisticated white-collar work in small towns. The long-predicted "death of distance" era has arrived.

In Culture

The sophistication gap between urban areas and smaller cities and towns has narrowed, thanks to technology (broadband Internet, cable television, satellite radio, overnight delivery, etc.). Yet smaller cities and towns remain vastly cheaper from a housing standpoint. They are also freer of the numerous "status competitions" (the social pressure to drive a fancy car, enroll the children in private schools, and take European vacations) that further drive up the cost of professional middle-class life in big cities and suburbs.

In Demographics

The median age of America's largest population bulge, the baby boomers, is now fifty. This age group is beset by time and financial burdens on all sides: college tuition, care for aging parents, and the need to save for retirement. (Most of us are way behind on that!) Many of America's 77 million baby boomers have reached the conclusion that they must reduce their household costs in order to meet their financial obligations and goals.

In Spirituality

America has entered what many observers think is a spiritual Great Awakening—touched off by a turbulent global economy, post-9/11 fears and insecurities, and an aging population (baby boomers in particular) that feels life's calendar winding down. I believe this search for meaning will beckon Americans out of pricey, status-competitive, time-robbing large population centers and toward more serene and pastoral places.

Okay, enough of the theorizing.

In *Life 2.0*, you'll meet real folks who are living larger lives in smaller places right now—people who have found a fulfilling Second Act for their lives. People such as these:

Connie Paraskeva, who for years had been on the road as a democracy specialist for the State Department. She now is doing her sophisticated global work from the unworldly outpost of Bismarck, North Dakota (so she can look after her aging parents).

Dick Resch, a Harvard Business School grad, who fell out of love with the materialism and morals of Wall Street. He took himself to Green Bay, Wisconsin, joined a furniture manufacturer, and became the laughingstock of his Harvard classmates. Now, as CEO, Dick's been able to implement a vision of making every employee in his company financially literate about the business, even though many have not finished high school.

Dave Barton, who once ran a most un-California-like business in California—a company brokering factory tool parts by telephone and fax. Dave was up against the wall economically when the landlord tripled the rent for his business and he couldn't pay his employees enough to live closer than a two-hour commute to the office. Dave closed the business, sold his 1,700-square-foot house for $895,000, and set off for the hills of Pennsylvania. There he discovered a remarkable high-tech answer to his problem.

Rick Randall, a self-made millionaire who paid a price for his financial success: not only a failed marriage but separation from the person he cared most about in this world, his daughter. When Rick married for a second time and embarked on a new series of entrepreneurial ventures, he decided to locate in smaller cities (Wilmington, North Carolina, during the school year; Lake Placid, New York, in the summer) where he could focus on both work and family.

Peter Scanlon, born, bred, schooled, and married on the East Coast in the New York area, a high-flyer at insurance giant Cigna until he burned out. Peter had three new job offers—two in New York and one in Des Moines, Iowa. The family has blossomed in Des Moines. Their cheaper, bigger, and more beautiful home is the material side of the Scanlon household equation. The qualitative is the stress-free drive to work, a dynamic church that even his kids like to attend, and a rich cultural life with events that take them no time to get to.

Andrew Field, who got the inspiration for transforming his life and his printing business while fly-fishing in the Yellowstone River. Printingforless.com locates idle printing press time around the country and brokers it to customers over the Internet. Andrew and his wife, Victoria, live like baron and baroness in their custom-built home on twenty-two acres near the Gallatin National Forest. Here's the irony: The Printingforless.com model was tried—and failed—in high-cost Silicon Valley.

Toni Sottak and her husband, Mike, both public relations professionals, were living in the Potrero Hill area of San Francisco and getting up at four-thirty to beat the traffic in the drive down to Silicon Valley. Flying back from a vacation spent scuba diving in the Caribbean, they played with an idea: What if we became full-time island dwellers? How would we make a living? Could we bring our black Labrador, Duke, without quarantine? Mike visited Providenciales in the Caicos and Turks, a lovely British island, just two miles wide, and said, "Screw it, this is the place." They sold everything in the Bay Area and started a freelance public relations business that has been a huge success.

Jonathan Weber, editor of the dot-com era's magazine sensation the *Industry Standard,* was exhausted from seventy-hour work weeks and in no shape to stick around for a tech recovery in San Francisco. He moved to Missoula, Montana, where he lectures part-time at the University of Montana's School of Journalism and writes reports about stocks of European wireless companies. A hyperfast Net connection and flights every six weeks to Europe allow Jon to write about the European scene from a small western university town.

I met these and many other people during personal visits over the last two years, when I set out in a small airplane to fly around the country and have a look at how Americans were coping with major structural changes in the economy. During this journey I met countless ordinary folks doing stunning, creative things with their work and lives in places you'd least expect.

My hope is that you will be inspired by their stories of personal reinvention and triumph—especially if you are among the millions of Americans who feel pressured by the costs, treadmills, stresses, and insecurities of post-boom, post-9/11 urban coastal living.

A tip on how to read *Life 2.0* . . .

In Part 1, join me as I learn how to fly a small airplane by instruments and then set out across America, starting in Lawrence, Massachusetts, and hopscotching to areas where

I could learn more about what I saw as the trend toward living larger in smaller places.

In Part 2, I attempt to pull together the meaning of these individual portraits of people and places and to examine the long-term economic, technological, and spiritual implications of the move to a saner style of life.

In Part 3, a resource section, I list 150 U.S. cities and towns you might want to consider as alternatives to your present locales. The key here is finding the best possible match of your needs to your choices. Take a look.

Some readers may think there is too much airplane talk in this book. Sorry; I just couldn't curb my enthusiasm. I hope you will look kindly on my aerial Jack Kerouac fantasies. However, if you are bored by the flyboy bits, just skip past those parts and go to the real meat of this book. Which is: A growing number of Americans are seeking a larger life in a smaller place. Many are finding it.

I live in rural southern Indiana in a small town of five thousand people. We moved here twelve years ago and tonight I was reminded once again of why we made that decision. I have just returned from a play performed in the cafeteria of the school where I am a guidance counselor. There are forty-two students in the senior class and eighteen were in the play tonight. Three hours of laughter and good food, all for $13 a person.

We moved here to get away from the city, a college town where parties, drinking, drugs, and other questionable activities are a common occurrence. We wanted to raise our son in a small-town atmosphere. When we looked for our new home, I remember telling the realtor that I hoped we could find something suitable for under $100,000. He was mildly amused and then told us that he didn't have any homes available for *over* that price. This is a beautiful area where a 2,000-square-foot home on twenty acres is affordable.

The wildlife is everywhere, so it's a challenge for this city gal to raise a garden that isn't eaten by the deer first! The winters are mild, making the bugs larger than where I had lived further north. It is the best-kept secret in Indiana, a place unknown, even to Mapquest!

Where do we go for culture? Where do we shop? We are fifty minutes from that college town, if we need its cultural and educational activities, and sixty minutes away from Louisville, Kentucky, where we can enjoy the southern charm and the riverfront. Even closer to home is a man-made lake and ski resort, the French Lick Springs, where entertainment is brought in from out of town. One of Indiana's finest wineries is located there and you can find gourmet cuisine. But honestly, the best cultural experience is the local culture. It is a world where people know their neighbors and care about each other. Our son attends school in California now, yet loves to come home and relax. I think the trend is to live where you can enjoy the most for your money. I know we are. We live in the most beautiful county in Indiana. For me, it is the American Dream come true.

CAROLYN HASH
Paoli, Indiana

While in grad school at Wharton, most of my classmates were contemplating investment-banking jobs in New York City, consulting jobs in Boston or Chicago, business development jobs in Silicon Valley—you get the point. My wife and I weighed the miserable hours, the expensive lifestyles, and the big-ticket salaries (many of which are now casualties of recent rightsizings) and said no.

I can see the allure of Boston or New York or Washington, D.C., but for our mid-thirties family of five, it doesn't work. So we trotted off to New Hampshire, where, for the price of our old tiny two-bedroom in suburban D.C., we got a six-acre idyll with a horse barn and small fruit orchard on a lake eighty-five miles from Boston.

By the way, I can sit in my two-hundred-year-old farmhouse listening to loons on the lake while I am on my wireless network through a broadband connection to the outside world. Pretty cool!

I have my choice of two airports—Manchester (cheaper and easier but with about half the flights) and Logan (well . . . you know). Manchester works out better 90 percent of the time. And for the Northeast corridor, the train out of Boston is always a better bet. So for transport, we don't even need the revolution in small-jet technology.

But there are definitely trade-offs. I joined a great opportunity with good pay and challenging work in a technology company that happened to be located in a rural area. That said, there aren't a lot of alternative employment opportunities up here if this turns out to be less than perfect.

A lot of my classmates would feel stifled out here. In fact they love to visit, but are always excited to get back to the city. But it's perfect for us.

Douglas Patteson
Rochester, New Hampshire

PART 1

CHAPTER 1

Trapped in a Cloud Cave

I push the throttle all the way forward to the airplane's instrument panel and begin rolling down Runway 31 at Fargo, North Dakota's Hector Field. The engine kicks in as my Cessna 172SP Skyhawk lurches forward and picks up power. At a speed of 60 knots, in response to a gentle pull on the yoke, the Cessna's wheels lift from the blacktop. I'm airborne.

Right away there's a bad omen.

Air traffic control says three National Guard F-15 jets are practicing touch-and-gos on the same runway, so I must keep a sharp lookout. A midair collision with a six-ton military kerosene burner capable of clipping along at Mach 2 would shatter my four-seat Skyhawk. The only thing left of me and my sorry encounter would be a four-paragraph story in tomorrow's edition of the local papers.

Ten minutes go by without incident, and finally I am out of harm's way. Across the Red River and into western Minnesota the air smooths out and I feel settled. First crisis averted.

What am I doing up here? That's a question I have asked myself countless times since taking up flying at age forty-five. Is this some kind of midlife crisis? Am I running away? Back on the ground, friends of my wife are asking the same question: What's he doing up there? I have left my wife and two young children for several weeks to fly a small airplane solo over the U.S. heartland.

Officially, there is a reason—an editorial mission. I'm looking for Americans who have fled high-priced cities and suburbs as a way of coping with a crummy stock market, a lousy economy, broken dreams, and post-9/11 terrorism fears. Americans "flying home" to their roots will constitute a major demographic trend of the early 2000s.

Or so I think.

———————

Today, I'm en route from Fargo to Green Bay, Wisconsin, on an instrument flight plan. I have chosen a path that will take me north of Minneapolis by forty miles. This morning I heard a report on the Weather Channel predicting late-afternoon thunderstorms moving up from Iowa. I'm anxious to avoid these troublemakers. This storm—the product of a summer cold front moving northward at 20 miles per hour—will contain lightning, hail, and possibly tornadoes. Such meteorological chaos is typical in the Midwest in the spring and summer. A river of warm, moist air collides with a solid wall of cold air. The roiling begins and in minutes thick gray vertical cumulonimbus clouds (thunderheads, they're called) can rise 50,000 feet or more. Hail is not uncommon, while severe updrafts, downdrafts, and 100-mph bursts of wind can toss a small airplane around like a beer can on a stormy lake.

Summer cold fronts are not to be mucked with. These nasties can even bring down a commercial airliner. On August 2, 1985, Delta Airlines flight 191, an L-1011 widebody jet, crashed near Dallas, killing most aboard. Among the dead was Don Estridge, the inventor of the IBM personal computer.

Whoa. Today is August 2.

Let's just forget about that.

Soon I'm cruising 9,000 feet over the town of Sauk Centre, Minnesota—hometown of novelist Sinclair Lewis, America's first Nobel Prize winner in literature and a deadly satirist of small-town America. My window is filled with deep blue sky, the sky of the mountain West, not typical of Minnesota. Below are cumulus clouds that look like snowmen, whose tops rise to, I'm guessing, 7,000 feet—2,000 feet below me.

The cloud tops will rise and grow tall as the afternoon rolls along. Summer weather in the Midwest is notoriously fickle. One sure bet is that cumulus clouds, once they appear, will grow taller as an afternoon progresses. It's also a rule of thumb that small plane flight under or through such growing cumulus clouds is to be avoided. The sudden updrafts and downdrafts can be teeth-shattering. But since I'm currently cruising 2,000 feet above the clouds, that's no worry. All is serene. With any luck I'll be landing in Green Bay in an hour and a half.

Not so fast.

Thirty minutes west of Minneapolis the sky changes from azure blue to battleship gray. A huge wall of clouds appears twenty miles off the right wing—it's that big nasty cold front. Damn; it looks closer than it is supposed to be. The Weather Channel said it would stay well south of Minneapolis. I am right now forty miles north of Minneapolis, and this thing is a lot closer than that. It is massive, solid, and gray—it looks the way a great battleship must appear if you're floating by in a rubber raft.

I think about asking ask air traffic control for a diversion to the north. A no-brainer, except that to my north sits another menace—a rising, blackening cumulus cloud, the type of angry formation that can quickly build into an isolated thunderstorm. It looks like Devils Tower in Wyoming.

But straight ahead, there is a large gap—a gap between the gray battleship and the Devils Tower. I decide to stay on my route and shoot that gap, working out the math in my head. My Cessna Skyhawk cruises at 120 knots. Ground speed according to the instrument panel's moving map reads 134 knots, or 154 miles per hour, thanks to a tailwind. The gray mass should be moving north at 20 miles an hour—isn't that what the Weather Channel said? If so, the math works. I'll easily shoot the gap. No problem, in theory.

In flying, you learn that the only weather forecast that matters is the one you see out the windshield. By the time I get to the gap a few minutes later, it has closed. Completely closed.

Suddenly I am in a big cloud cave!

Now I have to tell you, this is the oddest experience—terrifying and magical, like a scary children's book. I can't see daylight, and yet I can see in front of me for at least a half mile. A giant cloud cave! Swirling milk-shake hues of yellow and purple. To the left is that ominous gray wall, the giant battleship, closing in. Lightning bolts fracture the darkening sky.

I swallow hard at the lightning. My hands start trembling because now I've got another problem. The clouds underneath me, the floor of this damnable cloud cave, are rising like boiling soapy water and beginning to swallow me. I push in maximum power, pull on the yoke to climb. That brings the voice of air traffic control in my earphones. The controller is pissed at me. When you fly on an instrument flight plan you are supposed stay on your assigned altitude, no matter what. Air traffic's job is to separate you from other traffic, but the controller can't do his job if some amateur pilot is in the clouds freelancing. On the other hand, it's my sorry ass up there in the boiling clouds.

North of Minneapolis, exactly where I will encounter the heaviest traffic en route, I'm crazily busting air traffic control's assigned altitude. I'm climbing as rapidly as the little 180-horsepower plane will allow to avoid being swallowed by the floor. I plead on the microphone for air traffic's indulgence. The controller grumbles. At this point I no longer care, because I'm in big trouble. So I keep going up . . . 9,000 feet, 9,500, 10,000, 10,500 . . . and the whole cloud cave is closing in on me and there's lightning and turbulence, and I'm thinking this is really stupid . . . *what am I doing up here?* . . . how am I going to get out of this jam?

Then I see a patch of mist below.

I key the microphone and tell Minneapolis Approach: Cancel my instrument flight plan! I must get out of this cloud! I pull the throttle back to idle and start diving at a steep 2,000 feet per minute. I do about three full diving circles down, slip through that small misty hole—is that the Mississippi River down there?—then level out at 3,500 feet. That's where I stay: flying under this mass, flying for my life, flying all the way to Green Bay.

On the ground, I check into the airport Sheraton, sit at the bar, slug down two Jack Daniel's shots with Corona Extra chasers, go to my room, and watch the Weather Channel. The announcer is talking about that nasty cold front I jousted with in Minnesota only an hour ago. It indeed contained the classic brew of lightning, hail, and tornadoes. The storm now was in central Wisconsin upending trailer parks, shoving power poles through windows, inflicting the usual midwestern summer . . . hell.

In a sober moment before the booze transported me to a sodden slumber, I tried to remember just how I had got myself into this mess.

BOONYACK COMEBACK

I'm to blame, of course. My journey into the cloud cave began with a column I wrote in the April 15, 2002, issue of *Forbes* magazine called "Boonyack Comeback." In it I wrote that small cities could very well outperform larger cities, economically, over the next decade. If this happened, a trend that had favored large cities since about 1981—particularly those centers of tech and finance on both coasts—could reverse. The column quoted a headhunter from Heidrick & Struggles, David Pasahow, who said that he now recruits hotshot executives out of Chicago or Dallas and places them, amazingly, in Des Moines or Omaha. As recently as 1999, no dice. "What's the attraction?" I asked. His answer: "Great housing for the dollar, country clubs you can get into—and afford—public schools that work, and short commutes." As for culture, he said, "From the money they save on housing, country clubs, and schools, my clients fly to Paris when they want culture."

Normally I get thirty or forty e-mails in response to my *Forbes* column, usually short blurbs saying that I am a idiot and that Steve Forbes ought to drag me over hot coals and then fire me. Within a month of the "boonyack" column being published, however, I had received more than two hundred e-mails. These were not spitballs aimed at my head, but something much different. They were tales of the search for sanity and of the need to balance life and work. Many were sincere outpourings of deep life-transition stories. Most were from people who had undergone life-changing shifts in perspective.

Wrote David Marshall from Pittsburgh: "After living in Manhattan and working on Wall Street trading desks for over a decade, I packed up my bags last year and moved to the home-town of my fianceé—Pittsburgh. My commute is seven minutes. People actually say hello to me in the morning. Cars stop for me when I'm trying to cross the street."

Another, from Ray Ozyjowski in Portland, Oregon: "I am glad to be out of New York! The investment banking bloodbath continues. I have a real quality life in Portland at a small tech-nology research investment bank, calling on the same clients in New York I did when I lived there, and I still travel to New York once or twice a quarter. I now have a five-minute commute from a house in a prime community. I get to spend much more qual-ity time outdoors and with my boys."

Michael Stemo of Grand Rapids, Michigan, summed it up: "If folks start to take a tally of their lifestyle, cost of living, and the lack of leisure time, they'll realize that the quality-of-life cost is just too high."

On and on the e-mails ran.

Stories like these are fun to read. They evince something wonderful about the American character, the pursuit of happi-ness and the gift for reinvention. But do these highly personal stories tell us something larger? Might they also hint at deeper changes in the dreams and lifestyle choices of Americans?

MY MIDLIFE CRISIS

Oh, that. Okay, I admit it. I now believe (with perfect hindsight) that I was having a bit of my own crisis during the dark year of 2002 and needed a slap upside my addled head. As publisher of and a columnist for *Forbes* magazine, I had fallen into the nasty habit of theorizing my way through columns, rather than actu-ally venturing out into the world and seeing what was going on.

Working for a New York magazine and living in California's Silicon Valley during the Great Boom, this was an especially dangerous habit. If you hung around New York and Silicon Valley people—and nothing but New York and Silicon Valley people—you could swallow the idea, for example, that some CrazyFad.com might just wipe "brick-and-mortar" businesses off the face of the earth. You might swallow the Kool-Aid and believe that NASDAQ was going to overtake the Dow Jones Industrial Average on a numerical basis at any time, as was proposed by the respected consultant and venture capitalist Geoffrey Moore in March 2000. You might suppose that venture capital was perfectly, totally risk-free, as Geoff Yang of Redpoint Ventures gleefully told *Fortune* magazine that same month.

My own judgment lapses were no better.

Here is just one example: Four years ago I was introduced to Global Crossing chief executive Gary Winnick, not yet notorious. We met in a backstage green room at a conference. Winnick was that evening's keynote speaker. My job was to say a few introductory remarks about the promise of Global Crossing. This promise—that a new era of bountiful global capitalism would effloresce from fiber-optic lines strung along the ocean floors—was one I believed, and still do.

Backstage, Gary Winnick was giving me ghostly heartburn. For starts, he looked like no tech entrepreneur I had ever met. He had a fleshy, florid face. He wore a hand-sewn suit that probably cost more than an Apple G4 laptop—the wrong priority for an entrepreneur—and he was attended by an entourage that might have included a bodyguard. This picture of Winnick stood in contrast to every great entrepreneur I've ever known— guys like Bill Gates, Steve Jobs, Michael Dell, Larry Ellison— guys who had lean, hungry looks, particularly when their start-ups were new and their successes were no sure thing. Global Crossing was too new to be a sure thing.

I kept stealing glances at Winnick, trying to size him up. Standing with hands on hips in a wide stance and never far from his entourage, Winnick looked like a guy who devoted much thought to self-protection. Suddenly I had an intuition! Here's a guy with no apparent downside. That's why he flunks the real entrepreneur's test. He lacked that telltale entrepreneur's look—a half-feral, half-religious conviction you see in the best ones. Winnick projected a quite different look, powerful and self-satisfied, that of a mafia don or a four-term U.S. senator. In other words, the sort of person who could make poop run uphill and wanted everyone to know it. This I somehow intuited in only three minutes backstage with the guy. It was a moment of clarity and inspiration.

So of course I stayed up till 3 A.M. that night and typed out a column that would warn *Forbes* readers away from Gary Winnick—a predator in entrepreneur's clothing, certain to put his interests before shareholders.

The column, when it came out, exploded into controversy. It almost got me fired over the subsequent mountain of legal expenses needed to defend it from Winnick's libel charges. The column went on to win every major journalism award and landed me on *Lou Dobbs Tonight,* Neil Cavuto, and *Good Morning America.* The story ricocheted and reverberated for years after. Later in 2003 I was the frequent guest of Senate committee investigations hot on the trail of corporate fraud. My book advance on the fall of Gary Winnick was a bit more than $2 million.

Yeah, right. In my dreams.

No such column appeared.

My sense about Winnick was true and clear—he ended up selling $600 million of stock in a company that went bank-rupt—but I lacked the courage to write it that way. Worse, dur-ing the next few months I wrote the opposite! Piles of mush in praise of Global Crossing! How could I have done this? Apparently I had followed a line of cold, abstract reasoning—which posited that the Internet's full promise depended on broadband fiber-optic global highways connecting continents and here was the company and the man to deliver it. I had let this hopeful McLu-hanesque speculation of mine betray what I knew to be true in my heart. I had sensed a deeper truth about

Winnick backstage but did nothing about it. I rank this among the worst failings of my columnist career.

―――――――

Trust your instincts! That's one lesson I wish to impart to readers of this book. Except . . .

. . . Let me now take you to another intimate space where one's best instincts might be deadly: the cockpit of a small airplane. I have pointed my Cessna Skyhawk single-propeller airplane onto Runway 24 in Green Bay, Wisconsin, ready to depart for St. Cloud, Minnesota. A heavy fog sits just 100 feet above the tarmac. Visibility is described by the tower controller to be at one-quarter mile. Commercial jets are unable to land. They have resorted to flying endless oval-shaped holding patterns one to two miles aboveground, stacked in a line from here to Oshkosh. But I have filed an instrument flight plan. Legally I can go.

My instincts scream out: Don't go! You idiot, Northwest Airline jets can't land. A leather-faced turboprop pilot inside the Titletown Jet Center's green-carpeted pilot's lounge warns me not to go. No way in hell would he fly his King Air 90 out in these conditions!

But I knew if I could just stash my fear in a holding pattern, so to speak, I was perfectly okay to depart. My brain had calculated the departure risks to be low. There was fog, yes, but no other risk factors were in play. No rain. No wind. No thunderstorms or ice hidden within the fog. The fog layer itself was only 2,000 feet thick, which meant blue skies on top and serene flying in less than four minutes. My equipment worked perfectly. I was freshly trained to do it, having passed the FAA's instrument flight checkride only a month before. Let's go.

I did. The Green Bay tower controller issued a command I'd never heard before: Report when airborne. Wow, even the tower couldn't see me. I rolled down the runway, picked up speed, got the nose up, and for the next four minutes kept my eyes in a tight scan of the airspeed, artificial horizon, and the GPS moving map. Alone in the fog, blinded by it, my instinct naturally chose this moment to hector me like bad in-laws. What's that low rumble I hear? Did your engine just cough? Are your wings level? They don't feel level. Are you *sure* you're climbing a steady 500 feet per minute?

Evolution has not prepared us to fly through the fog in an aluminum can. My instincts were screeching to me like Woody Allen on crack. My twenty-first-century-attuned eyes and brain, certified by the FAA, calmly surveyed the instruments and told me everything was fine. All was fine. In precisely four minutes I was able to punch through the fog layer into God's blue sky, free of cloud caves and fear.

THE PARADOX

In his 1936 essay "The Crack-Up," novelist F. Scott Fitzgerald got off his famous observation about the test of a first-rate mind. Fitzgerald said an intelligent person should be capable of holding two opposing ideas in his head and still function. Fitzgerald never specified what he meant by this. Of course his quote endures because of its mysterious vagueness. Perhaps he meant to say something grandly philosophical, such as: For mankind to survive we must conduct our lives as if there was a God who would judge us for eternity, when the truth may be . . . well, who knows. Or maybe he was referring to the old paradox of our dualistic natures as human animals: part logical, part intuitive. Just maybe Fitzgerald was merely looking at his own unhappy life—and confessing to us how hard it is to pretend that one's work matters when one is beset by drunkenness and depression.

Another paradox: *Life 2.0* is about America's search for satisfying work styles. But it must begin with a sobering thought: This search will not be easy in the Turbulent 2000s economy. It may be especially hard if you, like me, are over the age of thirty-five, support a family and have a mortgage, and find that your capacity for risk is less than it used to be. I hope to show you that this very real psychological barrier needn't stand in the way of your happiness.

A generation of Americans between the ages of thirty-five and fifty-five will experience life in much the same way our grandparents experienced the one-two punch of the 1920s—a decade of promise that gave us skyscrapers, affordable cars and radios, and indoor electricity and plumbing for the majority—and the 1930s, its opposite. Novelist Saul Bellow writes that the 1930s were actually fun for young adults unburdened by family obligations and career dreams. In the deflationary 1930s you could attend a movie for a dime and buy a hamburger for a nickel. It was a time to indulge in radical politics, to overthrow Babbittry in art and culture. It was a good decade for bohemians. But the Great Depression was a horrible and humiliating experience for the family man. The stock market fell 87 percent from its September 1929 peaks. During the dust bowl year of 1932 American unemployment reached 24 percent.

The Turbulent 2000s won't turn out as bad as the 1930s in terms of raw deprivation. But in a relative and psychological sense the comparison is apt. America has just come through the greatest stock market lollapalooza in its history. It began in 1982 and saw the Dow increase fifteen-fold during the next eighteen years. Then it ended in 2000.

History suggests clearly that we won't see another monster wave like this for fifty to seventy years. By then it will be too late for anybody over thirty to cash in.

Even if you accept the New Economy premise that Moore's Law and communications technologies such as cable TV and the Internet have accelerated the cycles of history—a plausible argument—it's still unlikely that another sustained stock boom will emerge to compare with the 1982–2000 period. Not, anyway, until those millions of investors scalded by the 2000–2002 bust are senile or dead.

MEMORIES OF A BOOM GONE BAD

Broken dreams can permanently scar us, even if we don't want to admit it. Ever dated someone who was better looking, more athletic, smarter, richer, more sexually sophisticated, and just generally cooler than you in every way? Such mismatches do occur, often in your twenties. We all get lucky sometime!

Mismatches rarely last long. When the breakup occurs, the upper-hand partner, who was having a fling, who was slumming, recovers in about, oh, forty-eight hours and merrily goes on with his or her life. Meanwhile, the rejected partner is usually devastated for months and even then will remember the relationship (just a fling for the slummer) for years and always wonder if it might have worked.

In the early 2000s, millions of American knowledge workers are experiencing such a moment, not about past lovers but about the past boom. Legendary venture capitalist John Doerr called the 1990s boom "the greatest legal creation of wealth in history." For a while it looked as if perhaps Doerr was right. It was the best chance in our lifetimes to break the bonds from financial worry. Many of us did get rich, on paper, at least, for a couple of years. More had hoped to attain financial comfort. We had good reason to hope, with the stock market bounding up in 15 percent gains every year. But now it's gone. Like the upper-hand lover who was slumming, it will never return.

Consequently, some Americans have begun to doubt their chances of achieving the American Dream—which for the sake of brevity (and with apologies to Thomas Jefferson) let's define as *financial comfort* and *a job you love.*

Nobody should be surprised that we Americans are worried and confused. During the last four years we have lived through the deprivations of a stock market bust and a recession. We have suffered through the tragic events of September 11 along with its disquieting aftermath. Today we live and work amid an economic recovery that looks positively sparkling on paper. Yet it feels, because of its disruptive nature, unusually stressful.

Welcome to the Turbulent 2000s.

Mix into this turmoil the largest generation of Americans, those 77 million baby boomers born between 1946 and 1964. We boomers have arrived at an age when midlife reassessment might have kicked in anyway, triggering a midlife crisis in some. For boomers, one's personal stuff may be hitting the fan just at the time when the world's economic climate has entered a period of permanent instability and storms.

Sounds like a nightmare. In fact, now is a splendid time to rethink our own concept of the American Dream and perhaps embark on a Second Chance to pursue it.

THE WHERE OF HAPPINESS

As we grow out of childhood, we give up our dreams of playing center field for the New York Yankees or starring in a Hollywood thriller. Counselors call our new attitude "maturity." Likewise, the Turbulent 2000s will force millions of Americans to reassess our adult dreams of financial comfort and early retirement. How should we face this reassessment? Must we say adios to our dreams? No. But we might have to redefine them.

Philosophers since Plato have penned millions of words attempting to define what is happiness, fulfillment, and an idealized self. This is well-traveled turf.

Countless more millions of words have been written on the how of achieving these desirable ends. Think of all the how-to books published on money, career, health, diet, fitness, self-esteem, inner peace, six-pack stomachs, sexual pleasure. A huge bestseller, though you never think of it as such, is the Alcoholics Anonymous *Big Book*, which lays out the twelve steps to overcoming alcohol dependency. It has sold millions of copies since its appearance in 1940, spawning other twelve-step programs and books. The *Big Book* and its progeny aim straight at the very soul of the American belief in second chances. So, I hope, does *Life 2.0*. It is about the *where* of finding your place in the American Dream and attaining your "best self."

For some reason, *where* is rarely considered as an important ingredient to achieving the American Dream and one's best self, even as how—money, health, diet, fitness, self-esteem, spiritual contentment, sex, et cetera—is beaten to death as an angle.

Yet asking *where* makes sense, when you think about it. A polar bear is unlikely to find its bliss in a rain forest, no matter how many Second Chances its gets. We, too, are creatures of our environment. How many of us would prosper under Taliban rule, for example? Not many. Do you think you would thrive more in Shanghai or Tokyo? Assuming language was not the issue, you probably would prefer Shanghai if you shared its entrepreneurial mentality. Tokyo, like Paris, puts its faith in the dirigiste class of well-educated conformists. (Harvard M.B.A.'s, take note.)

Now let us count our blessings.

America offers by far the richest selection of location choices to work and to live—to pursue our American Dream. We can live in New York City, the one and only. We can live in other "dense" American cities such as Boston, San Francisco, and Chicago. We can choose our cities by size, by weather, by political tenor (Portland, Oregon, is very liberal, while Cincinnati, Ohio, is very conservative), by industry, by tax and regulatory scheme, by schools, by the art scene, by acceptance of racial and sexual minorities, and by cost of living. We can dwell in the mountains, put down on the beach, reside on a farm, or repair to the high desert. Within one city alone, Los Angeles, we can find a richer array of culture than is offered in some entire countries.

After traveling the United States by small airplane during the summers of 2002 and 2003 to gather material and stories for this book, I am convinced that the where of finding your American Dream might be as important as the how.

CHAPTER 2

Flying on Instruments

I can't explain what drove the need to start launching myself skyward in a small, single-propeller airplane. Perhaps there are deep biological reasons: My uncle, a radiologist, bought a Beech Bonanza V-tail and used to fly himself around the Great Plains to dusty small-town clinics. His father—my maternal grandfather—was a World War I aviator.

If you choose to take up flying, you'll be in for a shock when you visit the airport and inspect the fleet of trainers. Most are of 1960s and 1970s vintage—they remind you of cars in Cuba, says the writer and pilot James Fallows. The fabric seats are torn, the plastic is peeling, and quite a number of them smell vaguely of puke. The general aviation fleet is old because so few planes have been built over the last twenty years. From a high of 18,000 in 1978 to a low of 900 in 1994, the number crawled up to 2,500 in the boom year of 2000, then slipped back to 1,500 in 2003. The entire fleet of piston planes in the United States is estimated to be about 200,000, with crashes and rust depleting the stock more than newly built planes are adding to it.

For the last ten years one's flying options have come down to this: Buy a new plane—the most rudimentary will set you back nearly $200,000—or else stoically rent old junk. But now, thanks to the Internet, a middle way has been born. The idea is fractional ownership or leasing of new planes. Here is a perfect example of what the Internet does best. By speeding up information flow and lowering the costs of those flows, the Net can "make markets" in places that had been previously too expensive or inconveniently sticky to make. Net-based scheduling now enables a liquid market of brand-new airplanes flown by pilots who are not rich and may elect to own as little as one-eighth of an airplane.

In June 2001, I plunked down $8,000 to buy a one-eighth lease of a brand-new Cessna 172SP. I doubled up to a quarter lease a month later. For these modest sums I was able to fly 150 hours a year. On top of the down payment I paid about $800 a month in leases, fuel, and service fees. All said, I bought the equivalent of a weekly visit to a high-class Manhattan shrink.

BECOMING A PRIVATE PILOT

I earned my private pilot's certificate on October 10, 2001. The Federal Aviation Administration's mandated checkride consists of ninety minutes of oral quizzing and another ninety minutes of flight maneuvers that must be performed within the FAA's prescribed standards. These include making 45-degree bank angle turns for a full circle to the right, and then one to the left, without gaining or losing 100 feet (or the examiner's breakfast). The student must demonstrate a variety of takeoff and landing techniques and show that he can fly on instruments. A gut-check moment comes when the examiner tells the student to close his eyes while the examiner puts the plane in a dive, a stall, or a near spin. Looking solely at the instruments, the student is required to put the plane back on straight and level flight within five seconds.

At my airport, the word going round is that 60 percent of students pass on their first try. I passed my checkride on the first try, too, even though I bounced my short-field landing and momentarily forgot how to do radio tracking.

In the United States, it takes a minimum of forty hours of in-flight training to become a private pilot. The national average of hours-to-certificate is seventy hours. It took me more than a hundred hours. This does not count ground-school training for the written exam, which you can avoid (the training, not the exam) by buying a $300 DVD course from King Schools (www.kingschools.com). That's how I did it, spending long hours hunched over my Dell Latitude laptop studying aerodynamics and density altitudes during commercial jet jaunts from my home in California to *Forbes* headquarters in New York. Flight instructors run $25 an hour in rural areas and up to $60 an hour at airports near big cities. Toss in the cost of rental planes and figure on about $10,000 to obtain a private pilot's license.

If you can afford it, go for it.

With only a private certificate you can fly anywhere in the United States (outside of restricted military areas), cruise at any altitude below 18,000 feet, and land at any airport, except (post–September 11) those within a thirty-mile radius of Washington, D.C.

Three days after I got my private pilot's certificate, I took up my first willing passenger in my time-shared Cessna 172SP. Jeff, an old college roommate, was in town for our Stanford twenty-fifth reunion. I picked up Jeff at dawn so we might squeeze in our flying before the football game and festivities later that day. Out of San Jose Reid-Hillview Airport we climbed south and leveled out over Monterey. We continued south to Big Sur, steep-turned around the lighthouse, and got clearance from Monterey Approach to fly over Pebble Beach at 2,000 feet. The morning was so clear you could see whitecaps crashing the shore and golfers on the fabled seventeenth green at Pebble. I almost saw Tom Watson's ghost chipping in to win the 1982 U.S. Open— almost. We continued up the coast at 2,000 feet and circled the Santa Cruz amusement park and its 1920s-era mountainous wooden roller coaster, called the Giant Dipper. From there I shoved the throttle home and we climbed over the Santa Cruz Mountains at 4,500 feet, enjoying glass-smooth air and fifty-mile views. We floated on full flaps down into Reid-Hillview and, to make it a perfect day, flared to a landing that was feather smooth, a pure greaser, as we pilots call it.

Flying is a huge kick and a privilege, too, and before al-Qaeda or the FAA decides to take this one away for good, I intend to visit every American state in a small airplane. Level at 2,500 feet on a clear day, you can watch pass under your cowling the most God-blessed landscape that ever was or will be.

THE RISK OF FLYING

Flying a small airplane is said to be seven times more dangerous than driving a car and forty-nine times more dangerous than hopping on a commercial airliner. The risk is equal to driving a motorcycle. Mechanical problems with the airplane itself account for a small percentage of accidents. The rest can be chalked up to human error—usually the pilot's.

Most fatal errors are caused by flying into clouds or evening haze without a proper understanding of instrument flying. This is how John F. Kennedy Jr., his wife, and his sister-in-law met their ends on July 19, 1999. Beginning his descent from 5,500 feet into Martha's Vineyard in his new six-seat Piper Saratoga HP, young Kennedy lost the horizon in the evening gloaming.

This is frighteningly easy to do. Lacking an obvious reference point such as the horizon to check if the airplane's wings are level, the average non-instrument-rated pilot will lose control of his airplane in forty-five seconds. Flying by the gauges is a safer bet, but is counterintuitive. I know, because one day while flying with an instructor through the clouds overlying Los Angeles I became convinced we were nose down and losing altitude. All my instincts screamed at me to pull the yoke back and raise the airplane's nose. The gauges told another story. We were flying perfectly straight and level. Had I raised the nose, as every cell in my brain implored me to do, I would have slowed the plane's airspeed, perhaps to the point of a stall and a Kennedy death spiral.

I did not want this happening to me.

The pilot can, of course, restrict his flying to good-weather days. That's okay if his goal is recreational flying—hundred-mile jaunts before Saturday breakfast or a weekend's sightseeing trip over the Vermont mountains. But if you want to fly across the United States. on a schedule and visit people, you must learn how to fly in the clouds when clouds arise. That or sit grounded for days at a time.

I quickly figured out that I needed to earn an instrument certificate if I was going to fly around America and do research for this book. Good luck intervened. A *Forbes* photographer, Glen Davis, had recently earned his instrument flight instructor license and had called me in the summer of 2002 with a terrific idea. Let's fly across the United States, Glen said, hole up on the East Coast for eight days, and instrument-train with a monomaniacal fervor.

Why not, indeed?

Glen lives in Hoboken, New Jersey. The plan was for him to fly out on a commercial airliner and join me in San Jose. From there we would begin our trip back east in my Skyhawk.

DAY ONE

A rocky start. Clouds darken the sky over San Jose's Reid-Hillview Airport at 1,600 feet. Glen tells me to phone in my instrument flight plan to the local "Flight Service" station. This I do, but while waiting in the airplane for my official instrument clearance I get two pieces of bad news from the control tower. One, expect a ten-minute delay. Well, thanks, I'm already sweating. Two, here's your clearance to Reno and are you ready to copy? Yes, ready to copy, I say in my most professional pilot's voice, my writing hand poised over the yellow pad strapped to my thigh. Fake it till you make it, I figure. The controller spoils my carefully cultivated confidence, machine-gunning the instrument clearance in a voice that sounds like an auctioneer on speed—so fast, so jargon-filled, my brain freezes. My hand on the mechanical pencil freezes. Huh? I look forlornly at Glen who says: "You didn't get the clearance you wanted. Copy the one she's giving you. NOW!" I do. It takes three tries and I can hardly read it back to the controller my mouth is so dry.

It gets worse.

Two minutes after takeoff, we enter the clouds and are flying blind at 2,000 feet somewhere between Reid-Hillview and San

Jose International airports. By sheer bad luck, two Skyhawks, one of them mine, were observed by the control tower (using radar) to be on a convergent path, two miles apart. Our tail numbers are nearly identical, adding to the confusion. Skyhawk 987TW, turn left heading 220 degrees, says the tower. But my Skyhawk is 897TW, so is he talking to me? To the other Skyhawk? Who's on first? In the confusion I neglect my instrument scan and drop a wing 30 degrees. Just like that. Total panic. I would have started a graveyard spiral, Kennedy-like, in another five seconds. Glen calmly takes the yoke and sorts out the confusion. Soon we are flying serenely to Reno in clear sunshine, but I feel like a boob. An instrument rating seems a galaxy away.

Fortunately you can't self-loathe for long when sailing over the Sierra Nevada and blue Lake Tahoe. The altitudes are too high to fly instrument flight rules up here in my little Cessna bug smasher, so we cancel our clearance and lazily circle the West's largest freshwater lake. For centuries Lake Tahoe was occupied by the Washoe Indians, who hunted and fished in paradise before General John Frémont stumbled across it in 1844 during his exploration of the Far West. Today Lake Tahoe is home to casino gaming (on the Nevada side), alpine and cross-country skiing, golfing, water sports, hiking, fishing, and camping. Former junk-bond king Michael Milken recently built a $20 million home on the lake's southwest shore.

We cross Lake Tahoe over the north shore, aim for a gap in the Carson Range, and start a descent from 9,500 feet into the Reno/Tahoe International Airport. Luckily it is late morning. Jolting mountain winds have not kicked up yet. The landing is smooth.

At lunch Glen urges me to be more patient. Instrument flying is not learned in a day. Setbacks, including embarrassments and panics, such as this morning's, are a natural part of it. I listen and sigh inwardly. Patience is not my long suit.

The climb out of Reno is swaying and queasy. We climb to 9,500 feet on a visual flight rules plan. Unfortunately, that won't be high enough to escape the afternoon's thermal turbulence—caused by ground heat rising until it collides with cooler air above. I push the throttle forward, pull the yoke back, and climb as fast as the Skyhawk's 180-horsepower engine will allow, which is painstakingly slow at this altitude. It takes almost ten minutes to go up to 11,500 feet. At least the air up here is smoother. For awhile.

Nevada is a high plateau, the driest state in the nation, dominated by mountains nearly barren but for scant piñon and juniper groves that need little water to survive. From 11,500 feet Nevada looks like a moonscape. In the heat of the early afternoon, the rising thermal turbulence grabs and shakes us like a toy airplane. We are faced with a choice: go yet higher . . . or endure another two hours of nauseous pitching and yawing before arriving at our final destination, Ogden, Utah. We elect for higher and start a groaning climb to 12,500 feet.

The FAA mandates that pilots flying on a visual flight plan, as I am doing today, stick to "odd-numbered thousands plus 500 feet" when flying east (and "even-numbered thousands plus 500 feet" when flying west). Because we're eastbound, we should be flying at 11,500 feet or 13,500 feet, but not at 12,500 feet. However, Glen and I decide to assert our authority as "pilots in command"—a phrase that lets you violate an FAA rule for your own safety. We settle for 12,500 feet for two reasons. One, the chances of avoiding hypoxia and its consequences—poor judgment brought on by oxygen starvation—are better at 12,500 feet than at 13,500 feet. Two, Nevada and Utah are so big and sparse that the odds of crashing into a westbound airplane up here are nil. During the last hour of the flight, over Utah, we played dodge 'em with rising cumulus clouds. Glen and I are giggling like stoners, a sure sign that hypoxia is making sushi of our brains. Fortunately Ogden is only half an hour away and we begin our descent.

DAY TWO

I thought I would like Ogden, even speculating that I might return to profile this city of about 81,000, Utah's second largest. But the place, at least what I saw of it, strikes me as down at the heel, even sad. Glen and I checked into the Crowne Plaza, where a poor young woman at the computer talked to us like a 78 record playing at 33. It took her fifteen minutes to check us in. We were the only people lined up.

The next morning we had a cab scheduled to pick us up at six. I was up early and outside the hotel looking for the cab on the corner of Washington Boulevard and Twenty-sixth Street when I spotted a young man dressed like a tuba player in an oompah band. He wore hiking shorts hitched up to his navel, a long-sleeve white dress shirt, red suspenders, and a little Bavarian hat. He marched across Washington Boulevard, looked this way and that, adjusted his hat, and marched back. Then he repeated this, several times.

While settling our gas bill at the Ogden airport, I noticed the headlines in that morning's *Ogden Standard-Examiner*. A fourteen-year-old boy had been shot to death in a drive-by. Something very dysfunctional is going on here in Ogden.

I realize these are only glancing observations, but I wonder if Ogden is one of those small cities facing long odds. Salt Lake City to the south is a cosmopolitan center of 1.3 million people, the largest metro area between Denver and San Francisco; it's the state's capital city and home to the University of Utah, which is one of the world's leading research centers of three-dimensional computing. Salt Lake City is also, of course, the headquarters of the Mormon Church, whose adherents are a famously fecund and industrious bunch. But, surprisingly, only 51 percent of Salt Lake City's population is Mormon—a recent mayor was an Italian Catholic woman named Deedee Corradini. Thus a healthy creative tension and tolerance is in full flower in the state's largest city. Utah's other major universities are located thirty miles south of Salt Lake City in Provo (Brigham Young University) and twenty miles north of Ogden in the town of Logan (Utah State University).

Ogden lacks the cosmopolitan flavor of Salt Lake City and the youth and bounce of a university town. It remains mostly famous for an event that occurred almost 140 years ago at

Promontory Point, an hour's drive northwest of town. That was where the first transcontinental railroad was completed with the joining of the Central Pacific and Union Pacific Railroads in 1868. Today Ogden continues to struggle in Salt Lake City's shadow, and looks it. (If I have been unfair to Ogden, readers are invited to visit www.ogdencity.com for a more enthusiastic description of the city.)

We lifted off from Ogden at 7 A.M. The Wasatch Range air is cool this fine clear morning and the little airplane's engine is running like a top. Horsepower in my Skyhawk degrades about 3 percent for each 1,000 feet above sea level, but it still should produce sufficient oomph, we judge, to climb safely through Weber Pass at 9,500 feet. The sun over the Wyoming plains is glorious and we do a quick stop at Cheyenne. Again, the Skyhawk jumps off the runway at its maximum allowable weight and 9,000-feet density altitude. Gutty little plane. We follow Interstate 80 over southern Nebraska and watch in wonder as the landscape of the American West turns into the Great Plains. At North Platte, Nebraska, we veer north toward Iowa.

After landing at the Sioux Gateway Airport in Sioux City, Iowa, we fuel up on 100-octane low-lead "avgas" and sixteen-ounce bottles of Diet Coke and get serious about flying under instrument rules again. Over the mountainless Midwest, the Skyhawk now can easily make the Minimum Enroute Altitudes required of instrument flying. Besides, my checkride is only ten days away. Not a minute to waste dallying about on a joyride.

From Sioux City to Madison, Wisconsin, I am filed for instrument flying and truly navigating "in the FAA's system" for the first time, wearing fogged-up goggles (called foggles) to simulate clouds. I talk to air traffic control, fly assigned airways, and gain confidence with each mile. We fly the instrument landing system approach into Madison's Truax Field and I'm lined up with the runway perfectly when Glen tells me to shed the foggles at 1,000 feet. Hallelujah. The landing is smooth, but we have to taxi forever to get off the runway. Behind us, a Northwest Airlines 737 is ordered to abort its landing—FAA rules forbid a plane to land when another is on the runway. The 737 is told by the Madison tower to go around and try again.

"I'll bet we cost Northwest $3,000 in fuel," Glen says.

DAY THREE

I think I hear the voice of God calling us idiots as we go over Lake Michigan at 7,000 feet with no life jackets aboard and Glen now admitting that he swims like the New York City kid that he is. It's a long eighty miles from Milwaukee to Muskegon, on Lake Michigan's eastern shore. Good time to read the autopilot handbook. But the damnable handbook reads like the U.S. tax code. Why are these manuals written to torture users?

We fly over the hub and spoke that is Detroit and its freeways, a proper layout, one supposes, for a car town. Then it's into Canadian airspace, which seems exotic but isn't.

Buffalo Niagara International Airport is another dead-on instrument arrival, and I am beginning to think all this pilot yack about the IFR rating being aviation's toughest certificate . . . is a fiction. Fueled by club sandwiches, soup, and coffee, we take off for the east. Upstate New York looks beautiful from 7,000 feet, all finger-shaped lakes and rolling green hills. Hard to imagine that such economic devastation lies below. Perhaps now is a low point in the region's history, a perfect time to buy and rebuild. We sail over Vermont mountains and into Massachusetts during the afternoon, sweat through a bumpy approach in Lawrence, put down at Eagle East Aviation for the night, and toast our successful trip across the United States. I limit myself to two beers. Tomorrow we start eight days of solid IFR training.

DAY FOUR

Hell again. On a mission to record speeds for precise ascents and descents at various power settings, I can't seem to manage the simplest tasks, such as descending 500 feet per minute at 90 knots on a specific heading. I thought I had nailed this basic airmanship months ago. But now I can't do it for love or money. We try 45-degree banked turns while maintaining level altitude and I botch that, too. I snap at Glen and he tells me to chill.

DAY FIVE

More hell. We try our first radio-signal approaches. Not only is it hard and counterintuitive, the whole exercise seems so stupid. Why, in this age of global positioning satellites and onboard color moving maps, should I have to learn 1960s technology at all? Three thousand feet over Lawrence I launch a verbal tirade about the adjectival radio signals and the adjectival FAA's numb-nutted insistence that pilots learn radio signal naviga-tion . . . and holy cow, let's start a campaign to get rid of this very real threat to pilot safety, these adjectival radio signals.

Let's talk about it on the ground, says Glen.

The day is saved with José Gibert's arrival from Vero Beach. Cuban-born José is a friend of Glen's. José will join our IFR train-ing and attempt his own checkride on July 3, same day as me. My mood does not improve as José immediately transitions into my Skyhawk like a pro, even though he hasn't flown a Cessna in over two hundred pilot hours. It's obvious I am the weak link.

DAYS SIX, SEVEN, EIGHT, AND NINE

Miracle days! I begin to grasp radio signal navigation, holding patterns, procedure turns, published missed approaches, the whole darn menu of instrument flying. How? Well, sitting in the back of the plane watching José helps. Two students are defi-nitely better than one.

DAY TEN

Now it's José's turn to slump. He can't nail a 45-degree turn at altitude to save his mother, and the checkride is tomorrow. I'm feeling cocky again and go back to the hotel for a swim and a few ice-cold Coronas. Glen and José struggle against exhaustion and 97-degree heat to grease the steep turns, and in the early evening they finally do. Tomorrow's the big day.

DAY ELEVEN: THE IFR CHECKRIDE

Our examiner is a local legend, Allegra Osborne, a hearty sixty-nine-year-old whose nickname is Legs in the local aviation community. Legs Osborne got her private certificate in 1950. "She'll make you earn your IFR ticket," a local Lawrence pilot told us at the airport restaurant. "Damn, we want a Santa Claus," I said, and I half meant it. Legs tells us that during her oral test she probes for safety above anything else. If we bust a standard during the actual flight test, that's okay, as long as we identify it before she does and correct immediately. Legs Osborne is big on pilot self-talk. "I want to hear what you're doing and why at all times."

Self-talk—now that's something I'm good at. Filling the air with chatter must be something I picked up from all those sales calls as *Forbes* publisher. Anyway, Legs likes all the self-talk and I'm off to a good start with her. I nail the instrument approach into Manchester, New Hampshire, but then fly a sloppy radio signal full approach back into Lawrence, some kind of divine retribution for my temper tantrums. Legs assures me it is within test standards but I suspect she's cutting me a break. I do the steep turns on a rail and right the airplane within two seconds after Legs steers it into an incipient Kennedy spiral. Now I'm back in Legs Osborne's good graces and feeling good. In fact, I'm starting to feel giddy. Dear God, please let me land without incident! I do. On the ground Legs confirms the good news: a successful checkride. I feel as if I weigh only sixty pounds, like Neil Armstrong dancing on the moon! Two hours later José makes it a sweep for Glen Davis's first two instrument students. We celebrate in Legs Osborne's hangar, eating crackers and drinking bottles of Killian's Red from her fridge. Legs joins in— who can't love a lady pilot named Legs who slams down beer in the morning? It's 11 A.M., but the day's flying is done.

POSTSCRIPT

For the first time since San Jose, my mouth is dry. I'm in the airplane runup area at Lawrence, going through engine checks, about to commence my flight around America, solo, IFR. Glen is right behind me in his beautiful 1976 Grumman Tiger, giving me the thumbs-up. Over Hanscomb Field, Glen breaks off for White Plains, New York, I for Elmira. He calls Boston Approach Control to make a request. "Take care of the Cessna Skyhawk. The pilot just passed his IFR checkride yesterday." A lump appears in my throat. Glen is a prince.

For the first time I feel like a real pilot.

CHAPTER 3

Upstate New York Woes,
Twin City Triumphs

July 4, 2002. I'm a newly instrument-rated pilot by one day, and I'm celebrating at the bar at the Holiday Inn in Horseheads, New York, having flown into the nearby Elmira-Corning Regional Airport that morning from Lawrence, Massachusetts.

Swinging place! Uh-huh. I'm the only customer.

The bartender is a woman who looks ten years older than me, but in fact we must be about the same age. I, Sherlock Holmes, arrive at this brilliant deduction because the bartender has a ten-year-old daughter who sits in the corner and reads a Harry Potter book. Unless the woman adopted the girl, she can't be much older than fifty. She looks sixty. Working-class folks in small towns do appear to age faster.

I order the ham steak and peas. The ham is as tough as leather and the peas are half frozen, but the Coronas and limes are pure liquid gold. Enter a local man who's about sixty-five. He starts drinking vodka martinis fast, slugging down three, then switches to beer with raw eggs mixed in.

Since we're the only two people at the bar, I say hello. Turns out "Jack" is a lifetime employee of Corning. For more than 150 years, Corning has developed everything from the glass for Edison's lightbulb to television tubes and fiber-optic wire.

Corning Glass is headquartered in the town of Corning, fourteen miles up the road from the Horseheads Holiday Inn. The company is the lifeblood of the town and its closest neighbors, Horseheads and Elmira. As Corning has boomed and buckled, so have the three towns that depend on it, and if you happen to live in one of them, well, you had better enjoy the roller-coaster ride because there is little alternative unless you want to pack your bags. Corning's stock spiked during the 1990s thanks to America's fiber-optic splurge. It shot from $4 to $100. Then it sunk to $2, below where it started. (It climbed back up to $13 in early 2004.) But be careful whom you complain to. The walls have ears.

My new pal says he was a lifetime employee of Corning. Now slurring, he blames Corning's plummeting stock price on greedy Wall Street speculators, but he still has great admiration for the Houghton family that founded and still runs the firm. Jack has just retired, and his retirement, because of the $2 stock, is in shambles. He is much poorer and drinking heavily.

I sat there and listened to Jack grouse—and wondered whether he was just a down-market version of the executive dropouts I saw driving old cars and yanking their kids out of private schools in New York, Boston, Dallas, and California. I ordered another Corona and spent the rest of my July 4 talking to a small-town drunk and eating leathery ham steak and frozen peas.

I never did pinpoint what Jack did at Corning, but it sounded from his slurs and rants as if it was some kind of production manager job, probably midlevel. That's hardly a secure job in these Turbulent 2000s, even for younger, more sober workers. Three million U.S. manufacturing jobs have disappeared during this decade. The loss of jobs such as Jack's, which exist a step up the value ladder, are next. Marc Benioff, the CEO of Salesforce.com, which helps companies automate their sales operations, thinks 25 million white-collar jobs of the more routine nature (presumably like Jack's) could vanish into software during the next ten years, or else go offshore to cheaper places, mostly to India and China.

That's an astonishing figure, nearly ten times what most experts think, including the U.S. Labor Department. Could it come true? I put the jobs question to one of the smartest people I know, my *Forbes* colleague Robyn Meredith. Based in Asia, she has a front-row seat and told me this:

"Rich, whatever most people know about it is the tip of the iceberg. General Electric already has twenty thousand employees in India—most at the Jack Welch Center. American Express has ten thousand and counting. General Motors is doing computerized engineering models of crash-testing there. Every big American and European company is already in India or expanding—the tech jobs first and everything else on its way, at one-tenth to one-fifth the cost.

"The story is nearly the same in Malaysia—DHL Worldwide Express has a huge, high-tech room full of computers tracking packages and cargo shipments around the world. Electronic Data Systems and HSBC Bank and others are building human-relations back offices and credit-card processing units there.

"China is the biggest story of all. It is moving from just making cheap goods to having its bottomless supply of engineers research and design products to be made in the land of factories. The movement is huge. Some experts estimate 30 percent of all American white-collar work could be moved offshore at lower cost and equal quality."

Drink up, Jack.

ITS GREATEST RESOURCE
GOES UNTAPPED

Horseheads-Elmira-Corning was the first stop on my aerial boonyack mission. It would test my belief that smaller cities in pleasant settings with nearby universities strong in science and engineering would always succeed—America's answer to offshoring. Horseheads-Elmira-Corning possesses all these advantages, yet it is not succeeding. Maybe it's snakebitten.

On June 23, 1972, the city recorded one of America's worst floods. The cause was Tropical Storm Agnes, which was apparently headed out to sea when it pulled a U-turn and whacked Elmira. According to the Elmira city Web site, "the Chemung River rose to 17 feet above normal at the Lake Street Bridge.

The flood took 23 lives and caused an estimated $300 million in damage to the city."

Elmira's rotten luck has been running more or less the same way since. Rolf Pendall, an associate professor of city and regional planning at Cornell University, thirty miles to the north in Ithaca, recently examined Elmira in a Brookings Institute study, "Sprawl Without Growth: The Upstate Paradox." "Compound Elmira's falling population with the loss of manufacturing, and the problem gets more difficult to overcome," Pendall told the *Elmira Star-Gazette* in 2003.

It shouldn't be that way. The region that comprises Horseheads-Elmira-Corning, along with most of the Finger Lakes region of New York's southern tier, is blessed with rolling hills, fresh air, and clean lakes and streams. Eye-pleasing properties dot the area, from country homes to magnificent historic mansions. Picturesque farms and vineyards still help to support the local economy.

But the region's true asset is Cornell, one of the world's leading science and engineering universities, a mere thirty miles up the road yet a continent away for all the apparent good it does Horseheads-Elmira-Corning.

Cornell University's living alumni match the achievement levels attained by any college anywhere in America or the world:

Diane Ackerman (M.F.A. '73, Ph.D. '79): author, poet, and naturalist

Sandy Berger (A.B. '67): national security adviser, 1993–2000

Harold Bloom (A.B. '51): literary and cultural scholar-critic

Abby Joseph Cohen (A.B. '73): Wall Street stock analyst

Ann Coulter (A.B. '84): lawyer and bestselling author

Anthony Fauci (M.D. '66): director of NIH's National Institute of Allergy and Infectious Diseases

Ruth Bader Ginsburg (A.B. '54): U.S. Supreme Court justice

Jeff Hawkins (B.S. '79): inventor of the PalmPilot

Irwin Mark Jacobs (B.E.E. '54): cofounder, chairman, and CEO of Qualcomm; 1994 recipient of National Medal of Technology

Mae Jemison (M.D. '81): scientist, physician, and former space-shuttle astronaut

Bill Maher (A.B. '78): comedian

Toni Morrison (A.M. '55): winner of the 1993 Nobel Prize for literature

Douglas Osheroff (M.S. '71, Ph.D. '73): cowinner (with Cornell faculty members Robert C. Richardson and David M. Lee) of the 1996 Nobel Prize in physics

Tom Peters (B.C.E. '65, M.E.C. '66): management consultant-author

Richard Price (B.S. '71): novelist and screenwriter

Thomas Pynchon (A.B. '59): novelist and short-story writer

Christopher Reeve (A.B. '74): actor; activist for medical research

Janet Reno (A.B. '60): U.S. attorney general, 1993–2000

Jimmy Smits (M.F.A. '82): actor

Lee Teng-hui (Ph.D. '68): statesman; president of Taiwan, 1988–2000

Sanford Weill (A.B. '55): financier and philanthropist; CEO of Citigroup

Steven Weinberg (A.B. '54): 1991 National Medal of Science winner, and cowinner (with Sheldon Glashow, A.B. '54) of the 1979 Nobel Prize in physics

Paul D. Wolfowitz (A.B. '65): U.S. deputy secretary of defense, George W. Bush administration.

For all that, Cornell does not rest on its laurels. It prefers to look at the future—and what it sees (with an electron microscope, one presumes) is nanotechnology. In 2003, the National Science Foundation created a thirteen-member national consortium as the National Nanotechnology Infrastructure Network (NNIN), the world's largest nanoscale laboratory. The consortium will let university students and researchers, as well as scientists from corporate and government laboratories, have open access for studying molecular processes. Leading this effort is Sandip Tiwari, a professor of electrical and computer engineering at Cornell.

CLINGING TO THE PAST—
MARK TWAIN, 24/7

But as Cornell's magisterial visions of molecular engineering represent the future, poor Elmira carefully guards its past. Everything about twenty-first-century Elmira seems to center around America's most famous nineteenth-century author, Mark Twain, whose ties to Elmira date back to the 1860s.

In 1868—coincidentally, the same year Cornell opened its doors—Twain met his future wife, Olivia Langdon, at her Elmira house on the corner of Church and Main Streets. For many years, the couple divided their time between Hartford, Connecticut, and Elmira, New York. In a study at his brother-in-law's farm outside of Elmira, Twain wrote many of his most famous works, including *A Tramp Abroad, Life on the Mississippi, The Adventures of Tom Sawyer, The Adventures of Huckleberry Finn, The Prince and the Pauper,* and *A Connecticut Yankee in King Arthur's Court.*

According to the city of Elmira Web site, Twain "was often seen roaming the streets of the city looking for a billiards game, or someone to chat with."

The one thing the author apparently never did was swing a golf club, but that hasn't stopped Elmira from naming its public eighteen-holer the Mark Twain Golf Course, thus joining a long line of Elmira enterprises sucking off the author's white-suited, cigar-twizzling celebrity. Indeed, the name of Mark Twain appears about as many times in the Corning-Elmira-Horseheads phone book as it does in the phone book for Hannibal, Missouri, Twain's birthplace.

The collapse of upstate New York's manufacturing-based economy . . . from Buffalo to Syracuse . . . Schenectady to Albany . . . Binghamton to Corning-Elmira-Horseheads . . . has been well remarked, and I have nothing to add on this subject. Except to say that it has taken on a psychological element, as all economic depressions do (which is why they are called depressions, one supposes). The dysfunctional symptoms are seen in characters like Jack at the Horseheads bar, drinking his beer and raw eggs, and in Elmira's hugging of Mark Twain's ghost.

Still, if you take a contrarian view of this, you can't help but wonder if fortune won't favor Corning-Elmira-Horseheads in the coming years. It is, after all, a pleasant setting, tucked away in the Appalachian Mountains near the Finger Lakes. Housing prices are ridiculously cheap—30 percent below the national median, according to Coldwell Banker. If so inclined, you could swap your suburban Boston crackerbox for a ten-acre gentleman's vineyard in the Chemung Valley. And there is that huge intellectual capital gold mine of Cornell University just thirty miles away, if anybody down here bothers to notice.

P riorities change for people transitioning from their twenties to their thirties as they have families and become more homebodies. Therefore, fewer parties, shows, museums, et cetera, in lesser-known places doesn't matter that much since many would rather be home playing with children or doing yard work.

Having grown up in Westchester County, New York, which was more middle-class then than it is now, I knew back in the early '80s that I was better off remaining in the upstate Albany area where I was attending college than returning home and slogging away in New York City like most of my siblings were at the time.

Now, praise the Lord, I have a house that fits four children, with a two-car garage and a deck, on a full acre of property in Rensselaer County, just eleven miles from downtown Albany, with no Hudson River bridge tolls and children in an affordable parochial school. My visiting siblings from New York City, Washington, and L.A. had to spend considerably more for comparatively less in their respective metropolitan areas.

PETER MURPHY
West Sand Lake, New York

WESTWARD TO MINNESOTA

I departed Elmira with a plan to fly along the northern edge of Ohio, skirting Lake Erie and heading for Chicago. But, about twenty miles east of Cleveland, while cruising at 8,000 feet, I got a harebrained idea. I was feeling confident . . . which is not necessarily a good thing while flying a small plane . . . and I asked air traffic for an en route change, a fairly sophisticated thing to do. I keyed the microphone and announced my new plans; I now wanted to land in Muskegon, Michigan. From my view out the airplane's window at 8,000 feet, the weather had looked clearer up north than it did toward Chicago. The Skyhawk's 180-horsepower engine had been running like a top throughout the trip, so I felt okay about flying over Lake Erie. Air traffic control obliges—that's what midwesterners are, obliging—and tells me to stand by for a new routing.

Using a disposable mechanical pencil—the perfect writing instrument in a cockpit (because you can clip it to your shirt pocket, and it won't leak)—I write the clearance on a yellow pad. Then I get out my map, trace the new routing with a yellow highlighter, punch the waypoints into my GPS, and I am off and running.

Whew.

I sail over the southwest corner of Lake Erie at 8,000 feet, directly over Detroit's downtown, and then make a westward jog toward Muskegon on the shore of Lake Michigan. During the last hour of this four-hour flight to Muskegon I do math exercises, calculating my fuel burn against that which remains in the tanks. It's also something to do. It takes my mind off a more pressing concern—the need to pee. I have never run the Skyhawk's gauges this low, and when I touch down in Muskegon, only eight gallons remain in the tanks—about the same, it feels, as has accumulated in my bladder.

A satisfying leak and club sandwich later I hop back in the Skyhawk, depart Muskegon, and fly north along the Lake Michigan shore, climbing until 10,000 feet before turning left over the lake. The higher altitude will give the Skyhawk a longer

gliding range if the unthinkable happens and the engine quits
over water. Those eighty miles across blue water are nerve-
racking. Above Green Bay on the Wisconsin side, I take photos
of the Lambeau Field football stadium, home to the fabled
Packers. The stadium is undergoing renovation, and below I can
make out construction cranes and trucks.

But now it's midafternoon. Right on schedule, a few of those
puffy cumulus clouds directly ahead of me begin to grow taller
and darker by the minute—thunderstorms in the making—as if
ordained by script. The speed of Midwest weather change is
amazing to see. I ask for a diversion to the north to escape. The
new routing forces me to enter the jaws of a white cloud whale.
For the next ten minutes I'm flying blind. My hands sweat. My
butt squinches. The minutes pass slowly. Suddenly the clouds
shred apart and they're gone and I begin the descent into Flying
Cloud Airport in Eden Prairie, a Minneapolis suburb.

HOT SPOT IN COLD COUNTRY

Dinner tonight is with Graeme Thickins, a local technology
writer and consultant who makes it his specialty to connect the
high-tech Minneapolis crowd to the high-tech trade press and
rumor mills that mostly exist on the urban coasts. Graeme has
made us reservations at Redstone American Grill, which he calls
a "hot spot for the Minneapolis tech and entrepreneur crowd."

Did Graeme really call it a hot spot? Does that expression
apply in the bust year of 2002? It sounds so 1999 to my jaded
ears. But Graeme nails it. We walk into a joint that is loud and
crowded. We have to wait thirty minutes to get our table. It
indeed feels like a Silicon Valley or Manhattan or Boston Back
Bay restaurant in '99, yet it is happening during the very depths
of the Great Bust. Either Minneapolis has dodged a bullet and
the economy is good here or . . . or word of the tech bust has
been verrrrry slowwww to arrive, by dogsled perhaps.

I ask Graeme about it. He says Minneapolis is a balanced
economy, anchored by large companies in older industries, such
as General Mills and Cargill in food processing and 3M in office

products, but is also spiced by start-ups in such hot fields as medical devices and bioinformatics. This broad mix cushions Minneapolis when a bad cycle hits any one industry.

Even the tech meltdown, so ruinous to northern California, has hardly scratched Minneapolis. Graeme's explanation: "We didn't benefit from the IPO boom of the 1990s. We are not suffering a psychological defeat from its absence."

We order another bottle of pricey Chardonnay and Graeme reels off the names of a half-dozen Minneapolis-area entrepreneurs in the computer storage field alone. One is Gary Doan, a liver transplantee and founder of Edina's Intradyn. It makes a $1,495 storage device that lets small businesses too cheap to pay for an IT staff protect their data like big enterprises, both on-site and remotely. Another is Tom Kieffer, whose young firm, Agiliti, has acquired three hundred customers as a "managed IT services provider," exploiting the technology's latest trend: on-demand or utility computing. Then there is Phil Soran, who sold his previous firm, XIOtech, to California's Seagate for $360 million. After taking some time off, Soran founded another storage company, Compellent, which has already raised $23 million from venture capitalists, more than any other technology start-up in Minnesota during the past two years. Graeme says his favorite is Clint Jurgens, who was raised on a farm in Nebraska and attended a one-room school. Four years ago, Cisco bought Jurgens's first company, NuSpeed, for $460 million. Now Jurgens is chairman of NeuStream, a provider of open-systems storage software.

Small cities are the way to go. I graduated from the Stanford Graduate School of Business last spring, moved to Minneapolis to start a small investment business with two family members, and bought a 4,200-square-foot house in a high-end, near-downtown neighborhood for less than a shoe-box starter home in Palo Alto, and am loving it.

I'm glad I moved from California back to the Midwest. My second child is due in six weeks, and the natural thoughts that percolate through a father's head continue to support the move I made.

I'm thrilled to be in the one place that has ever felt like home to me, thrilled about the environment I've created for my family, thrilled about professional challenges I'm able to pursue here, thrilled with the friends we've reconnected with and made, and thrilled about being close to my extended family. Mostly I am thrilled to be able to define a life for myself that lets me prioritize, properly, all of the above.

Finding one's best self, in my opinion, is one of the most important quests a person can pursue, and is obviously a prerequisite to being one's best self as often as possible. Even as a thirty-year-old entrepreneur and Stanford B-school alum, I still wrestle with choices I've made, and think actively about how I might mold my path to allow new expressions of that best self to emerge.

I married a social worker, and have started to appreciate the divergent value systems that honor the businessperson very differently than the highly personal, sometimes life-changing impact of a social worker. Obviously the financial honor in our society is widely divergent (appropriately so, I might add, just so you don't think I spent too long in California). But after learning from my wife's example and experience, and experiencing the joy I get from teaching and being with my three-year-old son and his friends, I'm not sure that I, as a rational, utility-maximizing capitalist, might not need to reassess whether my personal utility gets maximized by making a few wealthy people a few hundred extra basis points of return on their capital, or whether it does by changing the lives of a few young children.

I don't mean to imply California wasn't an environment in which I could pursue these same kinds of questions. But centers of wealth tend to place undue emphasis on wealth as a measure of status. The Bay Area in 1999/2000 had reached an excess in that respect I found quite disturbing. At least for me, in my circumstances, the Minneapolis community is where I feel much more able to consider paths in the quest for my best self that would have been difficult for me in the Bay Area.

JEB MORRISON
Minneapolis

All of Graeme's examples are so-called serial entrepreneurs—business start-up junkies. They made their first pot of money in Minnesota and elected to *stay* in Minnesota for subsequent attempts. Which says a lot about Minnesota.

"Yes, it does . . . they like it here," Graeme says. "None of them pulled a Ted Waitt and headed immediately to San Diego when they had made the big bucks."

I ask Graeme, a Californian who has ended up working most of his career in Minnesota and who now divides his time between the two states, to elaborate.

"The differences in the business cultures of the two states are marked. California is about starting trends," he says. "Minnesota is about making sure they're for real before getting too carried away. California has highly mobile tech employees, who are always tempted by an array of new opportunities. Minnesota is more about stability and longevity, identifying strongly with the vaunted Midwest work ethic."

Coffee arrives and Graeme continues: "On the other hand, California's start-ups know how to actively communicate the benefits of their technologies, early and often, to their advantage. Minnesota has a surprising conservatism in that regard, and almost an aversion to what they might think of as overly aggressive marketing. Which is too bad—because California's tech start-ups have the advantage of proximity to the powerful industry resources and influencers of Silicon Valley, not the least of which is a considerable force of media focused on its every move. Minnesota, on the other hand, has the geographic misfortune of being in flyover land, where most media people wouldn't be caught dead. The term Silicon Tundra comes to mind."

Graeme says he spends most of his effort working with Minnesota tech start-ups (more than seventy-five and counting) in helping them understand the brutal reality of needing to either (a) spend more money on travel, promotion, and media and analyst relations, or (b) come up with a marketing strategy that can somehow outsmart or outmaneuver their Silicon Valley competitors.

"Neither is an easy chore," he says.

"An overriding concept I try to teach them is that 'Silicon Valley' is, essentially, a mind-set. And, no matter where your tech start-up is located, you had better understand and be prepared to live that mind-set. Spend as much time there as you can, and continually network into it—with abandon. For the world of technology start-ups, the Valley sets the bar. You can only learn about it by being a part of it.

"With today's technology, if you can understand what the Valley mind-set is and live it, you can physically be anywhere." And, in fact, if a company can combine the spirit of Silicon Valley with the attributes of the Minnesota lifestyle and Midwest work ethic—along with a great technology, of course—I firmly believe it has a very unfair advantage indeed.

NO BAD DOGS

Minnesota is a famously liberal and tolerant state. A story surfaced in 2003 about a Fergus Falls drunk driver who'd killed four teenagers. The driver had twenty-four previous DUI convictions and still held his Minnesota driver's license! That's because Minnesotans believe in the "no bad dog" theory of human behavior. The Scandinavian Americans who populate Minnesota are deeply and existentially pessimistic yet paradoxically sweet-natured; they believe in blizzards of bad luck but not in bad people. It's no coincidence that the country's first successful treatment center for alcoholism and drug abuse is located in Hazelden, an hour outside of Minneapolis. Other places are quicker to give up on the troubled.

Taxes run high in Minnesota, but residents don't seem to mind too much because the taxes consistently show up in bicycle trails and parks—public amenities that outdoorsy Minnesotans love and use. But Minnesota is liberal in a midwestern-Lutheran-Scandinavian sense, which is far different than the hostile ecotopian attitude held by, say, coastal Oregon or Vermont. Minnesotans are too close to their rural heritage to not think work and enterprise are good. They like growth and vitality. But unlike stock-market-minded New Yorkers and Californians, Minnesotans take a very practical view about how growth happens. "Living here, you just expect that the goal of a company is to go forward one step at a time and attempt to make a profit," Graeme tells me at dinner. "We don't live for Wall Street events—IPOs and acquisitions."

Speaking of liquidity events, the restaurant patrons, I noticed, were ordering expensive bottles of wine—Silver Creek Merlot for $70. Graeme said that even in the tech bust years there was a tremendous sense of excitement. Not just in Minneapolis but in smaller towns nearby, such as St. Cloud, Brainerd, and Marshall, or in some of the towns of western Wisconsin—towns within a two-hour ring around the Twin Cities. Graeme says lakefront properties at some of the more popular resorts are just soaring in price.

Half a million dollar vacation homes.

In Minnesota!

Ya!

I am a lawyer who had lived in Southern California for twelve years (some up in L.A. and some in San Diego). For the past couple of years, business was getting tougher and more competitive, traffic was getting worse, and the cost of living was spiraling up. Worse, the school violence was getting out of control with two shootings in the last year alone. I have a daughter I was keeping in private school for kindergarten because I had no trust in the public schools. Earlier this year, it was reported that the average cost of a modest home went over $400,000. Not a fancy home, mind you, but a modest two-bedroom one.

My wife is from St. Cloud, Minnesota, which has a population of about 130,000 (including the surrounding communities). We vacationed here last Christmas, and I was introduced to an attorney who was looking to expand his practice to include my area of expertise. My wife and I talked about it between ourselves and with our daughter. It did not take long for us to decide to get out of the insanity of Southern California and move to the humble town of St. Cloud.

We love our decision. I am working for a small firm where everyone enjoys coming to work. My wife made a lateral transfer from her national telecommunications company and is working the territory that includes the northwest portion of the Twin Cities, stretching right to St. Cloud. My daughter is now going to the same school as did her mother and aunts and uncles (and has three cousins in the school as well). We are near my wife's parents and two of her siblings and their families. We recently bought a home and will get two to three times what we could have gotten in California for less than half the price. The people are friendly and a handshake actually means something.

What we like about St. Cloud: Being close to family, seeing my older daughter thrive in her wholesome learning environment, having the time and space to adopt two new children, not having to deal with the daily hustle and bustle of Southern California traffic (my commute is now 1.5 miles on residential streets), a much more relaxed atmosphere that has reduced stress greatly, the change in seasons, the helpfulness of Minnesotans instead of the selfishness I saw so much in Southern California.

What we don't like about St. Cloud: Our first winter in Minnesota was cold but not too snowy. If we are going to have one, let's have both! I miss my Southern California friends and have not had much opportunity to make new ones here (it seems to be much more family- rather than friend-oriented here), and I miss looking out my office window to San Diego Bay and the Pacific Ocean.

When I went back to San Diego (I was just there last month), it was terrific seeing my friends and my dad, who lives up in Long Beach and due to his health is not able or willing to come to the northern cold. I stopped in at a pub I used to frequent and saw many of the people I hung out with, and after the additional catching up, it was as if I had never left. I was happy to see some of my favorite restaurants and eat the food that was so familiar. On the flight home, I reflected and thought: I do have the best of both worlds!

I think moving to St. Cloud has greatly encouraged me to become my best self, both spiritually and circumstantially.

On the spiritual side, I am much more at peace with my beliefs in God and have become an active participant in the church choir. Lori and I both see the same thing happening with Annie, our seven-year-old who came with us from San Diego, and are trying to teach religion to the new ones. In St. Cloud, the church and such personal beliefs/morals are much more prevalent than they were in San Diego. I think I can attribute that to the slower pace as well as a much more cohesive feeling of togetherness and stronger family values (What can I do to help you? Instead of, What can I get for me?).

Financially, in San Diego, we would have never been able to afford our wonderful 2,700-square-foot two-story house in a nice neighborhood. Though we had a short setback with Lori changing jobs and me being the sole breadwinner, that is now solved with her new job. We had enough tucked away in savings to get through it.

I think Lori and I are much closer than we ever were in San Diego, and that our now-completed three-child family will grow and thrive together. She loves being close to her mom and dad, who though still relatively young and active (late sixties) are getting up there. She also spends more time with her two siblings who live here. I have a new little brother (brother-in-law, actually) and we get along wonderfully.

I have taken to the Minnesota lifestyle of fishing and hunting—though in the thirty-plus hours I sat in my tree, I never even saw a deer! All in all, we are very happy with this move to the rural environment, and feel we made what can only be considered a terrific decision. As I said, stress is down, weight is down, peacefulness is up, and I do have a much better sense of accomplishing something in this life.

J. R. SPANGLER
St. Cloud, Minnesota

CHAPTER 4

You *Can* Go Home Again

W hen I set out to write this book, I had a hunch that some adults who had grown up in small towns and subsequently had moved away to a big city—for the usual reasons of college, stimulation, opportunity, et cetera—might love to move back. Who doesn't feel the nostalgic tug of home and native soil now and then? But is such a move really practical? When I looked into this a bit further, I was amazed at what I found, starting in my own hometown at my thirtieth high school class reunion.

Sometimes, moving to places like Bismarck, North Dakota, can actually broaden your horizons, as I discovered when I met up with my classmate Connie Paraskeva, a former U.S. Department of State employee and now a self-styled "global democracy specialist." Thanks to information technology, in North Dakota Connie can focus on both career and family, and do so in spectacularly unique ways.

MOVING HOME TO SAVE MOM AND THE WORLD

In high school I was deathly afraid to talk to girls like Connie Paraskeva. Connie was blond and bouncy—perfectly located on the babe scale between cute and pretty. She was a varsity cheerleader as a junior in the glamour sports of basketball and football. None of this B-team, pom-pom-girl crap for Connie. She was A-team all the way. Not long ago I was sitting at home with my eleven-year-old daughter, watching one of those movies featuring the Olsen twins, Mary-Kate and Ashley. The twins were in Rome, all blond and bouncy—perfectly located on the babe scale between cute and pretty. That's what Connie looked like in high school.

She still does at forty-eight! Sometimes when you go to a high school reunion and you haven't seen classmates for thirty years, a guessing game takes place. Is that so-and-so? Gee, I think the bald fellow in the corner is the kid I used to throw snowballs at cars with in the seventh grade, but I'm not too sure. With Connie, there is no doubt. She looks exactly the same, except for some crinkles around her eyes and a voice that is oddly raspy and old-woman-like, maybe a delayed effect of her days as a cheerleader yelling in crowded gyms and on cold October Friday nights outdoors. Same taut swimming-pool lifeguard's body, though. Same blond hair hanging to midback and parted in the middle, as if she had walked out of a 1972 high school yearbook to be here.

I know this may sound funny, but I had to work up my courage to speak to Connie. Two stiff drinks helped. Courage, boy!

Parenthetical thought here: where did shyness go? It seems like shyness was epidemic among teenagers a mere generation ago and for millennia before that. Then, starting about, I don't know, 1993 or some damn year (too late for my nerdy adolescence) a tectonic shift occurred in American culture, and afterward not a single teenager has been afflicted with this crippling social disease. At least that's the impression one gets from meeting today's teenagers or seeing them depicted in movies or on television. I must admit, I am jealous as hell.

———

So here I am, forty-eight years old, a fairly worldly and accomplished guy (and with nothing at stake in this anxious flirting game as I am happily married to a cute and pretty babe myself), yet terrified out of my gourd at the thought of walking up to a high school cheerleader and . . . talking? Only talking? Come on! Courage, wimp!

Then I remembered that just the day before I had piloted my own airplane from Eden Prairie, Minnesota, to Bismarck, North Dakota. Departing Eden Prairie's Flying Cloud Airport that morning I had shown a remarkable courage that had bordered on insanity. Fog enshrouded the Eden Prairie airport, with sky conditions officially listed at one-quarter-mile visibility and ceilings of 100 feet. No planes were permitted to land. Very few had decided to gamble on a takeoff. Inside the Executive Aviation briefing room, pilots crowded around the computers looking for any hole in the satellite pictures, any hint the fog might be lifting.

I announced to the room: "Screw it, I'm going."

Me. The two-week-old IFR ace.

After obtaining my instrument routing from Flying Cloud Ground Control and taxiing out, I lined up, sucked in my breath, and pushed the throttle forward, thinking, *This is it. As of today, you're either a real IFR pilot with cojones or not. If you're not, you'll be dead in four minutes anyway.*

At 60 knots I lifted the nose and departed Flying Cloud's wet tarmac. Almost immediately I was in the fog, with no visibility. I kept the scan on the instruments, feeling calmer than I had any right to feel. Precisely at 3,000 feet the fog broke into white wisps and I was on top of what appeared to be a giant down comforter that stretched to the horizon in all directions. The sky was brilliant blue. I was indescribably happy.

Being in God's blue sky, floating above a giant down comforter, having just cheated death, took me to a very happy place—lying on a rug at home watching *Teletubbies* with my five-year-old son. I can't remember exactly, but I might have even sung the *Teletubbies* theme song as I piloted the Skyhawk on my way to my thirtieth high-school reunion in Bismarck, North Dakota.

Over the hills and far away.

"That was gutsy," said my instructor, Glen Davis, on the phone that night. "I don't know if I would have recommended that."

Preparing to talk to Connie Paraskeva at the class reunion, I let myself remember this wonderful immortal feeling, let it swirl around, let it send happy endorphin chemicals flooding into the cortex of my brain and say hello to the two vodka tonics already there. I suck in my stomach and walk up to Connie.

Where was that confidence in high school?

A WOMAN ALONE IN THE WORLD

At lunch the next day Connie told me her story. It's a strange story that nevertheless has an impeccable logic to it.

After high school, Connie did an unsurprising thing and went off to the University of North Dakota in Grand Forks, 240 miles away. Until she was a senior in college, all her life's dots seemed to connect in a predictable way. Summer lifeguard, cheerleader, solid A-student, University of North Dakota, and from there…well, from there she had no doubt gone off to law school, met a guy, got married, whelped three children, moved to a nice Minneapolis suburb like Edina where she joined a country club and campaigned for liberal goo-goo Republicans. Had Connie been a little less bright, I might have pegged her as the girl who married the quarterback, moved back to Bismarck, and helped her mate build a career selling insurance, managing a Chrysler dealership, or even running for mayor.

But Connie didn't do any of that.

Not long after Connie graduated from college she got lost in a blizzard in Grand Forks. When the snow stopped falling, her heater fell off her Subaru. Some larger force was telling her: Get out of North Dakota! She moved to Oregon and worked for the U.S. Labor Department, counseling migrant workers. But that didn't float her boat, either. One day Connie had an epiphany: "All of a sudden, I saw my life as a series of boxes. I lived in a box—an apartment. I commuted around in a box with wheels—a car. Every two weeks I got a box-shaped paycheck."

Connie says she realized right then and there she wanted a life of "constant change." She bought a book called *The Art and Adventure of Traveling the World Cheaply.* "The catchphrase I remember from that book is that real travel means you stop and buy, not just window-shop." With $2,000 of savings,

Connie set off on a global journey that would last three years. She bicycled around New Zealand for five months. She sailed from Australia to Indonesia as a hired crew hand on a sailboat. In Nepal she climbed a 21,000-foot mountain. She returned to Oregon from her trip three years later with $1,800—only $200 less than she had started out with.

"Were you ever afraid as a young woman alone in the world?" I ask.

"No," Connie says, "you follow a few simple rules. Leave yourself plenty of daylight. Walk with a sense of purpose. Never carry more in your backpack than you can run with. I had calculated this to be eighteen pounds. The money belt never leaves your waist. My eyes had been trained by my lifeguard years to spot trouble—who's loitering, what's out of place."

She is using these skills again. Up until May 2002, Connie worked for the U.S. State Department, in its U.S. Agency for International Development, working mostly in Africa and the Middle East to build institutions that foster democracy. Her actual title was "democracy specialist." She took armored cars to work in political trouble spots such as Kinshasa, Congo, and Monrovia, Liberia. In the Congo she saw the utter breakdown of family life because of AIDS. "There are orphans everywhere," she said. She shook hands with Yasir Arafat on the West Bank in Gaza. That particular experience would shake her world. "I am very pro-Palestinian," she says. "I have never felt safer than when I was among Arabs." Her stance was costly. "I used to get into the worst kind of arguments with my Israeli friends in Tel Aviv and even my conservative father back in Bismarck."

Listening to Connie at lunch I'm full of conflicted emotions. The crush I had on her has returned—Lord, has it!—yet Connie is someone whose politics I would skewer if I didn't know her. She's a wide-eyed idealist who "has looked into the eyes of Arafat" and come away trusting. Really, now? Speak that to the gravestones of the 1972 Israeli Olympic athletes. She professes admiration for billionaire do-gooders like George Soros, whom I regard as a pompous meddler. Months after our lunch I will learn from another Bismarck classmate that Connie went to New York during the spring of 2003 where she protested the Iraq War, was briefly detained, and called George W. Bush an idiot on TV—an impressive "three-fer" when you think about it . . . a sort of hippie hat trick. Then again, this is Connie Paraskeva the soulful cheerleader eating veggie burritos with dweeby old me. That counts for something. I decide I want to run away to Egypt with Connie and ride horses alongside the Pyramids at midnight.

GLOBAL DEMOCRACY SPECIALIST— OPERATING FROM A SMALL CITY

Today Connie subcontracts her "democracy specialist" services through a Washington, D.C., outfit called Pact to Booz Allen Hamilton and other firms that contract directly with the USAID. She travels the world as a consulting democracy specialist. Her first freelance gig after retiring from the State Department was with Booz Allen in Egypt. The astonishing thing is, Connie these days performs her sophisticated work from the utterly unworldly outpost of Bismarck, North Dakota.

"Yep, I've moved back home. My parents are getting old. My mom is sick a lot. I bought a duplex in Hillside Park, where I was a lifeguard."

Connie adds: "I spend roughly four months of the year each in Bismarck, Washington, D.C., and various overseas locations—but usually no more than about six weeks consecutively at any one place. This arrangement works for many reasons, not the least of which is that I keep a bike and pair of Rollerblades in both Bismarck and Washington so they're always on hand. Only wish I could do the same with my cats."

I ask: "Could you have done your work in Bismarck in the old days, pre-e-mail and pre-Web?"

"Absolutely not," Connie says.

Connie's work in international development involves as much communication with people located around the United States and the world as it does with her Pact headquarters office in Washington. In other words, it almost doesn't matter where she physically is when working. All she needs is an Internet connection "whether . . . in Bismarck or Beirut."

How does Connie keep up with world events?

"I pick up the *Economist* at newsstands since I am not in one place long enough to receive it at home. The *Washington Post* and *New York Times* online fill in a lot of the rest. Even in Mongolia I was able to keep up with the news."

What's it like working from good old Bismarck?

"I love looking out over my backyard in Bismarck while on the phone with a colleague in Madagascar, discussing a project for Mali, and then e-mailing a colleague in Indonesia, before turning my attention to another project in the Middle East or China. And then it's time for lunch and I go outside to see if my cats are up for some fun. Then I return to phone calls and e-mails that further jump me back and forth across time zones and datelines. When I have in-depth, analytic writing to do, I relish the quiet workspace, but for the odd cat strolling across my keyboard. And then, of course, the calls come from a few blocks away, when it's my old high school friend Jennifer checking in to plan a walk along the Missouri River or an evening at her log cabin—the simple pleasures rooted in history for which I longed when I lived so far away."

"I PREFER A LIFE OF A THOUSAND DIFFERENT DAYS"

Before Connie moved back to North Dakota, she was lucky to see her parents twice a year. Now she sees them at least every six weeks. The value of this to her is priceless, particularly given that her parents are in their eighties. Nothing beats turning off her laptop at the end of the workday and heading over to her parents' house to talk about the little things that never seemed to make their way into conversations because of expensive overseas phone calls or short visits home. They also talk about the bigger things.

"Although my dad deserves a lot of credit for mellowing with the years, I'd like to think that this additional time we've had together helped us," Connie says.

"On my last trip home, we held our first-ever discussion about U.S. foreign policy in the Middle East (and it was even after the U.S. had invaded Iraq) from which neither of us stalked out in a disgusted rage. We actually discussed the issues calmly and heard each other out, which speaks volumes for two passionate Greek-Americans on opposite ends of the political spectrum."

Connie says her parents' health still permits them to remain quite independent. Still, her mom in particular says she feels more secure just knowing that Connie is in town and available for anything she might need.

"They have their own lives and are happy for me to stop by for a visit several times a week, but they don't need me with them every day. That's the beauty of it. With me around more often now, we don't feel the pressure to spend every moment together. We know there's plenty of time to spend together on weekends, and catching a few of Mom's favorite TV shows with her on weekday evenings now and then."

Connie continues on about her mother.

"My most exotic overseas adventures pale in comparison with the excitement I take in being able to do little things for my mom—the kind of things you can't hire someone to do while you're away—like picking up some of her favorite soup from the Wood House restaurant and bringing it home for her lunch."

It's comically bizarre to think of Connie trundling off to the Bismarck Municipal Airport on a cold windswept January morning, lining up at the Northwest Airline counter, checking her bags with some Swedish Meatball blonde who says, "You betcha!" every two minutes, boarding the plane . . . and emerging in Cairo, Egypt, eighteen hours later. But that's her life. Tilt your head as if there is something unorthodox about her life and Connie just looks at you and throws the challenge back.

"Do you want to live a thousand days, all the same? Or a thousand different days? I prefer a life of a thousand different days."

I'm a thirty-something, stay-at-home mother of four. I have lived in Dallas, Mexico City, Hawaii, Omaha, Southern California, Jinan (a medium city of three million on mainland China), and, finally and most happily, in Fort Worth.

Here we can manage cheerfully on a single $65K income. My husband, a programmer, turned down an $85K job in Dallas. It would take a much bigger salary hike than that to even tempt us to move.

Our house is 2,200 square feet, with four bedrooms and two baths, and a great yard with big trees (a necessary feature when raising three boys). We have great neighbors and live in a pleasant established community that is in a convenient location for the family, with only an eleven-mile commute to downtown for my husband. The house cost less than $110K (and, thanks be to God, there are less than four years left on the mortgage).

We like Fort Worth because it is convenient and affordable, but we LOVE Fort Worth because it is a terrific place to raise a family. We have incredible (and mostly free or very inexpensive) museums and lots and lots of parks. Our new Bass Performance Hall is rated as one of the top ten opera houses in the world. There are junior sports leagues of every variety, strong churches, and so on.

For educational reasons, Fort Worth has been a great blessing for our family. We homeschool our children, and Texas has the most liberal (in the old-fashioned sense) proparent educational laws in the country. There are large homeschool support groups in the area and major curriculum fairs each year, and homeschoolers are perceived as a positive segment of the population. Here it is Cool to Homeschool. Even the local public high school treated us with great respect and consideration when I needed to register three of my kids to sit for the PSAT exam.

Paula Olson
Fort Worth, Texas

CHAPTER 5

Smashing Small-Town Stereotypes

The middle-aged man with shoulder-length hair, a T-shirt, cargo shorts with big pockets, and Teva water sandals sharing a pizza with me looks like a guy who follows the Grateful Dead around in a VW bus and earns his keep selling brownies laced with marijuana.

In fact, Doug Burgum is:

1. Head of Microsoft Business Solutions Group
2. Boss to 3,800 Microsofties from his most unlikely base of Fargo, North Dakota
3. A centimillionaire
4. Half nuts

Doug's current hobbyhorse is to persuade state legislators to drop the North from North Dakota because he thinks North gives folks the misbegotten idea that his state is forlorn and freezing, an American Siberia. Well, no kidding! But irrepressible Doug, who built a scrappy, world-class software company in North Dakota, took the company public, and sold it to Microsoft in 2001, insists his state is a hot place to launch an intellectual capital business such as software. Depends on how you define "hot," of course, but the Stanford Business School grad who returned home to North Dakota to make his fortune may be right.

No, Doug Burgum doesn't fit the stereotype of the typical button-busting corn-fed midwestern businessman. He wears no suit jacket and no tie. He is not dressed in that Nordstrom casual cookie-cutter look typical of a Microsoft executive. Curly hair cascades around a rawboned face. Doug seems more like a guy who'd be selling puka shell necklaces on Duval Street in Key West than one who's running a subsidiary of Microsoft that sells accounting software to small businesses.

Doug certainly doesn't look like the guy who runs the joint, nor does he sound like it. Despite the fact that Doug leads the largest Microsoft workforce outside of the company's head-quarters in Redmond, Washington—3,800 employees, and seemingly growing by the hour—Doug's competitive strategy does not drip with images of eviscerating the competition. Instead, he speaks of feeding the soul.

"Ultimately, what people really want is to have meaning in their lives," he says over lunch.

This from a Microsoft boss?

ARTICHOKE PIZZA ON THE GREAT PLAINS

I had flown in to see Doug that morning, having departed from my hometown of Bismarck. The route took me straight east over Interstate 94, and the ride was eerily smooth in the July morning air. Over the town of Jamestown I circled its small Presbyterian school, Jamestown College, which fancies itself as a kind of prairie Princeton, down to the same orange and black team colors. This is where my dad finished college in the early 1950s. It is also where I ran several track races in high school, most of them poorly except for one redemptive 4:36 mile that qualified me for the state track meet . . . which happened to be in . . . the next town east, Valley City . . . over which I now find myself fifteen minutes after departing Jamestown. I look down and see the aqua-colored 400-meter track of Valley City State College. My one appearance in the North Dakota state boys' track meet, in 1972, ended in disaster on that track. I finished last in the mile, or almost so. Up front, three boys smashed the old state record of 4:20 (including one of my Bismarck teammates, who finished second in 4:19). I ran about a 4:48 or something. My memory still suppresses any further details of this derelict performance.

The landing in Fargo was tricky, thanks to a direct crosswind of 12 knots. Proper crosswind landing technique is not easily learned. You turn the plane's yoke into the wind while simultaneously depressing the opposite rudder pedal with your foot. That keeps the airplane aligned with the runway you intend to land on, even though you are banked over 15 degrees or so. The feeling is like driving along a ditch. The problem is, you can't actually land the airplane banked like this. If you do, you will scrape a wing on the pavement. So just before touching down, you take out the bank in one smooth motion—turning the yoke back to level while releasing the opposite rudder while pulling the power to idle while holding the airplane's nose high. That's a lot of stuff to do in one smooth motion.

On the ground, I gave myself a C+ for the Fargo landing. It was ugly—a series of little serrated motions rather than one smooth one—and the tires screeched a bit. But both the pilot and airplane escaped the ordeal unhurt.

Now I'm sitting in Doug Burgum's corner office next to a wooded area in the southwest part of Fargo. Doug and I are eating some kind of fancy deep-dish pizza with chicken and artichokes.

Microsoft made Doug an instant centimillionaire the day in 2001 when the software giant purchased his company—then called Great Plains Software—for $1.1 billion. While Doug's own vast riches came from Microsoft's acquisition, vast numbers of Microsoft employees back at the software giant's headquarters in Redmond got moderately rich just by doing their jobs and sticking around. Some ten thousand of Microsoft's fifty thousand employees are thought to be millionaires today, thanks to Microsoft's wild stock ride in the 1990s.

Doug himself has ambivalent feelings about those riches. "Money is nice," he says. "Money gives you options. Money can sometimes take away worry. But ultimately at the end of your life what you're happy about is whether your life had meaning.

Did you influence people? Did you make a difference? Did you pursue the thing that was your best talent?

"The worst tragedy of life is you lived your life as an accountant when you could've been a great artist," Doug says over a bite of pizza. "Imagine if you had sidelined those plans because you didn't have faith it would work out or you just didn't know you had the talent. That would be horrible."

This seems like odd talk from a Microsoftie. But Doug's perspective was built in the forge of entrepreneurism. He's seen the hard times, as well as the flush. He knows both the putrid feeling that invades your body when there's a real possibility of losing your company, as well as the delirious high acquired when the world's biggest software company offers you $1.1 billion for it. It's given him some good perspective.

Or maybe this attitude owes to Doug being an outsider, a roll-up employee who never worked at Microsoft headquarters near Seattle. Doug is a native of Arthur, a farming community of four hundred people, mostly of Norwegian descent, some thirty miles from Fargo. He earned a degree from North Dakota State University before heading out to Stanford University to get an M.B.A. After graduating in 1980, he took a job with McKinsey & Company, the world-renowned consulting firm, in its Chicago office. It was a world-class job and Doug loved it. He liked the cosmopolitan aspect of Chicago. His biggest client, Steelcase, was an easy trip across Lake Michigan in Grand Rapids. He had a great time for two years until he woke up one morning and felt . . . lonely. In particular, lonely for North Dakota. Doug loved growing up in Arthur and he loved North Dakota. There were vast tracts of land on his farm and he and his brothers fished, hunted, and raced snowmobiles. As much as he loved Chicago, he realized that North Dakota was home.

In 1983, Doug left the Windy City and headed back to Fargo. He'd been reading about the burgeoning personal computer revolution, and he joined up with some friends who were running a retail chain of two stores, called Great Plains, that was selling the Apple II personal computer. Doug was so pumped at the sales potential of the chunky beige machine that he bought

4 percent of the chain for $250,000. In a symbolic shift from the agrarian to the tech economy, he mortgaged the family grain elevator in Arthur to get the cash. It was a spectacularly dumb move in many respects. By paying a quarter-million dollars for $\frac{1}{25}$th of Great Plains, Doug had bizarrely calculated the two-store chain was worth $6.25 million. Perhaps Stanford should have refunded the money on his business degree.

DOUG'S GAMBLE ON SOFTWARE

The move seemed even crazier a year later when Apple introduced the breakthrough Macintosh computer and orphaned the Apple II. Not only had Doug wildly overpaid for his share of Great Plains, but the store's product line was now irrelevant. "We were in a world of hurt," Doug said, looking back with the bemused comfort of knowing that everything eventually turned out fine. But Doug had an idea. All along, Great Plains had written its own software to handle inventory management, accounting, and bookkeeping. It was good, efficient code, so why not sell it as a software application to other small businesses struggling with similar problems? The other owners wanted no part of the scheme and backed off. Doug bought control of the company, further mortgaging the family's luckless grain elevator. He rechristened the company Great Plains Software.

For the next several years, Great Plains made slow, steady progress. It didn't set the world on fire. It didn't crush the competition. It didn't get featured on the cover of a business magazine with Doug in a grim Superman pose, arms akimbo against a background of wheat. It didn't do any of that, but it also didn't go out of business, like most small companies do. In 1997, with Great Plains generating more than $100 million a year in revenue and making a profit, Doug took the company public. The stock opened at $14, doubled to $28 that day, and for the next four years never fell below its end-of-first-day price. When Microsoft bought the company in 2001, it renamed it Microsoft Business Solutions. Doug's operation in Fargo is now Microsoft's beachhead for small business software applications. Microsoft itself is enormously ambitious about this market. (Senior vice president Jeff Raikes told me recently, while we were scarfing down hot dogs in the owner's suite at a Seattle Mariners baseball game, he thought the market size for small-business software would soon reach $10 billion.)

The roller-coaster ride of Great Plains would never have been possible in Silicon Valley, Seattle, Boston, or New York. "We wouldn't have survived the hothouse environment," Doug says. "No way. If today's venture capitalists had invested, there would have been no patience for our growth, which was sometimes one step forward and two steps back."

FROM WEALTH TO PERSONAL FULFILLMENT

One of the great upsides of free-market capitalism, beyond the fact that it makes societies prosper more than planned economies, is that it allows people to pursue what they are good at. Capitalism means that people or companies can bring their skills—that which they are most passionate about—to the marketplace and then trade with other people or companies who are passionate about their skills: growing food or making clothes or building houses and cars. Capitalism doesn't always work out perfectly, and it never will, but it unquestionably offers people the most chances to find meaningful, rewarding work. It's easy to say that free-market capitalism creates soul-sucking organizations that are the antithesis of meaning. Not true. Capitalist organizations can have great spiritual meaning, as well as increase one's professional worth.

Today in the Turbulent 2000s, Microsoft, like many companies, is struggling to figure out what motivates the most talented employees within a free-market system. Microsoft, of course, had no such problem figuring that out during the Great Boom. Microsoft CEO Steve Ballmer liked to call the old motivational carrot The Deal. That arrangement worked like this. Come and work for Microsoft. Make do with a so-so salary but partake lavishly of stock options. Sure, you might be forced to grind away on eighty-hour workweeks for six or seven years. You may have to sacrifice health and family. But you'll get rich—wildly rich.

Then in July 2003, Microsoft announced it was chucking stock options in favor of restricted grants. An army of Microsoftologists parsed the move for deeper meaning. One analysis had it that Microsoft was merely acknowledging what Bill Gates's good friend Warren Buffett had asserted—that the early 2000s mostly likely would produce subpar returns in the stock market. If that turned out to be true, stock options would only disappoint employees and lead to bad morale at Microsoft. Another school of thought had it that Microsoft's move to restricted grants meant that that company now was fat and middle-aged, incapable of outgrowing the S&P index.

Doug Burgum offers a third interpretation. He thinks The Deal was always a regional phenomenon—a significant carrot for employees living in high-cost Seattle. Doug believes that many high-IQ workers in lower-cost cities would gladly trade wealth for personal fulfillment. Thus he thinks Fargo and places like it could become small hubs of new economic activity that's paired with personal fulfillment.

In California or New York, such talk of personal fulfillment is hastily dismissed as New Age or worse. But I think Doug is onto something.

Doug is the prodigal son who went out to get a better education, then returned home to build a local business. Microsoft founder Bill Gates did the same when he returned to his hometown of Seattle in the late 1970s when the local economy was in the pits. Michael Dell, too, kept his insight and entrepreneurialism in Austin, not far from the dormitory he lived in while an underclassman at the University of Texas, when he founded Dell Computer and created the made-to-order personal computer market. Like Gates and Dell, Doug Burgum has returned as the greatest asset to and proponent of his region. Great Plains, for instance, has a beautiful headquarters, built shortly after the company was acquired by Microsoft in 2001. The building designs are wonderful—two stories, lots of wood and glass. All the raw materials came from North Dakota. Doug insisted on that. Quite remarkably, Fargo now hosts the second-largest Microsoft workforce in the world, trailing only the company headquarters in Redmond.

Doug's employees are mostly local kids, the grandchildren and great-grandchildren of austere and hardscrabble Norwegians and Germans who immigrated to the northern central plains a century ago. Until just a few years ago, the state had a hard time keeping young ambitious people. The employment opportunities in the Dakotas weren't that compelling compared with Minneapolis, Chicago, or Denver. The featureless expanse of North Dakota pales when compared to the electricity of New York City or the cocoa butter beaches of the West Coast. North Dakota doesn't have the cool factor of Alaska, or any nationally recognized recreation spots like Montana. No Hollywood actors or tech billionaires make their vacation homes in Fargo. The one movie of recent note that even mentions North Dakota is *Fargo*, which spoofs the region's whole character. You can't think of a more obscure state in the public's imagination than North Dakota. Subsequently, the population of North Dakota reached the mid 600,000s in the 1920s—and it's still there. It hasn't gained a net person in eighty years. The four largest towns have grown in population, the next three or four towns have more or less held steady, and everywhere else there has been small-town carnage.

That wasn't always the case. For nearly two centuries, one of the cornerstone American dreams was to settle the heartland. In the 1840s Horace Greeley, the founder of the *New York Tribune*, encouraged his readers to "turn your face to the Great West and there build up your home and fortune." In 1851 John L. Soule, editor of the *Terre Haute* (Indiana) *Express*, wrote the clarion call of the day—words later erroneously attributed to Greeley—when he penned: "Go west, young man." Hundreds of thousands of people took his advice. One of the most famous images of the Anglo expansion of the day was an 1861 painting by Emmanuel Leutze (himself, ironically, a German national) that showed excited Eastern emigrants, some in midwhoop and others poised like heroic Greek statues, surveying the noble distant land from a hilltop. It's title: *Westward the Course of Empire Taken Its Way*. The advice was still being greedily devoured a century and a half later by a new generation of people, this time packing computers and AOL accounts, instead of cornmeal and gunpowder.

That philosophy, however, also gutted the country's interior. Today, much of the Great Plains is undergoing a catastrophic demographic collapse. The Great Plains stretches 1,600 miles from central Texas to the Canadian border. It's 750 miles across at its widest point, and contains all or most of ten states. This vast heartland accounts for one-fifth of the land area of the United States, but only 4 percent of the population—about 12 million people. To put this in perspective, the population of metro Los Angeles is greater than that of the Great Plains, though the latter comprises an area five times the size of California.

But 60 percent of the counties in the Great Plains declined in population during the last decade. Many heartland communities face the prospect of becoming ghost towns, as older inhabitants die and younger residents move away. Some of these areas have even reverted to what the Census Bureau calls frontier territory, designated as an area with no more than six inhabitants per square mile.

The spread of tech and people like Doug Burgum could change that. In a second inland movement, wired professionals and well-paid service workers might make new lives in the Great Plains. The high-tech pioneers of the twenty-first century, unlike their agrarian predecessors, might be able to reconcile the myth of the heartland with the American dream.

In recent years, Fargo has reversed the inclination of talented young people to move away, suggesting that they stay because they now realize the long-term potential of the region. That's a big deal. The city's population grew 20 percent in the 1990s; its populations of young people ages twenty to thirty-four and those under seventeen rose by roughly 10 percent. Concurrently, a *Forbes* magazine study identified Fargo—as well as Sioux Falls and Lincoln—as among the twenty-five best smaller cities for high-tech companies.

FORTY THOUSAND STUDENTS
AND THE ROLLING STONES

Over lunch, Doug said that between North Dakota State in Fargo and Moorhead State across the Red River in Moorhead, Minnesota, he has access to twenty thousand college students. Include the University of North Dakota in Grand Forks, an hour's drive north (if you nudge the speed limit) and the student pool doubles to forty thousand. Recruiting hasn't been a problem. Software jobs are good-paying jobs. An annual salary of $80,000 is decent anywhere. In the relatively inexpensive northern plains, it's kick-up-your-heels phenomenal. Several Great Plains shareholders who did particularly well in the Microsoft buyout own summer cabins on nearby Pelican Lake, fishing the shallow waters in search of walleye. The success of Great Plains has even revived the local yacht club.

To the local community, Doug is a real hero. Not only has he given entrepreneurial glamour to an unlikely place like Fargo, but he's pumped up the local economy and quality of life. He donates huge amounts of money to North Dakota State. Fargo now also has a little panache, and has become more than a punch line. The Rolling Stones played there on a recent tour, as did Bruce Springsteen. Much of this snap and pop is because of Doug. The place would not have the economic vitality or be growing if Doug hadn't showed people how it could be done, and on a grand scale. He created a world-class company and proved that he could do a pure intellectual content business in the sticks. Not only that, he proved you could build to scale. He did this to the point that he could take it public and sell to Microsoft.

The key here lies in retaining what are increasingly rural America's most important assets: its distinctive quality of life and its young people. The Great Plains and Upper Midwest today are a kind of "brain belt," boasting one of the nation's highest levels of literacy and scholastic achievement, with Minnesota, North and South Dakota, Iowa, Nebraska, and Kansas almost invariably ranking at or near the top in national science test scores and in bachelor's degrees per capita.

These areas have spawned a series of successful technology firms, from Gateway 2000 to Great Plains Software, as well as a large array of smaller start-up companies. (A hot California start-up, Alien Technology, the leader in radio frequency identification chips, moved its manufacturing and R&D to Fargo in 2003.) Although these burgeoning communities are no longer really rural, they help prop up the economies of the surrounding rural areas and help keep younger people and their families close to home.

Too many regions try to set themselves up on a national scale, comparing themselves to the Silicon Valley or Wall Street. They spend a lot of money trying to do that, and generally it never works. Instead of trying to be the next Silicon Valley, they need to find out what works for them, and create a business and a lifestyle that reflect the pride and possibility of the area.

Role models in the United States tend to be athletes and entertainers—Phil Mickelson, Barry Bonds, Oprah Winfrey. But they can also be people like Doug Burgum, someone who looked out his window and discovered that gold doesn't always lie in the most distant of hills.

I live in Granite Bay, California (outside Sacramento, near Folsom Lake). After residing at 3000 Sand Hill Road in Menlo Park for a number of years, I moved my money-management firm, Legacy Capital Management, to nearby Roseville in 1996. We moved here for family reasons. The Eureka School District in Roseville/Granite Bay is one of the best public school districts in the country, when the return on investment is considered—test scores per dollar spent per child.

When I moved up here in 1996 the area was a financial backwater. Since our clients ($1 million minimum) come from referrals, I introduced myself to some of the local professionals (C.P.A.'s, attorneys). They didn't know the difference between a registered investment adviser and a stockbroker!

Have times changed in Sacramento!

In March 2000 I attended a conference in Sacramento put on by the Golden State Capital Network. Its goal is to replicate the "secret sauce" of Silicon Valley (networking the resources necessary to support organic entrepreneurship—attorneys, financiers, infrastructure providers, et cetera) in a series of conferences around northern California. Attendance was huge!

Entrepreneurialism is breaking out everywhere, including a third-tier financial town like Sacramento. When my friends at Sand Hill asked me in 1996 why I moved to the "hinterlands," my reply was . . . because I can. Many wish they had.

JOE MILAM
Granite Bay, California

DICK RESCH—A VEGETARIAN IN PACKER TOWN

As tech professionals move wherever they like and set up shop, they may be upending long-held beliefs about the critical mass needed to establish tech centers. They are also revising the typical thinking of what an organization looks like.

Those ideas were bouncing around my head as I departed Fargo and headed for Green Bay's Austin Straubel International Airport on a two-hour flight to see Dick Resch, who runs an office-furniture manufacturer called KI Industries.

I'm not exactly sure what the chief executive of a furniture company is supposed to look like, but I know it's not Dick Resch. Dick looked like he'd just breezed in from Marin County, California. He's an ultra-marathoner, a mountain biker, and a vegetarian, though he admits to sneaking a bit of salmon. What he doesn't eat is cheese—and this in a guy from Wisconsin—nor does he eat red meat. When we met, Dick was munching on soy nuts, drinking a vegetable protein shake, and massaging his thighs, sore from an eighty-mile bike ride the day before. He looked like the owner of a health-food-store chain, not an industrial furniture maker. He talked like one, too—he had a calm, a real serenity about him, none of that backslapping personality you think of when you're an urban coastal sophisticate picturing a midwestern CEO. For all I know, Dick is a Green Party member, for God's sakes. Everything about him said that you can't make these stereotypical assumptions anymore.

Dick was born and raised in Minneapolis. He went off to MIT in 1961, got his degree in physics, and polished off his education with an M.B.A. from Harvard Business School in 1963. During the so-called Go-Go Sixties Wall Street was exploding with activity—the Dow first hit 1,000 in 1966—and Dick had a front-row seat. But he didn't like it. It somehow didn't feel right to him on a physical or spiritual level.

A few years later, Dick discarded the J. Press suits and J. Lobb shoes of Wall Street to join something on the other end of the glamour spectrum: Krueger Metal Products. He was the laughingstock, one imagines, of his Harvard Business School class for abandoning the easy riches of Wall Street. The job took him to the backwater of Green Bay, Wisconsin. Krueger was a family-owned business and Dick got an outsider's 3 percent token ownership in the company. But over the years, he worked his way up and won the trust of the family. And when Al Krueger, the founder, died and the heirs of the company wanted to sell it, Dick stepped in and did a leveraged buyout in 1979. That's when he tapped his old Wall Street friends, raised a bunch of financing from a big-league roster that included Kohlberg Kravis Roberts, Citicorp, and Clayton, Dubilier & Rice and bought out the company. Dick then renamed the company KI Industries.

In 1988 Dick Resch and his managers did another leveraged buyout to win complete control of KI. Once more, Dick pledged his entire net worth. He now says these personal trials by fire are the basis of KI's financial discipline today. "I had a picture in mind of my family's going bankrupt if I failed. That's of a different magnitude than seeing your options underwater."

Today, management and employees own 100 percent of KI. Dick makes everyone buy their shares with real cash. Stock options do not exist at KI. An internal market governs the privately held company, and, happily for the employee-owners, the accounting firm KPMG has calculated a rising valuation for KI during each of the last twenty-three years. This despite KI's sales having slipped 5 percent a year during the 2000–2002 bust.

Having customers in a broad swipe of industry segments—education, government, and health care—ensured KI's relative success in a business-furniture market that collapsed in mid-2000. KI itself had a big exposure to technology clients. "Sun Microsystems did eighteen million dollars with us in 2000, and four million last year," says Dick. But KI's larger competitors, such as publicly traded Steelcase and Herman Miller, were hit much worse by the tech falloff.

TEACHING FINANCIAL LITERACY TO HIGH-SCHOOL DROPOUTS

Dick is no rube who just fell off the turnip truck. He isn't a guileless Pollyanna devoted to Green Bay just for the sake of it. He believes there is something extraordinary about the heartland worker. His manufacturing plans, too, show a similar sophistication. Some even take a page out of the work of Friedrich Hayek, the Austrian economist.

Hayek was the great libertarian who wrote *The Road to Serfdom* in 1944, and received the Nobel Prize three decades later. Hayek began thinking of companies and how they're put together, particularly the tiered big-company model. Hayek observed that small teams often work better than big teams. He mused that people are naturally socialistic within smaller groups. Hayek fixed the ideal size at about twenty, an amount not too dissimilar to the size of extended families, start-up teams, and military squads. At this size, everyone looks out for one another. They share knowledge. Time isn't spent making sure everyone is staying on the same page; rather, energy is spent making the music. More than twenty people, however, and that inner support begins to break down. This is one reason why socialism never works as a way of organizing a nation's economy—it can't be scaled up. Hayek thought it was a natural human impulse that small teams work the best. Consultant Tom Peters, too, has written about small-team efficacy in great length, particularly with design teams, innovation teams, tiger teams, and turnaround teams. When units grow larger than twenty people, individuals begin to start looking out for themselves more than the group, and managers need to motivate people differently.

Dick has organized Hayek's teachings into what he calls cell manufacturing. After Dick threw the Teamsters Union out in the 1980s, he restructured KI from an assembly-line structure into a design where a dozen or so people do everything on a piece of furniture within a cell. Team members—Dick has the good sense not to call them cell mates—wear colored T-shirts so they feel like part of these small teams. Every cell has its own little profit and loss statement. Every cell receives daily figures on quality, rejects, and even comments from angry customers.

"It creates a team," Dick says. "I think it's important that people work in units where they all know each other's names."

Dick took me on a tour of the factory floor. It's a spotless place. There are neatly arranged pathways and shipping lanes, which are given cornball monikers. It's "Quality Way" in one corner; "On-Time Express" in the next. Some cell groups may wear funny purple T-shirts. And their financials and quality-control information is posted outside of each cell. If a cell flubs it on customer complaints or by not using available scrap metal, the sin is posted! Monthly bonuses to cell members, called gain-shares, are based on each cell's results. "It puts a little competitive pressure on them," say Dick, "which they seem to enjoy."

The methods may be odd, but the financial results aren't. KI now boasts more than 3,500 employees and gross sales revenues of more than $600 million. It's got manufacturing facilities in Wisconsin, Mississippi, Kentucky, and California, as well as Canada, the United Kingdom, Germany, Malaysia, and Bene-lux. Dick says that KI gets more revenue per square foot of factory than any other company in its field.

The stunner about KI's workers is that they are, to a person, financially literate, although some didn't finish high school. Dick obsesses about financial literacy. Monthly, he makes team cell leaders attend classes on P&Ls, balance sheets, inventory turns, and the like.

By coastal urban standards, KI is not a spectacular success. It is a solid one, led by a New Age–sounding chief executive who fled New York and somehow turned up in Green Bay. Dick

Resch believes in the eternal values: fiscal discipline, worker education, community responsibility, the long view.

In short, the stereotypes are wrong. It's simply dated thinking that small-town people are narrow-minded or autocratic or that small-city business leaders resemble a warren of Babbitts. Surely there are dinosaurs out there, but that's not the type I saw. That's not what refugees fleeing the urban coast are looking for, either. They are looking for Doug Burgum and Dick Resch.

Since September 11, 2001, I'm even more convinced of the wisdom of relocating from Washington to Knoxville.

Let me give you some examples.

Our kids were young when we first moved here but not so young as to express their extreme displeasure at leaving the Washington, D.C., area for Tennessee. My son said that as soon as he was old enough he was going to go to college in California and never set foot in Knoxville again.

My daughter had dreams of going to college only in Boston or New England because her personality was much more northern than southern.

As years went by the kids began to actually savor the quality of life and the simple pleasures of Tennessee. To make a long story short, my son is now a senior at the University of Tennessee and is trying his hardest to find a position in marketing in Knoxville or close by. He can't imagine living anywhere else.

My daughter spent spring break of her junior year in high school touring the big-name private colleges and universities in Boston and environs—Boston College, Tufts, Wellesley, Holyoke, Skidmore, Middlebury, and Dartmouth. Then came 9/11 and suddenly being closer to home mattered. She applied early action to Vanderbilt and was accepted.

Which raises another issue.

Although terrorism can strike anywhere, it is my contention that terrorists like to perform high-profile acts in high-profile locales. Furthermore, in a town like Knoxville outsiders are more likely to be noticed . . . to stand out. It's likely to be a subliminal form of profiling but I assure you it is equal-opportunity profiling down here. These folks can spot a Yankee at ten paces. So there is a sense of safety and security here that really was underscored when the D.C. snipers were busy with their murder spree. My relatives and friends back in the D.C. area were frightened during that time and I felt comforted being here in this backwater.

Along those same lines there is a concealed carry law in Tennessee and a goodly percentage of the population is armed . . . especially at home. It makes the bad guys think twice.

There is another aspect of life here that I've not talked about; for want of a better term, I'll call it the "birds-of-a-feather" syndrome. There is a great deal of comfort to be derived from interacting with and living among people who share common values, ideals, ethics, et cetera. Sure, the people of Knoxville are a bit old-fashioned, particularly if they possess such quaint characteristics as gratitude, respect, sincerity, loyalty, and patriotism. If their preferences run more toward Bud and Nascar than foie gras and the Metropolitan Opera, well, so be it. Who is to judge?

But keep in mind that these are the descendants of the folks who came over the sea and the mountains and tamed this land, whose hard work and determination continue to make America great and whose sons and daughters continue to fight to preserve our liberties.

NAME WITHHELD BY REQUEST
Knoxville, Tennessee

We have most of the same stores you do in New York. I can get my Jaguar serviced in thirty minutes, and I have access to the largest wine collection in Texas, the largest cheese collection in the United States, and the best damn tortillas anywhere in the world. Want good meat? How about Buddy's chickens, which are grown thirty minutes from here. Fresh milk? There is Promised Land Dairies. Good steak? Well, this is Texas, after all. The absolute best. Fresh fish for your grill? The best red snapper, flown in fresh from the Gulf of Mexico daily. If you ever come to San Antonio, go to Central Market, which puts Zabar's to shame. Concerned about not being Jewish enough? We've got Chabad, Orthodox, Conservative, Reform, and a brand-new Jewish Community Center.

ALAN WEINKRANTZ.
San Antonio, Texas

CHAPTER 6

Searching for the Winning Formula:
A Tale of Two Cities

In the ancient world, the Library of Alexandria in Egypt was a special place. Like Aristotle's Library in Athens, it was designed to hold the collected knowledge of the world. For several hundred years it did just that. Its more than 400,000 scrolls were the first systematic and serious collection of documentation on physics, literature, mathematics, medicine, astronomy, biology, and engineering. The only trouble, of course, was that you had to physically *be* in Alexandria in order to tap into its resources. That meant either walking across untold miles of waterless desert or hauling yourself there on a donkey. Plus you had to be an accredited scholar to get in. No library cards were issued. It just wasn't that convenient.

While subsequent learning centers achieved a similar celebrity for their expansiveness—the Celsus library at Ephesus, the library of the Vatican, Oxford's Bodleian Library, the Library of Congress, and the New York Public Library among them—they all were tough to access for the average guy. Until the Internet came along. The Internet has created the greatest assemblage of knowledge the world has ever seen. From the highest philosophizing to the dopiest political rants, from ancient books to silly blogs, every form of information is available to anyone at any time.

That's done a few things. It's opened up our minds and widened our consciousness. It's expanded our knowledge and our compassion. It's narrowed the sophistication gap between the most urbane city center and the farthest desolate crossroads.

But access to information does not necessarily mean it will be readily absorbed. I discovered this on a humid summer day as I pointed the plane diagonally across Indiana toward Cincinnati. It's a town that made me realize that there are thousands of communities that will not be successful in their bid to gain new transplants from urban areas.

"A CARICATURE OF MIDWESTERN RECTITUDE"

My friend Rick Segal offered to show me around his hometown, Cincinnati. Segal founded and runs an advertising agency, Hensley Segal Rentschler, which performs work for so-called B2B, or business-to-business accounts. A big client is GE Aircraft engines.

Rick's talents have landed him several awards for his work. *BtoB* magazine has named Hensley Segal Rentschler its national agency of the year three times. Rick also was an early booster of Internet advertising, adopting a California-like fervor about the Net back in the 1990s. Maybe it's only coincidental, but 55 percent of Rick's advertising clients come from outside of Cincinnati, from places like Detroit, Boston, and New York. Could it be that Rick's vision about interactive B2B advertising is too far over the horizon for the locals? "Travel outside Cincinnati is a big expense for us," Rick admits.

I thought Rick Segal would be representative of an emergent, new Cincinnati, which is why I took up his offer to come visit. Too often, Cincinnati is the butt of disdain by the urban and liberal media. Novelist Sinclair Lewis used Cincinnati as his model for the city of Zenith in *Babbitt*. More recently the *New Yorker* and *New York Times* have taken endless delight in throwing spitballs at Cincinnati. Sensitive liberals back east were aghast when Cincy protested the display of publicly funded gay erotic photography by the late Robert Mapplethorpe. Yet more scandal fodder was provided by a former baseball team owner Marge Schott, who called her black ballplayers, including Ken Griffey Jr., "my slaves." In late 2003, an African-American man, Nathaniel

Jones, died after being beaten by police outside of a Cincinnati restaurant.

On the other hand, if Cincinnati didn't exist, the liberal eastern media might have to invent it. "We are a caricature of midwestern rectitude," Rick says.

———

My journey to Cincinnati began in Green Bay. I flew across the white-capped waters of Lake Michigan at 9,000 feet, praying my lone engine wouldn't burp and cause me to deadstick the airplane into the cold lake. Over land again, I continued down the western side of Michigan, home to chic furniture manufacturers such as Steelcase and Herman Miller, fine examples of the light manufacturing renaissance occurring in parts of the Upper Midwest, and Dick Resch's competitors.

Leaving Michigan, I crossed into Indiana. The skies remained perfectly blue as I flew atop Fort Wayne, a declining city of 175,000 that once hosted a National Basketball Association franchise (the Pistons, 1948–1957). According to the *New York Times*, the most expensive house in Fort Wayne sold for $800,000 in 2003. In Manhattan, those 800 g's might buy a two-bedroom condo in SoHo.

I was headed for Cincinnati's Lunken Field, nestled among the hills of the Ohio River Valley. Afternoon cumulus clouds by now had gathered and the descent below them into Lunken Field was bumpy and nerve-racking. I landed on Runway 21R, 3,800 feet of asphalt and 100 feet wide—a sweet landing salvaged from a choppy approach. Lunken used to be Cincinnati's main airport. It is now an FAA designated "reliever" airport, a cute throwback overshadowed by the bigger and more sprawling Cincinnati/Northern Kentucky International Airport fifteen miles south. (Flying a little four-seat airplane, I was part of the Lunken proletariat.)

Cincinnati boasts plenty of good attributes on paper. Christened the "Queen City of the West" by Henry Wadsworth Longfellow, Cincy has a nice midrange population of 380,000 with a real urban downtown, while the greater area population measures about 1.5 million. Cincy sports two major-league ball clubs, the resurgent Bengals in the NFL and the legendary Big Red Machine, the Reds, playing professional baseball. Sparkling new stadiums house both teams.

Lying on the southwestern edge of Ohio, Cincinnati enjoys a welcome southern breeze coming up the Ohio River Valley that eliminates the icy claw of the north. The Ohio River provides recreation, and low hills cover the landscape, relieving Cincinnati of the dreary flatness of the plains. House prices mirror the national average. Universities dot the region. The University of Cincinnati and Xavier University are within city limits, while the University of Kentucky and Miami of Ohio are each about an hour away. In total, more than a hundred thousand four-year college students reside within sixty minutes of Cincinnati, a hopeful sign of future growth. Anchor companies include Procter & Gamble, Kroger, and GE Aircraft Engines.

The Cincy locals are said to be hardworking and industrious, a product of the German-American culture that loves making things. Cincinnati borders Kentucky, so there's also a hint of the South, both in the accents and the attitudes. But, oddly, it's not the New Information Age South—the high-powered, integrated, and forward-looking South that Atlanta or Research Triangle in Raleigh-Durham invoke. The more time you spend in Cincinnati, the more you come to realize you are in the old conservative South, implausibly retreated all the way up into the Ohio River Valley. Cincinnati thus can appear slow to accept new changes, never on the cutting edge. At least that is its image. Perhaps, as Segal said, it's an unfair one. I wanted to check it out myself.

THE VILEST RACIST JOKES
YOU CAN IMAGINE

I made plans to meet up Rick Segal the next day. After checking into the Holiday Inn Crowne Plaza downtown, I needed to unwind, so I hit the hotel bar for a few Corona-and-limes. The availability of cold Corona beer served with a slice of fresh lime wedged into the bottle's neck is my own admittedly narrow test of urbane sophistication. Ah, here they come, liquid gold! Cincy passes its first test. I'm feeling good about the Queen City.

Pretty soon a guy walks into the bar. He's good-looking, thirty-something, healthy—a guy straight out of an outdoor clothing catalog, with a stunning girlfriend to boot. He sits down and announces to everyone and no one that he's a former Indy race-car driver. I can't tell if he is kidding or not, but he looks the part. He buys drinks for everybody and within five minutes he starts telling . . . the vilest racist jokes you can imagine. The jokes involve apes and black women. The whole episode is outrageous, provoked by nothing. Bar patrons laugh nervously, but no one leaves. So I do. I don't mind jokes with a racial edge if they have a kind of irony about them or if there isn't a hatred or ignorance lurking beneath. But that wasn't the case with this yahoo. The jokes were crass and insulting, and the incident made a bad first impression.

It also had me wondering about the zeitgeist of Cincinnati. How could a guy just walk into a bar and launch into insulting jokes without expecting to be shown the door? We were not drinking in some backwater American Legion outpost, or on a southern plantation turned dove-shooting club. No, these were all strangers in a public place. I'm not saying that the average Cincinnatian approves of this, but the bar certainly didn't cre-ate an atmosphere that would disapprove it in a way that it would preempt it. I walked out of the bar, rattled.

The next day I met with Rick. I didn't mention the episode in the Crowne Plaza bar, preferring to hear about the good side of Cincinnati. Rick ticks them off. You hop a Delta Airlines jet for a day's work in New York City and return that evening to your $324,000 five-bedroom mansionette in the leafy suburb of Hamilton—in time to tuck in the kids.

Procter & Gamble gives Cincy a world-class marketing aura. If you have a choice between getting your M.B.A. in marketing from Northwestern University or working in the P&G trenches to launch a new breakfast cereal, take the P&G stint every time. You'll learn more. Three billionaires in the high-technology field can attest to their superlative on-the-job training at P&G: Steve Ballmer, chief executive of Microsoft (P&G: 1976–1978); Steve Case, founder of AOL (P&G: 1980–1981); and Margaret Whitman, chairman and CEO of eBay (P&G: 1979–1981).

Yes, Rick, I say. But they all *left* Cincy and made their names and billions in Seattle, northern Virginia, and Silicon Valley. Rick counters that Cincy has plenty of local entrepreneur heroes, such as Dick Farmer of Cintas. Farmer started his business by picking up dirty rags at gas stations and washing them. Today Cintas is America's largest uniform rental company. Another hero is Carl Lindner, current owner of the Cincinnati Reds. Lindner began his career selling ice cream cones. Now he runs a global empire of grocery stores, insurance companies, and banks. "That's the local entrepreneur model," says Rick. "Shirtsleeve guys, big philanthropists."

Rick says that in his field, B2B advertising, coastal glamour is not an asset, but a distraction. What clients want from Rick is straightforward help in selling products, not glamour—industry to industry, mano a mano. Rick calls it narrow-minded marketing, a neat bit of irony meant to play upon East Coast prejudices about Cincinnati.

What about the snooty New York perception that Cincy is redneckville? Any truth to that?

Rick says, "A lot of it is a bad rap. We are extraordinary about keeping pornography out. Notice that Larry Flynt does not live here anymore. Sheriff Simon Leis Jr. is a hero to most people. He's the guy who ran the Mapplethorpe exhibit out of town."

What about race relations? Rick folds his arms and doesn't speak for a minute. He's heard this rap before—and he doesn't like hearing it again from me. Finally Rick says, "People around here work hard. They don't buy into the victim culture." What about Marge Schott, the one who called her black ballplayers "my slaves" and was a collector of Nazi memorabilia and Doberman pinscher dogs. Was she representative of Cincy?

"A loose-mouthed old drunk is closer to it," Rick says.

Well, maybe. Rick is a good friend, blameless, and I don't press the issue.

The next day I walked to Riverfront Stadium, in its final season before a teardown, and bought a scalped ticket to the Reds baseball game. I sat in the third row behind the third-base dugout. Curiously, I noticed that there were no blacks sitting in the better seats. Later, I strolled around the downtown. I saw very few African-Americans who weren't doing some sort of menial job—shining shoes, opening doors, and so forth. And a nasty thought began to creep into my head: Why would an immigrant want to live in Cincinnati? Why would an Asian or an East Indian or a West Indian or anyone who wasn't white-bread like me or Rick Segal want to live here? Why would a gay man or woman select Cincinnati of all places in the glorious American tapestry? Why pack your bags for Cincy when you could go to Columbus, which has a Big Ten university and is more open and tolerant?

Indeed, what to make of Cincinnati? Good on paper. Full of intelligent, bighearted people, like my friend Rick Segal. I would include the maligned Sheriff Leis. We should applaud Cincy's gutsy attempt to declare war on slime merchants like Larry Flynt and push porn off the streets—yes, even the arty kind found in Mapplethorpe's photos of bullwhips shoved up men's rectums.

Then again, don't you detect that Cincinnati seems a little too eager to link pornography with gay lifestyles? Perhaps the city leaders should take a page from New York's former mayor Rudy Giuliani, an ardent porn fighter himself. He supported gay rights.

That's an important distinction. The bad press emanating from New York media no doubt is responding in kind to the antigay vibes radiated by Cincinnati during the Mapplethorpe dustup. The eastern press is less than honest about its real reasons for constantly attacking Cincinnati. Shame on them. But on the whole, I think Cincinnati has further to go than its critics. Minneapolis, to pick a city of similar size, enjoys a more robust and diverse economy. Minneapolis, like Cincy, is full of midwestern rectitude. In fact, there are not many places in the urban United States where you can hear a religious invocation delivered before a civic lunch. Minneapolis is one of them. But Minneapolis also is tolerant, even accepting, of racial and sexual diversity. In a competition for talent, Minneapolis will have an edge over Cincinnati, especially for the talent needed in the twenty-first century: cognitive, creative, and courageous enough to challenge the status quo. To the degree that Cincinnati repels such talented people who happen to be dark, foreign, or gay, the city will lose out. Thus good Cincinnatians like Rick Segal will discover that more than half their business always seems to come from outside of the Queen City.

———

After the Reds ball game, the pregnant dark clouds broke open and poured rain for the next two days. I am willing to fly the Skyhawk in light rain, but not in the heavy stuff, and so I sat around the hotel for most of the day, pondering the "Cincinnati question" and wondering if I had evolved into yet another one of those hated coastal liberal snoots, despite my own conservative leanings and midwestern roots. Then I remembered a story I was told about Cincinnati and Henry Ford. In 1915, the Detroit car mogul was considering Cincinnati as a secondary manufacturing center. Ford's plan was to create a vast integrated car manufacturing facility here, and he believed that he should pay his workers enough to buy one of the cars they built. In his early years, before he become a crank and an anti-Semite, Ford was progressive.

As it turns out, too progressive. The Cincinnati town fathers ran the inventor out of town because Ford's plan was going to hobble their current pay structure, which was barely above slave wages at the time. So Ford went back to Michigan and put the plant along the Rouge River west of Detroit. The River Rouge plant ultimately included virtually every element needed to produce a car: blast furnaces, an open-hearth mill, a steel rolling mill, a glass plant, a huge power plant, and, of course, an assembly line. Ninety miles of railroad track and miles more of conveyor belts connected these facilities, and the result was mass production of unparalleled sophistication and self-sufficiency.

"By the mid-1920s," wrote historian David L. Lewis, "the Rouge was easily the greatest industrial domain in the world" and was "without parallel in sheer mechanical efficiency." Ford did create a branch sales and manufacturing presence in Cincinnati, but the real plum got away. The giant assembly plant could have been Cincinnati's, but it wasn't.

WINNING CIVIC FORMULA—
OPTIMISM AND AN OPEN MIND

American cities best poised to win the battle for talent will have, I think, a mix of centrist politics with a pro-growth attitude. By centrist I mean moderate southern Democrats like Bill Clinton (minus the obvious baggage). Or supply-side Republicans like Ronald Reagan, Jack Kemp, and Steve Forbes. Or even cheerful libertarian nut cases like Jesse Ventura and Arnold Schwarzenegger. What matters is that the politicians don't take politics too seriously and screw things up. Better to embrace the future and do so with a smiling optimism, an inclusive approach, a light touch on taxes and regulations, and a rakish glint in the eye.

A city that is both oppressively liberal and antigrowth—Portland, Oregon, for instance—is going to have a harder time. Instead, the Portland suburbs right over the border in Washington might become a real boom spot because Washington isn't afflicted by the ecotopian religion that damages Oregon's economy. Moreover, Washington doesn't have a state income tax. So entrepreneurs fleeing California's high costs and structural breakdown might never hit the brake in Portland, but instead continue on into southern Washington. This region could boom in the same way that southern New Hampshire communities like Peterborough grew in the 1980s when they welcomed entrepreneurs fleeing the Boston region.

Closer to the Silicon Valley, Berkeley, California, is antigrowth to a famously silly extreme. When you look at all the high-tech companies located in the East Bay, you soon realize that none are in Berkeley. That's really odd, considering what a rich resource the University of California is in town. Instead,

East Bay tech companies are sprinkled in nearby towns like Emeryville and Alameda, or down the road in Pleasanton, and San Leandro. But Berkeley is so hostile to capitalism that it routinely cuts off its nose to spite its face: I have a feeling Berkeley would bar trendy-lefty Ben & Jerry's Ice Cream from moving in if Ben Cohen dared to utter a word about displacing a derelict building that happened to be a place where homeless people slept.

Likewise, a town like Cincinnati is too conservative, in the hidebound sense of that word, for its own good. Cincinnati has all the attributes to boom—nice weather (if a bit wet in the summer), central location, major hub airport, a moderate tax and regulatory burden, German-American industriousness, a hundred thousand university students close by, and local success stories such as P&G, Dick Farmer, Carl Lindner, and Rick Segal. For all that, Cincinnati is not the star it could be. I have doubts that it ever will be. Instead, nearby Columbus and even comebacking Cleveland will do better. Cincinnati needs an attitude adjustment for the twenty-first century.

JONATHAN MURRAY— CLEVELAND MAKEOVER FOR CALIFORNIA FINANCE GUY

When the rain stopped, I hopped in the Skyhawk and flew from Cincinnati to Cleveland. If there is ever a town that gets a continual bum rap worse than Cincinnati, it's Cleveland—the punch line to a thousand jokes, the epitome of a Rust Belt town. There was a point when Cleveland's seedy reputation was richly deserved. The city was incredibly polluted, so much so that the Cuyahoga River—brown, oily, bubbling with subsurface gases—caught fire on June 22, 1969. A spreading oil slick ignited and two railroad trestles were scorched. Oddly enough, it wasn't the first time the river caught fire. A fire in 1952 on the Cuyahoga caused nearly thirty times the amount of damage, but the 1969 blaze landed on the front page of both Cleveland papers, and even *Time* magazine picked it up. Eventually, the river fire, with its seeming implausibility, became a rallying point for the environmentalists in their fight for cleaner water. The Clean Water Act passed three years later in 1972, while cleanup of the Cuyahoga River continues today.

Thirty years after the fire, however, Cleveland's image is still scarred. The fire was a metaphor for Cleveland's meltdown, the problems of an industrial Rust Belt town that was being left behind in the 1970s and 1980s.

My journey to Cleveland began that morning from Cincinnati's Lunken Field, the old main airport southeast of the city near the Ohio River. A forest surrounds this picture-book airfield, now home to corporate jets and single props like mine. I get my clearance, line up on Runway 3L pointed to the northeast, and go.

Flying toward Cleveland to see for myself, right now I'm 7,000 feet over Ohio's state capital and now largest city, Columbus . . . suburban and sprawling, not really a city at all. Under my left wing sits the massive Ohio State campus and its famous football stadium. I have an urge to push the Skyhawk's nose down, fly a few lazy circles, and take a closer peek at Columbus, but I can't. That's because today I'm flying an instrument plan under the guidance of air traffic control. I chose to fly IFR (instrument flight rules) not because of clouds, but because the airspace surrounding my final destination, Cleveland, will be a hornet's nest of activity—big jets coming and going into Hopkins International by the minute. Wishing to avoid jet traffic, I will happily trade my freedom for a professional air traffic controller's telling me where to go. As I enter Cleveland's thirty-mile radius "Class B" airspace, the controller directs me east of the city then out over the choppy whitecaps of Lake Erie before a final approach into the Burke Lakefront Airport.

The landing path takes me directly over the Cleveland Browns Stadium, the Great Lakes Science Center, and the Rock and Roll Hall of Fame and Museum. Man, is it windy! Only 500 feet above the ground, the Skyhawk pitches and yaws like a kite, and I have a brief thought that if I were to flip over and spiral in here, straight into the Rock and Roll Hall of Fame and Museum, my name might become immortal. I might live forever with Buddy Holly, another air crash victim, as the bozo who made the music die, if only for a day and only in Cleveland. But seconds later the wind dies, thank God, and I sail placidly onto Runway 6R at Burke.

One's initial impression of Cleveland is that it is a mini-Chicago . . . the lakefront, the urban density . . . with an emphasis on *mini*. Cleveland is small! In an hour of walking one acquires a feel for the whole downtown. It's tight, it's close in, it's vertical—when you're in it, you know you're in a real city, unlike sprawling suburban Columbus or midsize Cincinnati, which resembles another river city touched by the South, St. Louis.

Jonathan Murray, the object of my visit to Cleveland, grew up in Washington, D.C., and worked in New York City and eventually in Silicon Valley. In 1997, amid the froth of the tech boom, he and his wife and two children were living in Mountain View, a California suburb. It happened to be one of the most expensive cities in the country, for no other reason than that it was in the very heart of boomville, Silicon Valley. The Murrays' dinky three-bedroom condo with its '70s-style appliances and shag carpeting abutted a low-end shopping mall anchored by discount clothiers and a 7-Eleven convenience store. For all that, the Murray condo cost $395,000.

"THE IDEA OF PULLING UP STAKES DID NOT SEEM EXTREME"

Worse, Jonathan also had a nasty fifty-minute commute each day across the Dumbarton Bridge to his finance job at Spectra Laboratories in the gritty East Bay suburb of Fremont. When Spectra Labs was sold in 1997, Jonathan began looking around. But unlike most of America's job-worried, Jonathan saw it as an opportunity. He and his wife had not participated in the IPO Boom anyway, had not gotten rich. They wanted out of insanely priced California.

"It wasn't a hard decision," he says.

"Growing up in Washington, D.C., I never had a sense of belonging. So the idea of pulling up stakes did not seem extreme."

We are sitting in his downtown Cleveland office on East Ninth Street, where Jonathan Murray today is a venture capitalist with Cleveland-based Early Stage Partners. It's summer, but Jona-than, the newly minted financier, is wearing a dark business suit. He looks good in it, like he's been doling out money his whole career.

Jonathan continues on the theme of geography.

"I never thought location to be of overweening importance," he says. "After Liz and I decided to leave California, we decided we could make a life anywhere." Yeah, but why Cleveland, for crying out loud?

Jonathan explains. "Well, any city we chose had to be reasonably priced. My wife wanted to stop working. Second, we really like Cleveland."

"You like Cleveland?" I ask.

"Sure. Its problems are overrated, while its assets are vastly underrated. The symphony is world class. The art museum is world class. Case Western Reserve University and the Cleveland Clinic form the basis of cutting-edge medical technology."

Cleveland as an emergent medical technology center tickles Jon's investment buttons. His venture capital firm is small, with only $32 million under management—a peashooter by California or New York standards. It therefore has to focus, and it does, in life sciences and medical technology.

"Sounds good, Jonathan," I say. But then I repeat the cliché that while the Midwest may hold vast treasures of intellectual property and is virtuous and hardworking, it lacks entrepreneurial talent.

Not true, he says. Cleveland had a burst of entrepreneurialism a hundred years ago. Jonathan sees it coming around again. Echoing Graeme Thickins's words about Minnesota entrepreneurs in Chapter 3, Jonathan says the ethic among Ohio entrepreneurs and venture capitalists is "build to break even."

"That's an attitude the Midwest has always had," Jonathan

says. "It got to be old hat only because of the cheap money available on the coasts during the boom."

Jonathan says Cleveland has become a destination for other Californians sick of the high costs. A local start-up called Athersys, the first to create synthetic chromosomes for use in treating obesity, asthma, and cancer, recruited its entire management team from California. Its CEO, Gil Van Bokkelen, a Cal-Berkeley grad, was able to pull the top scientist in the field, Dr. Hunt Willard, from Stanford University. Another top scientist, Dr. John Harrington, was recruited from MIT in Cambridge, Massachusetts.

How has Jonathan Murray's midlife dash to Cleveland worked out? His new venture capitalist career hasn't provided the big payoff yet and it's too early to know if that will ever happen. But in the meantime, the Murrays have settled into a six-bedroom Georgian house in Shaker Heights.

They bought it for $350,000.

THE MURRAYS—ONE YEAR LATER

A year after my visit to Cleveland, I contacted Jonathan and asked him if he and Liz were still happy about their move to Cleveland. He wrote back a long e-mail.

"My circumstances haven't changed much, though my subconscious and conscious mind have continued to digest events. Cleveland and the Midwest in general are running contrary to national trends in areas in which I focus, including early-stage venture capital formation, entrepreneurship, and increasing support for entrepreneurship. This is a good trend for me and our business in the medium and long terms, but hard work in the short term."

Jonathan said that many Cleveland-area institutions, including Case Western Reserve University, the University of Akron, and the City of Cleveland, have brought in new leaders who are focused on technology-based economic development. Pension funds, banks, foundations, and wealthy individuals have seen the benefit of venture capital and are either investing in funds like his or plopping cash into early stage companies. Consequently, Jonathan's venture capital deal flow has increased. "The quality of business plans is very high. In a few years, the statistics will show that now is the time when this region became focused on creating more high-tech early stage companies."

As for his personal and family life, Jonathan listed the pros and cons.

"Cleveland is a good place to raise a family. Housing is plentiful and affordable. Family values predominate. Schools are good. Commutes are acceptable. The region has a strong sense of history and place that people who grow up here relate and return to. The arts scene is spectacular, including the symphony, the Museum of Art, and the theater scene (much better in all three areas than the Bay Area).

"Cleveland's business community operates like a small community and it takes time and effort to break in. But once you are in, you are in. Of course, this can cut both ways.

"On the downside, the health climate is not as good. Smoking is rampant and rudely public. Many people are overweight. The lengthy winter makes outdoors activity more difficult. The quality of produce is much better than it was in the Midwest a decade ago, but still not on par with California. The restaurant scene is improving, but not up to par yet. Property taxes are high and are used to fund public school systems that are serving the needs of teachers and administrators as much as of students and their families (I'm not sure that's different than anywhere else).

"I'm less negative on the weather than others are. I don't mind cold and snow in winter and in summer Lake Erie provides a mild, moderating effect that is not dissimilar from what the Bay Area gets from the Pacific."

Jonathan says he and Liz were not alone in their dash from California.

"Our firm gets résumés and business plans regularly from people and companies fleeing the coasts who want to return to their roots. Some are motivated by security and family concerns, and others by the economy. We have been in a dialogue with a serial entrepreneur who left Ohio for Silicon Valley ten years ago, participated in three prominent Internet start-ups, formed his latest tech company on a second mortgage against his inflated Bay Area house, and is now seeking to return to Cleveland to implement his business plan and reconnect with family and friends here."

I asked Jonathan if he had any nostalgia for California.

"I have been back to Silicon Valley twice since 1998. The strongest impression I had was of returning to St. Nicholas Church, in Los Altos, where Liz and I were married, which we attended for seven years. There had been an almost complete turnover in the congregation in just four years. I no longer knew anybody who was there, with a few exceptions."

I recently moved from the San Francisco Bay Area to Tucson, Arizona.

BACKGROUND

I am forty-four years old, married for nineteen years. My wife has not worked in sixteen years. We have three kids, ages sixteen, twelve, nine. I've been an investment banker for fifteen years, a money manager/financial adviser for the last three.

OUR REASONS FOR WANTING TO MOVE FROM THE BAY AREA
The Crowds

Long ago we gave up doing anything on the weekends due to the crowds. But in the last couple of years, the crowds during the week have pretty much ruined most recreational activities. Tahoe, Yosemite, Carmel, all the things we moved to the Bay Area for. The one time we chanced Angel Island was during Super Bowl Sunday when we knew it would be quiet.

The Cost of Living

During the bull market when money fell from the sky, I didn't pay attention. Last year or so, I paid attention. I needed about $300,000 before-tax income to live. Just to basically pay the bills. Could we live on less than that? Sure. But we don't want to. Private schools cost. Mortgage, $400 water bill, every aspect of daily living in the Bay Area is ridiculous. When I was young and building a career, I didn't mind. At forty, you get tired of making good money and just living.

Social Considerations

This is a harder one to explain. We lived in an affluent area of Walnut Creek. Our kids went to private school. The changes were subtle. My son complained that we were not spending the summer in Europe like a friend of his. My wife made comments about who had a new $50,000 SUV. All our activities seemed to revolve around shopping. Financially, I'm fine with this, but I was not sure it was a terribly healthy environment.

Partial Midlife Crises

I was bored out of my tree.

Because I Could

Once I became self-employed, I didn't have to stay here. Why Tucson? We looked at areas outside of the Bay Area. The kids and schools were top priority. We eliminated most areas in northern California because (a) the schools were crummy, (b) the cost differential was modest, (c) the weather was wet or there was another disqualifying factor. We finally decided that if we were going to do this, we wanted to really do this.

SO WHY TUCSON?

1. I have a lot of family there and was quite familiar with it.

2. The change of culture and landscape was dramatic enough to intrigue us.

3. It's right next to California, which is where all my business is and where I would have to run back to frequently.

4. It's big enough to have good schools, infrastructure, airports, etc.

Now that we've made the move, here's what I think about Tucson:

The Cultural Environment

One trade-off I assumed we'd make is that we'd leave the center of sophistication of San Francisco and move to the sticks of Tucson. Nothing could be further from the truth. The culture in Tucson is fascinating, with the whole southwest/Mexico influence. There is a thriving artist community here—writers and painters in particular. I'm collecting local artists in a way I never could have in San Francisco. Spend a little money on your house, and you can afford exotic stone and other material quite unaffordable in the Bay Area. A terrific sushi bar is four miles from the house.

Social Considerations

Our previous town, Walnut Creek, was boringly homogenous. Everyone is a doctor/lawyer/financial something. The women look the same. The men look the same. In Tucson, it is much more diverse. The socioeconomic floor is much lower, the high end is no different. You can live in a safe neighborhood with good schools in a $200,000 house. Or you can live with other Brahmins in $1 million to $4 million neighborhoods. There are more people from the Midwest here. It is more conservative, more religious, much friendlier. We have made better friends in four months here than in eighteen years in the Bay Area. After dinner, our whole neighborhood takes a walk, and we all socialize. Now that I'm away, I can say there is something weird about California perception of the rest of the United States.

Business Culture

Mañana is the norm here. I don't know how anything gets done. Businesses don't return calls and don't keep appointments. You have to beg a contractor to make a bid. I don't get it. I hear Phoenix is different.

Family Life

I feel far safer here raising kids. Here the kids can ride their bikes without fear. The neighbors watch for each other. The kids at my son's high school look normal. I don't see the kids in a new BMW, and I don't see the kids with tattoos or dressed weird. There are none of the overt sex and drug issues prevalent at our old public high school. The kids ride a school bus, which thrills them. That was out of the question in the Bay Area. My wife and kids love it here.

The Cost of Living

There's an astonishing difference! I estimate that I save at least $100,000 a year by living here versus in the Bay Area.

Trends

A ton of people like me, who don't have to show up at an office every day, are making this move. I believe Tucson has statistics to bear this out. The local cable company told me they get a dozen Bay Area transplants a week. The Internet and cheap airfare make all this very easy.

In fact, as an investment adviser, I believe this is very fore-boding for the Bay Area. I am incredibly bearish on Bay Area housing. As Silicon Valley matures and disperses, I believe that this engine of growth for twenty-five years has ended for the Bay Area, and will have a disastrous effect on pricing.

My office is still in Danville and I am in the Bay Area once a month. In fact, none of my clients have any idea that I've moved. I've told them I have a house in Tucson. I am afraid I'll lose busi-ness if I'm not perceived to be a local.

I was a little homesick at first, but now I love the contrast of bouncing between two locations. Actually, now I like the Bay Area better. Before, I always ran home to the family. Now, I see and do more things as a visitor than I ever did as I local. Typical, I guess.

If I were single, or part of a childless couple, Tucson would be too boring for me. If I did not travel, if I were to become a Tucsonan, or raise my kids to be Tucsonans, the answer would be no, because it's too backwards here. If I had to make a living here, the answer is a resounding no, because the money simply isn't here like California.

NAME WITHHELD BY REQUEST
Tucson, Arizona

CHAPTER 7

How Technology Closed
the Sophistication Gap

Afternoon breezes dance on the Nittany Mountain ridges. When the winds exceed 20 knots, the case today, currents called mountain waves can form and toss a 2,550-pound Cessna Skyhawk around like a leaf. Steadying my hand, I reach for the digital camera. Final approach into the State College, Pennsylvania, airport will put the Skyhawk directly atop Beaver Stadium, a 106,537-seat football palace. I snap a few shots.

Whoops. Pay attention! My landing on the short Runway 34 is ugly—two hard bounces and a rubber-burning skid to prevent an "off-runway" slide into the gravel.

Dave Barton is waiting in his new Dodge Ram pickup. A few months before, Dave, a very pissed-off California businessman, had introduced himself to me by e-mail. Dave said he was moving to Pennsylvania to enjoy the state's four seasons, lower costs, and shorter commutes. He said he would *not* miss this about California:

- "Having to cosign a car loan when negotiating with a college intern for a summer job.
- "The overweight boys riding their motorized Razor scooters down my street at six in the morning.
- "Listening to ten-year-olds discussing their favorite German road cars at recess.
- "Seeing a line of brand-new cars pulling into a high school parking lot, each occupied by a single sixteen-year-old talking on a cell phone."

We are driving from the little State College airfield toward Dave's research-park office on the Penn State campus, trying to avoid hitting deer, a constant local hazard in these parts. Dave starts telling me about the two biggest disappointments in his life.

The first came at age nineteen, when his pro baseball dreams died. Dave was one year out of high school and playing utility infielder for the Class A Newark, New York, Copilots of the Instructional League. Though a .400 hitter as an all-star high school shortstop in California, Dave now found himself on the other side of the country, at the bottom rung of professional baseball, batting a pitiful .218.

"I remember facing a pitcher who was six-six and threw a hundred miles per hour on the radar gun," Dave says, while steering his pickup along a back road. "He was wild, like Tim Robbins in *Bull Durham*. None of his warm-up pitches were strikes. They bounced into the dirt or sailed over the catcher's glove. I was the first batter up. I stepped into the batter's box, terrified. There was a glaring light from a building past center field across the street, just at the pitcher's release point. This big fella winds up and ... *whoosh* ... here comes the pitch. I can't see the ball against the light so I covered my head and hit the dirt. The pitch goes right over the plate. I'm still in the fetal position in the dirt when the umpire yells 'Strike one!' The fans are laughing."

Not Dave. He felt like crawling home.

Fast-forward to the spring of 2000 and his other big disappointment. This time, Dave is a middle-aged businessman based in San Jose, with a wife and two children. He had always thought his life would get easier at this point. Instead, that old gut-wrench feeling was back, evoking his minor-league failure. The business Dave had founded, owned, and devoted his life to for the previous twelve years—a factory tool parts brokerage—was going downhill fast, batting the equivalent of .218. Dave felt he was mired in the worst slump of his life. He felt powerless to make his business better, almost as if some large force had changed the playing field to his permanent disadvantage.

The playing field had changed! In Silicon Valley, where Dave and his wife owned their 1,700-square-foot home on a quarter acre, business was rocking and rolling as never before—ten thousand new millionaires were being coined every thirty days during the early months of 2000, according to the *San Jose Mercury News.* The Internet boom was being called the greatest gold rush of the century.

Only one problem. It wasn't Dave's gold rush.

GREED, SOARING PRICES, AND MORE GREED

No, not even close. Dave's business was as far removed from the hopped-up Silicon Valley business climate as Akron or Altoona. He ran a business that was almost embarrassing to talk about in Silicon Valley in the spring of 2000 . . . brokering factory tool parts! My God! What kind of business was that? Brokering parts by . . . telephone. Hey, Dave—haven't you heard of the Internet? The name of Dave's company, American Machine Supply, practically evoked rotary phones and Rotary lunches.

Funny thing is, American Machine Supply might have survived into Dave's old age had it actually been located in a backwater like Akron or Altoona. But it was in San Jose, and this was the worst place in world for an old-style business like his. In one year alone, 1999, Dave's landlord tripled his office rent to $28 per square foot. American Machine Supply's office was in a crummy manufacturing park of one-story buildings with roll-up aluminum doors—and still the landlord wanted $28 per square foot. All of Silicon Valley was like this in 1999: greed, soaring prices, and more greed. Why, up the road in Menlo Park some venture capital firm had set an American record for office rent, plunking down $240 per square foot, triple net, three times the fanciest space in midtown Manhattan! The trickle-down effect fell all the way to San Jose industrial parks and rained on Dave's small profits. Suddenly, with rent tripled, American Machine Supply wasn't profitable.

And the people problems! American Machine Supply had once employed twenty-five but was down to fifteen. The workers spent their days on the phones and faxes. They brokered precision drill bits, mills, and lathes from the outfits like Haas Automation in Oxnard, California, to Silicon Valley machine shops servicing the chip industry. A fluid market of factory tool parts is not something the average person thinks about, but tooling is an $8 billion business in the United States, a riotous anachronism of phones and faxes and bids and offers.

To run a business like Dave Barton's, you needed shifts of people willing to stay on the phone for eight hours and remain alert and cheerful. Problem was, Dave couldn't keep anybody for the salaries he could afford to pay them. Families couldn't live in San Jose when the breadwinner made $45,000. Not when little 1,700-square-foot houses like Dave's were going for $800,000—the case in 1999.

So Dave kept hiring, then losing, his best people. They would take the job, commute in from cheaper Gilroy or Tracy, ninety minutes of freeway crawl each way, do solid work for three months, and then burn out and quit. The best phone brokers in the Valley never even applied to Dave's shop. Not when nearby Cisco, Sun, and Oracle were showering $60,000 salaries and stock options on top phone reps. Little guy Dave Barton and his American Machine Supply were priced out of the market on all levels.

CALIFORNIA EQUITY BANDITS

After two more lousy years of trying to keep their factory tool business alive in Silicon Valley, Dave and his wife made a break in May 2002. With their older daughter off to college, they liquidated their two major assets. They sold their dying business, American Machine Supply, for $210,000, and their 1,700-square-foot home, which they owned clear, for $835,000. After taxes, the Bartons pocketed just shy of a million dollars. Not bad for a couple in their mid-forties with one kid in college at Ohio State and another in grade school. Then again, not enough to retire.

Dave thought about relocating American Machine Supply to San Diego, where rent and mortgage would go twice as far. "I was astonished to discover I could buy a house on Coronado Island for half the price of one in San Jose," he says. But Dave knew that manufacturing businesses were fleeing all of California, not just overpriced San Jose. His wife suggested moving east. Good idea. Rent and mortgage payments would stretch five times further in Charlotte, North Carolina, Lansing, Michigan, Columbus, Ohio, and State College, Pennsylvania. In June 2002, Dave flew back east for a look-see and visited the local Chambers of Commerce in each of those cities.

While visiting State College, Dave walked into a Chamber of Commerce office and explained his plight. Within twenty-four hours, State College had found Dave office space in a Penn State University–sponsored research park. That settled it.

Here's the deal Dave made in a nutshell: He sank $500,000, half his net worth, into Blueswarf.com, his new company. Penn State granted him a no-interest loan of $125,000, payable in three years. Dave pays the university a yearly rent of $10 a square foot for space in a brand-new research park, located one mile from Beaver Stadium. Dave, in turn, pledges to hire Penn State grads. He'll need those Penn State engineers, too. His new company is pure high tech.

Blueswarf.com (the name joins *blue*, Penn State's team color, with *swarf*, a factory tool term) uses software and the Web to automate the old American Machine Supply way of business. So instead of twenty brokers working the phones and faxes, Dave now has a team of seven Penn State software geeks. They've written some fancy "expert systems" code that lets Blueswarf's customers find their own tooling parts on the Web. Let Dave explain.

"I knew starting around 1998 that online markets would kill traditional distributors. I was a Web believer," he says. But a rather cautious believer, for Dave had seen the early carnage of

Internet pioneers, too. "Millicron launched a big e-commerce site in 1999. It failed miserably. Millicron didn't count on a backlash from its sixteen hundred distributors."

Dave goes on: "Then you had companies such as Machinetools.com in Chicago and Red Spark, a spin-off of California's Autodesk. Together they raised hundreds of millions of dollars. Even Lee Iacocca got into the act as a front man for a San Diego firm called Online Machine Exchange. All failed."

"Why?" I ask.

"Some were too early for broadband. Some pissed off their distributors. Some were run by M.B.A.'s who didn't understand the factory tool business."

"And why will you succeed?" I ask.

"One, everybody has bandwidth now. Two, I can't know the tooling business any better than I do, including the politics of distribution. Three, the software created by these Penn State geeks blows you away. Penn State is a huge asset. I'll bet you didn't know that *U.S. News & World Report* ranked Penn State's engineering school the fourth best in the country, behind Caltech, Stanford, and Georgia Tech. Four, customers who have tried the product, such as Haas Automation [of Oxnard, California] love it. Haas says we can become the Orbitz of our industry."

DEPARTED SILICON VALLEY TO FIND CUTTING-EDGE TECHNOLOGY

In the heart of Silicon Valley during the Great Boom, Dave Barton was old economy—wrong place, wrong time, and going broke. Now in the Pennsylvania hills during the Great Bust, he's new economy—not a mere tool broker, but a software company! Life is challenging but good.

In Pennsylvania, Dave's personal expenses are as low as it gets. He, his wife, Elizabeth, and their eleven-year-old daughter, Kelli, have settled into a 3,800-square-foot house on two acres, a fifteen-minute drive to work. They bought the house for $235,000—with cash. Dave owns the truck free and clear, too.

His only significant expenses are paying for daughter Kirstin's Penn State tuition and funding Blueswarf.com, which is not yet profitable.

Not profitable? A worm in the apple, here?

"What's Blueswarf's burn rate?" I ask.

"Our expenses are thirty-five thousand a month. We take in fifteen. So we're burning twenty a month."

"Whoa. That's a quarter mil a year. You worried?"

"Some. I'm very bullish about our prospects. Understand, America has just come through three straight years of declines in capital spending. That will turn around. When manufacturers start to buy tooling again, they'll see they can do much better with a Web service like Blueswarf.com."

I don't say anything.

"Look, it's a risk," Dave says. "I know that. But I'm energized like I haven't been in ten years."

"What will you do if you run out of cash?"

"Could happen. I don't think so. But if it does, we have our house and cars and everything paid for. Our expenses are low here in State College. So if Blueswarf.com tanks, I will consult for a living. I can drive two hours and visit seventy percent of American's manufacturing businesses. We will be just fine."

I ask Dave a question about geography. "Now that you've lived in the Pennsylvania hills for fifteen months, are you still happy?"

"My wife loves it. Me, too. Personal safety never crosses our mind. We let our eleven-year-old set off on her bicycle and don't worry if we don't see her for several hours. We went to the Pennsylvania State Fair last month and I said, 'Let's hurry and get out of here before it turns dark.' I am so used to thinking gangs come out after dark. But that was in California. Not here.

"The lack of time pressure amazes me. Back in California, if my daughter had a recital at seven-thirty, I'd start looking at my watch at three-thirty, thinking about traffic. Here, you just hop in your car fifteen minutes before you need to be there.

"Finally, and I don't know why this is true, but the cost of medical treatment is like night and day. Much cheaper here."

"Any downsides to Pennsylvania?" I ask.

"I go crazy if I don't get to New York or Philly or Boston once a month, if only to eat sushi. It's like a dose I need every month. But after a couple of days in the big city, I'm ready to come back. The other downside is mowing our two-acre lawn in the summer. It takes forever. Last Sunday I drove around in circles all morning. I felt like Forrest Gump when I got off the John Deere."

In the spring of 2004, Barton moved Blueswarf thirty miles down the road to an even smaller town in central Pennsylvania—Clearfield, population 6,631. Dave explained: "I followed the fiber-optic lines along the railway to Clearfield and am on the site of the brickyard that my wife's grandfather and uncle worked. I negotiated space for Blueswarf (at $4 per square foot!). While I fear my mother-in-law, whom I love dearly, pulling an Aunt Bee and showing up at my new office with a basket of lunch each day, and I worry about creating unreasonable hopes or false expectations to a town that needs some, it feels right. Really, really right. I think I am home."

DEATH OF DISTANCE— LONG PREDICTED, FINALLY HERE

Dave Barton moved to Pennsylvania for price relief. What keeps him in Pennsylvania are the opportunities afforded by technology. Dave is not alone. The last twenty years have brought an incredible array of "distance-shrinking" technologies to middle-class Americans: overnight delivery services, cable television, personal computers, fax machines, cell phones, high-speed Internet access, satellite radio, wireless home networks.

Irony from my own neighborhood in Silicon Valley, thought to be the center of sparkling information technology know-how: It is a *terrible* place to get high-speed cable or DSL Internet service. Intel chairman Andy Grove, a guy who ought to have clout, says it took him three rescheduled meetings with Pacific Bell (now part of SBC) before he got his high-speed line installed at his home in Los Altos Hills. Keep in mind that Grove's neighborhood sports an average house price of $3.2 million. Customers in cheaper Boise, Madison, and Charleston often have a far easier time of it.

Technology's spread into the American boonyack is a hugely democratizing force. It means that opportunities to create meaningful work are limited only by the imagination.

During my solo airplane travel across the United States I saw this every day. I drank beer with a small-town Montana entrepreneur, Andrew Field, who created a profitable Web commerce site with a national presence (see Chapter 10). I had lunch with a long-haired software executive, Doug Burgum, who wears cargo shorts and Teva sandals to the office. Sounds like a California guy. But his company is located in the American Siberia—Fargo, North Dakota (see Chapter 5). One night I stayed at the house of a spinal surgery catheter entrepreneur, Rick Randall, who was running his business out of Lake Placid, New York, during the summer (see Chapter 8).

These stories aren't anomalies. America is rapidly becoming a broadband nation, closing the technology gap between large and small places. "High-speed data is now the hottest product we have," says Brian Roberts, the CEO of Comcast. "The volume and quality of Internet usage has been far beyond anyone's expectation." At least three-quarters of American homes have cable modems or DSL service available to them. Comcast alone boasts 3.6 million subscribers to its high-speed Internet service and profit margins that would be the envy of any business.

Broadband penetration grew rapidly even during the economically lousy years of 2001 and 2002, partly fueled by the growth of telecommuters and home-based businesses. Almost anybody in a town of more than twenty-five thousand can get broadband service within days of making the call to his or her local phone company or Internet service provider. Rural areas are next.

H. L. MENCKEN WOULD BE SHOCKED

In the 1920s it became fashionable for American writers and intellectuals to bash the small communities from which they came. Sinclair Lewis, the first American novelist to win the Nobel Prize in literature, skewered his hometown of Sauk Centre, Minnesota, in *Main Street*. Lewis next satirized a middle-sized city (presumed to be Cincinnati) in *Babbitt*, portraying the backslapping Rotarian realtor George Babbitt as an American archetype.

Led by Lewis, social critic H. L. Mencken, and novelist Sherwood Anderson, America's emergent intellectual class of the early twentieth century set a tone that prevails to this day. An urbane San Franciscan easily imagines that all towns in Georgia or Alabama are overrun with toothless jabbering yokels and the Ku Klux Klan. A die-hard New Yorker is fully convinced you can't buy a good newspaper or cup of coffee in Rapid City or North Platte.

More recently, writers and intellectuals had a field day with the 2000 presidential election. While the popular vote split evenly between George W. Bush and Al Gore, the county-by-county results showed a sharp geographic—and by implication cultural—divide. The "blue" counties of the urban coasts went solidly for Gore, while Bush swept the heartland "red" states. Much, too, was made of press coverage following the death of NASCAR race-car driver Dale Earnhardt in 2001. It seems that only a dozen people in Manhattan had heard of this hero of Daytona and Talladega, who had already achieved legendary status in the hugely popular world of stock car racing. The great outpouring of grief following Earnhardt's death on the last lap of the Daytona 500 left many in the urban coastal centers scratching their heads, yet his demise moved America like no other athlete's death ever had. Into 2004 the culture war raged, over issues such as gay marriage, Mel Gibson's *The Passion of the Christ*, and the venomous Kerry versus Bush election campaign.

Are we still living in the era of the *Green Acres* television show—sophisticated New Yorkers and San Franciscans versus redneck hicks of rural America? No. If my trip is any indication, the gap is overstated, and narrowing at the speed of a cable modem.

My own story is rather typical.

When I left North Dakota in the 1970s to attend Stanford University, I quickly saw that the distance between the two was not only thousands of miles, but several decades as well. Everything in North Dakota seemed rooted in the dull and distant past, from people rooting for Woody Hayes–style grind-'em-out football to the lack of television stations and newspapers to the painfully long lag of fashion trends from New York and California.

If you were a teenager in North Dakota, you felt that you were at the ends of the earth. Sixties hairstyles hit my high school yearbook in 1973. One day in 1966 a snowstorm knocked one of our two television stations. The survivor was reduced to playing four episodes of the Adam West version of *Batman*, over and over. (Pow! Bam!) If you subscribed to the *Wall Street Journal* or the *New York Times*—and nobody I knew did—you got your paper a day late. There was no *USA Today*. All of this is changing. When I visit North Dakota today, it is astonishing to see how much the sophistication gap has narrowed. It's not completely erased, of course, and never will be. Plenty of teenagers will still want to leave to pursue dreams that the fly-over states can't fulfill. But it's remarkable how much more current the area feels than when my voice was an octave higher.

Today there is no difference between the cable television you get in North Dakota and the cable television you watch in Georgetown or Santa Monica—Fox News, BBC America, CNN, the History Channel, everything imaginable. And today it is just as easy to get a broadband connection in Bismarck as it is in Brooklyn, maybe easier. In the boonies it's a lot simpler to schedule an installation appointment.

One consequence of this change is that the boredom factor, so crippling to rural areas, is shrinking. It used to be incredibly stultifying to grow up in some of these hick towns. Now with TV and the Internet and technologies you don't even think of as technologies—indoor shopping malls, indoor arenas, movie multiplexes, twenty-four-hour fitness centers—that's changed. Even the weather isn't such a daunting force. Clothing technology has advanced to such a state as to seriously defuse the subzero temperatures that mark the northern plains. Cars can be started and heated remotely.

I am continually surprised when I go back to North Dakota now; it seems to be much more connected and, as such, more tolerable and even fun. An indoor shopping mall may not seem like such a remarkable thing in Miami, but it is an entertaining place to go in Minot in the middle of winter. It has added significantly to the quality of life.

Technology is only going to get better. The most efficient and productive place to hold a meeting in the twenty-first century is right on your desktop. Video desktop conferencing services like WebEx and Polycom, for instance, allow you to do just that—work remotely and communicate easily with others who are thousands of miles away. It's also not uncommon for businesses to use Instant Messaging to communicate with clients and coworkers in real time.

In 2001 we sold our home in the San Francisco Bay Area (a twenty-five-year-old tract house) for more than $500 per square foot and bought a brand-new house in Katy, Texas, for less than $100 per square foot. Twice the size for one-third the price. In the two years and a day that we owned the California home, the selling price increased enough (from $700,000 to $1,100,000) to actually pay for the new house in Texas outright.

Thanks to the Internet and the wonders of Virtual Private Network technology, I took my job with me and work from a dedicated home office that is nicer than any company has ever provided for me. The technology is only getting better. My wife may go back to work . . . or she may not. We can make it on one salary now! Lifestyle options can be better than stock options. The lack of a state income tax also translated into an instant 10 percent raise!

The local school district is rated the best in Texas and number four in the country (our kindergartner has started to say "Yes, sir" and "Yes, ma'am" to us). The Houston ballet, museums, live theater, and grand opera are first rate and we don't miss the parking hassles we used to endure on our cultural outings in San Francisco. We do miss the Bay Area's weather in the sweltering July and August of southeast Texas, but instead we have wonderful warm evenings to sit gazing over the new pool and gardens listening to the frogs and crickets.

Texas pros: The house we live in now is by far the nicest one we've ever lived in. There are good schools with lots of parental involvement (the key to learning!) and excellent museums and theaters (we have season tickets to the Alley Theatre downtown). Shopping (which runs neck and neck with high school football as the state religion) is convenient and of good quality (Nordstrom's opened last week at the Galleria)! Minute Maid Park (né Enron) is just as nice as Pac-Bell Park and the parking is better.

Texas cons: Southeast Texas weather is nowhere near as clement as California's. Houston gets twice as much annual rainfall as London (but we get it four or five inches at a time rather than half an inch per day for eight months).

Neither pro nor con but different: Religion plays a larger role here in people's lives. We were active at our church in California; I was the sexton (handyman) and my wife chaired a couple of committees. That made us not really odd, but did put us in the minority. Here in southeast Texas, the churches mostly seat in excess of two thousand and the sermon comes with a PowerPoint presentation on rear-projection screens on either side of the altar. We still haven't found a church we can stomach, although we've heard some good things about the Methodists up the road. Their minister has been quoted as saying, "You will never see my face on a billboard!" Might be worth a visit.

Politics are different, too. In California, my small "l" libertarian leanings made me a bit of a right-winger. In Texas, the right wing is soooo far right that I find myself leaning left to compensate.

I was just in the Bay Area last month. I noticed in the Bay Area the houses now seemed smaller and closer together. I noticed that even with the slower economy, the traffic was still horrendous. I'd forgotten how cold it gets after dark. Everyone seemed just a bit frazzled and hurried.

Working from home is what's given me the extra time to spend with family or picking up and pursuing new hobbies or just sitting and reading, which my wife and I love to do but seldom had the time for when we were commuting for two long hours, high-stress jobs to afford a lifestyle in the Bay Area.

My best self doesn't respond well to pressure!

My best self wants moderate stress for moderate success, and has found a place where he can afford to do that.

DAVID SCOTT
Katy, Texas

TWENTY-FIRST-CENTURY SUCCESS
SECRET—GEOGRAPHIC ARBITRAGE

As these technologies click into place, more American white-collar workers can engage in what I call Geographic Arbitrage. Let me explain: If you move to a small city like Bismarck or Biloxi and then insert yourself into the local salary structure, you really haven't gained much. You may have lowered your cost of living dramatically, but your paycheck shrinks, too.

But what if you can enjoy the best of both worlds:

- Live in a small town
- Get paid like you're in a big city

That's precisely what a Cisco Systems manager named Christian Renaud chose to do. Christians's job at the Silicon Valley telecommunications giant is to find new, offbeat markets for Cisco technology. Wireless routers for delivery trucks came out of his thirty-person group. But Christian doesn't live or work in Silicon Valley. Nor does he live or work anywhere near Cisco's East Coast technology development center in Raleigh, North Carolina. No, Christian rises in the morning and pads across the carpet to his home office in pastoral Johnston, Iowa, ten miles northwest of Des Moines.

As Christian explains: "My wife, Janeen, and I met at Cisco. We lived in an eight-hundred-square-foot condominium in Palo Alto, which was fine while we were childless. But in 2001 we had a baby girl, and Janeen didn't want to go back to work. Suddenly our eight-hundred-square-foot condo seemed like a closet."

In search of an affordable house suitable for kids, the Renauds thought about Bay Area exurbs such as Livermore and San Ramon, where houses cost half as much as those closer to Cisco. But the commute along Highway 680 is clogged and long. "I would never have seen my daughter during the week," says Christian. That's when he decided to risk a chat with his boss about moving out of California and telecommuting. The boss agreed—why not, he said, since Cisco makes products that permit just such remote work—and the Renauds got out their U.S. map.

Next they went on the Internet to evaluate home prices, school quality, recreation, and the local arts scenes. Janeen, a software engineer, even went so far as "data dipping" into the FBI crime files, since safety was a high priority for the Renauds. In March 2003, the young family bought a 5,000-square-foot house with a 1,500-square-foot finished basement on one acre of land. The house cost $600,000, just a tad more than their 800-square-foot condo in Palo Alto.

"We feel like feudal lords," says Christian. "My home office is larger than our former condo." Better equipped, too: The Renauds installed a three-megabyte cable modem, a Cisco IP phone, and a Polycom Via Video conferencing system that he uses to confer with his team members in Silicon Valley, Raleigh, Austin, and Missoula. Once a month, Renaud hops on a plane and spends three days in Silicon Valley or Raleigh.

Not everyone is cut out to be a Geographic Arbitrageur, of course. It takes buckets of moxie and self-motivation to work hours (or even time zones) away from the main arenas. It takes a certain knowledge and sophistication about how the main arenas operate. I have seen some professionals play the GeoArb game without ever having lived in the economic powerhouses, but it's rare. It helps enormously to have lived on the urban coasts, put in a few years, met people in your field face-to-face, and established a professional reputation and a contact list.

In this decade of Great Busts and Jobless Recoveries, GeoArb could become a way of life for millions of knowledge workers. Suppose you lost your high-paying white-collar job in a big city. What would you do? File for unemployment? Probably not. Show up at a bogus "jobs-retraining" program and be taught by a social worker who knows diddly-squat about the way business really works? No. In all likelihood you'd set up a home office and try your hand as a consultant. That's what 250,000 Americans have done since 2000.

The catch? Surviving as a freelance knowledge worker—where you sell your time—is extremely tough in high-priced joints like New York, California, and Washington, D.C., especially if you are the sole family breadwinner. It is cruelly difficult to generate enough income to make your $3,000-a-month mortgage payments, keep the cars and professional wardrobes up, take clients to dinner, maybe send the kids to private schools, give to charities, and try to save money.

Most competent freelancers past the age of thirty with big-city connections in fields such as product design, public relations, software, and sales and marketing can make $100,000 a year if they put their minds to it. Trust me, it's not that hard to do if you're smart, you're a pro, and you're pulling those bucks from California or New York. What's hard for a freelancer to do anywhere on the planet is earn the *second* $100,000. Yet that second $100,000 is what your household needs to swing a comfortable middle-class family lifestyle in the urban coastal areas.

But $100,000 a year, or even $75,000, buys a nice life in most smaller communities. Presto: Geographic Arbitrage.

In Chapter 11 you'll encounter Toni and Mike Sottak, two of the smartest Geographic Arbitrageurs I met during my research. They earn their income from California and the Far East. They spend their dollars in ski-country Vermont and on a Caribbean island.

THE GROWING HIDDEN-TECH MOVEMENT

Drew Massey, a New York magazine entrepreneur, recently moved back to Denver and sent me this e-mail:

"Although I am a media entrepreneur at heart, I have always longed to return to my home state of Colorado. Life is very good. Nice to have a 102-year-old 2,600-square-foot house for the price of a one-bedroom apartment in Harlem. Not to mention saving enough money on my monthly parking bill to buy a vintage '55 T-bird to put into my 4-car garage. Even splurged on the rights to 4 season tickets to the Broncos—a 10-minute walk from my house. Rockies baseball is a 15-minute bike ride (joked with my buddies to try *that* in the Bronx). Ditto for Avalanche hockey and the famous lively LODO scene. Airport is 30 minutes door-to-door (no tunnels, no O'Hare or SFO highways). And the best benefit is the access to my favorite skiing. Casually leave at 8:30 on a weekday (after checking the 7:30 market opening and reading the *Wall Street Journal*) and I'm on the chair lift by 10:00. Tell me again why I should be packed like a sardine on the 4/5/6 or 1/3/9 subway in New York City?

"P.S. I kept my NYC cell phone to fool everyone."

Drew is not unique. Five years ago, if you wanted to be in the middle of the most lucrative opportunities, you had to be in one of the great urban centers. No longer. Suddenly, smart and ambitious entrepreneurs like Drew Massey can set up shop wherever there's a high-speed Net connection. A number of experts like Joel Kotkin, author of *The New Geography*, have identified an emerging tech industry in parts of the country that provide lifestyle opportunities to knowledge workers.

This "hidden-tech" movement, a term coined by author Amy Zuckerman, refers to a clustering of like-minded tech professionals far removed from urban environments. In *Hidden Tech and the Valley*, Zuckerman says the hidden-tech economy includes hard-core "techies"—people like software programmers or hardware developers—but it also includes lawyers, patent agents, jewelry retailers, management trainers, content providers, graphic artists, Web designers, and marketing specialists. They may be professional telecommuters, freelancers playing the GeoArb game, or entrepreneurs who develop and sell products or services from a home or small office. What these "hidden techies" do is leverage the Web to expand their reach.

The "hidden" portion has two meanings. Sometimes, as in the case of home offices squirreled away in a spare bedroom, den, or attic, they are literally hidden from sight. More often, though, they are hidden from government, private sector, or academic statisticians because many are not incorporated. That means they may not be captured by any government reporting service.

Author Daniel Pink in his book *Free Agent Nation* counts at least 18 million Americans who are sole proprietors or operating their own small, home-based companies. He believes this is just the beginning of a significant trend toward self-employment. The Great Bust and the subsequent export of white-collar jobs to India and Asia can only accelerate this trend.

Joel Kotkin also cites a "critical shift" in the population that is moving into the countryside. "In the past, it was often less educated people and the elderly who flocked there," he writes in *The New Geography*. "But now a growing percentage of the new population consists of knowledge workers. For the first time, vocational choice has expanded to allow these elite workers the option of locating not only outside the city, but outside the metropolis itself."

AIR TRAVEL TO THE BOONIES

When discussing the factors that bestowed riches upon the urban coasts during the Great Boom (see Chapter 12), we talk mostly of access to a large, talented workforce and capital availability. But there's another factor, and it's not so obvious: air travel. The deregulation of the airline industry in the 1970s seriously hurt the attractiveness of rural America for the busy executive. Before deregulation, travel to small towns was effectively subsidized by coast-to-coast business flyers. Then came deregulation, which created the hub-and-spoke air travel system that we know so well today. The efficiency resulted in plummeting airfares between New York and San Francisco. The flip side was soaring costs and roundabout routes for trips that start or end at spoke airports—that is, most American cities under 250,000.

Try getting from Boise, Idaho, to Birmingham, Alabama. You might spend half the day because you first will have to fly to Salt Lake City, then to Dallas, and only then to Birmingham. For journeys of five hundred miles or less, door-to-door travel by car is almost as fast as flying. Things are likely to get worse: The Federal Aviation Administration expects air traffic to double by 2010.

Still, there's hope. The solution lies in a new generation of small, high-powered yet fuel-stingy airplanes that may be the greatest transportation innovation since interstate highways. These "cheap jets" are designed to fly into thousands of local airports, thus bypassing the snarls at the dozens of hubs and hundreds of spokes now served by the major airlines. This approach, which is laid out in detail in James Fallows's wonderful book *Free Flight: From Airline Hell to a New Age of Travel*, could cut travel time in half.

Direct flights on such flying marvels as Adam Aircraft Industries' A700 could put an air-taxi service only a phone call away. The five-passenger A700 will zip along at 400 mph, cruise above the weather at 41,000 feet, nestle passengers in comfy seats, and cost only about $1.9 million, about a third of today's comparable jets. Of course, you and I may not be able to write a $1.9 million check for a personal jet, but that's beside the point. What matters is whether an emerging industry of air-taxi operators will buy them. If they do, good news. You, the passenger, will pay the price of a business-class ticket to ride on them. That's still not dirt cheap, of course, but it's fast and direct, with the added benefit that air taxis may help you avoid the overnight stay that hub-and-spoke routing often necessitates. Vern Raburn, founder of Eclipse Aviation, another cheap-jet contender, figures air taxis could grab 20 percent of the business-travel market during the 2010s—and generate sales of perhaps thirty-five thousand tiny jets.

The effect of these small, cheap jets on rural communities could be electric. If you are trying to get a business going in a small community that has a national clientele, as opposed to just serving the local community, travel may no longer be the rude hassle it once was.

CHAPTER 8

Sometimes, Material Success
Is Not Enough

Would you have made this trade? You get to pocket millions of dollars before the age of forty. But you pay a high price for your financial success—your marriage fails. Worse, the person you most care about, your daughter, now lives on the opposite side of the country. Rick Randall knows the difficulty of explaining this kind of psychic torture to the 99.996 percent of people in the United States who don't have millions of dollars lying around. (He grew up in a blue-collar family himself.) But in Rick's mind, the journey from poor to rich doesn't add up to much if losing your family is part of the deal.

So when Rick married for the second time and embarked on a new set of entrepreneurial adventures, he struck a far better trade. He has learned how to combine work and family in an incredibly creative way. Not only that, but thanks to technology, he and his family live and work in captivating places and own two splendid homes for the price of one executive-style house in Boston or Southern California.

Let's find out how he did it.

I departed the western Massachusetts city of Pittsfield, late on the morning of August 9. I am slow getting away from my hosts, George Gilder and his wife, Nini. They live in a red farmhouse in a valley in a village called Tyringham, close to Stockbridge, where Norman Rockwell lived and painted.

George, a writer, economist, and futurist—a famous one for having written books such as *Wealth and Poverty, The Spirit of Enterprise, Microcosm,* and *Telecosm*—is my mentor. We became friends shortly after I cofounded a technology business magazine called *Upside* during the late 1980s. Then in 1992, at the beginning of the Web revolution, we convinced Steve Forbes to launch *Forbes ASAP,* and in those pages George did some of his finest work. As we drank coffee and watched the dairy cows outside of the Gilder farmhouse, I marveled at how George was able to pull off writing about developments in Silicon Valley, Singapore, and South Korea from a red house in the valley of the Berkshire Mountains.

It is nearly noon by the time I pull the Skyhawk's nosewheel up and allow the miracle of air traveling fast over the wings to lift the plane over the Berkshires. Hard, jolting turbulence over the peaks somewhat wrecks the picturesque flight, but not completely. This is indeed lovely country. I would prefer to fly as low as possible over the Berkshire ridges up to Vermont, stick it on autopilot, and look out the window, but the air bumps force me up to 4,500 feet, then 6,500 feet to find smoother air. I cross into Vermont, the college town of Bennington to my right, the Hudson River to my left.

I had e-mailed Rick Randall that morning from Gilder's office. Rick agreed to meet me at Lake Placid Airport. I said I would phone him when I got there. This may sound like common courtesy to the person picking you up, and it is. But I do this for more selfish reasons. I want the option of not showing up at all, or showing up very late, just in case the weather turns bad or I have problems with the airplane. This afternoon, I do have a problem of sorts. I have not brought the New York Sectional air map, which depicts Lake Placid Airport on it. No, that can't be true! The New York Sectional is right here on the plane's right seat. I grab the map, fumble with it, but can't locate Lake Placid.

Where is it?

Oh, jeez—Lake Placid must be off the map. It must be on the Montreal Sectional! It is that far north!

Not having the New York Sectional map is a bit of a worry. That it is illegal is of minor concern. The bigger worry is that my onboard GPS map shows Lake Placid Airport to be in a bowl surrounded by the highest peaks in New York State. That almost certainly means a tricky arrival. What to do? I push the throttle forward and climb up to 8,500 feet so I can get a better look. As the Skyhawk nears Lake Placid, the correct strategy reveals itself. I will descend into a valley, level off at 6,500 feet, then chop the power and drop rapidly into Lake Placid's airport. While parallel to Runway 32, I see that I must make a base turn before reaching the end of the runway threshold, to keep from barreling into the mountainside rising abruptly at the threshold. I make a steeply banked turn left and keep it going round for a full 180 degrees, level the wings, line up on final approach . . . and see that I'm way too high. The choice now becomes (a) go around and try again, or (b) try a "slipping" maneuver—turn rudder one way, wings banked the opposite—to lose altitude fast and get down on the runway. I go for the slip. It works. Not a bad piece of flying for a rookie.

THE PRETTIEST VILLAGE IN AMERICA

Rick picks me up in his Range Rover. Fifty years old, he talks in that quick caffeinated patois common among people in bigger cities. We drive through the village of Lake Placid, a stunner if you've never been there, a jewel of a Swiss-like village, nestled up to a small lake, which is not Lake Placid at all. "It's Mirror Lake," says Rick. "Lake Placid is much larger and over there, to the north." Mirror Lake lives up perfectly to its name—glassy smooth, rippled only by swimmers and canoes. No powerboats are allowed. Normally I am for powerboats, on principal, because Republicans like me are known to derive a near sexual pleasure at the roar of fossil-fuel machines. Seeing Mirror Lake makes me rethink my position.

Soon we are driving along the village's Main Street, past restaurants and shops, and around a bend. Rick's home is on a lot that runs down to Mirror Lake. The home is large and rustic, with bright yellowish brown logs and stone and vaulted ceilings inside. A rich man, with false modesty, might call it a cabin, but it was the kind of cabin similar to what millionaires own in Jackson Hole and Lake Tahoe. The place looks western to my architecturally uneducated eyes. Rick says it is Classic Adirondack.

We grab Cokes and head for his Mirror Lake–facing porch. I am parched and really would have preferred to suck down that sixteen-ounce can of Miller draft beer I saw in Rick's fridge, but I stay silent. During the course of my flying adventures I have noted with some alarm that I have been drinking a lot of alcohol, starting earlier in the day than usual. My nerves are so taut in the airplane that I feel the need for a comedown on the ground. Also I'm thirsty as hell, because I don't drink much fluid before or during flying, a strategy that helps me contain my squirrel-size bladder during a three-hour flight. Thus I typically finish my flying very tense and very parched. Never has a cold beer tasted so good as when I'm safely on the ground after the last flight of a summer day. Problem is, my last flight of the day during these trips often concludes at 2 P.M. to avoid late-afternoon summer thunderstorms. That means I'm lusting for my first cold beer—ideally a tall one, poured into a big frosty mug, with maybe a shot of Jack Daniel's on the side—at around 3 P.M.

I immediately like Rick Randall. He describes his childhood growing up in Appleton, New York, outside of Buffalo. His father was a tinsmith at a General Motors plant. Tinsmith! Must have been the last tinsmith in America. His boy was blessed with brains and ambition. Young Rick loved science and biology and wanted to be a veterinarian. He went off the University of Houston, calculating that the U.S. draft board might not be able to find him in Texas. Then Houston raised tuition for out-of-staters and Rick came back to the State University of New York at Buffalo. He managed to escape the draft, and spent his summers working at the General Motors plant to pay for college.

"The best business education I had was working on the GM factory floor," Rick tells me. "It was very alienating. You'd ask yourself: 'What does this part mean? Where does it go? What happens if it breaks?' But you'd never get any answers from the foreman. It was a stupid way to run things. I could see the Japanese invasion of the auto industry a mile off."

After college, Rick got a job teaching high school biology in Syracuse. "The salary was ninety-six hundred dollars a year. I was a good teacher—I knew how to connect and communicate." During summers, Rick drove an ice cream truck. "I took a route nobody else wanted—the black neighborhoods of Syracuse. I drove the truck from ten A.M. to ten P.M. every day. Pure commission job. It went poorly at first. Then I realized the music coming from the truck was all wrong for a black neighborhood. It was 'Turkey in the Straw' or 'Dixie' or some damn redneck thing. I rigged the bell to make a jazzy beat. Pretty soon the business turned around, and I made more money that summer than I did teaching for nine months."

Around that same time, Rick's first wife to be, Janice, was scheduled for a medical sales job interview. The job, if she got it, would put Rick's teacher's salary and ice cream truck driver wages to shame—$30,000 plus bonus! The day of the job interview, Janice was sick with the flu, so Rick asked if he might go to the interview in her place. During the interview Rick told the story about changing the jingle on the ice cream truck and was hired on the spot. Janice's reaction? "She was pissed! I don't think she ever forgave me."

Rick is now remarried to a woman named Lori, and they have two children, Alec, nine, and Hailey, four. An hour into our interview on the back porch facing Mirror Lake, the three walk in, all bubbly. Rick excuses himself to talk to the children. Nothing could be more important to him.

Lori and kids have planned to watch a movie that night with another mother and children, leaving Rick and me to fly solo. We decide to walk into town. I don't want to exaggerate, but Rick's rustic/modern lakeside house, the sumptuous guesthouse where I have tossed my bags and will be staying tonight, his pretty wife and two children, the village of Lake Placid, the 75-degree light mountain air—the whole package—are as close to perfect as you can get on this mortal coil. Rick has really made it. At dinner, I hope to get the rest of the story.

BIG PROFITS FROM SMALL HOLES

The walk into the village from Rick's is half a mile. We settle on an outdoor café called The Great Adirondack Steak & Seafood Co. Ah, cold beer, at last—more precisely, a dark brew called Wee Heavy Scotch Ale, which the menu calls strong. Ah, that's the ticket! While I tipple my ale, Rick continues with his story: After cheating his first wife, Janice, out of her medical sales job, Rick rapidly climbed up the medical sales rung, but soon topped out on commission. One night over drinks, he pressed a colleague for career-move tips. The guy told Rick, "If you get on the ground floor of a paradigm shift, it's an elevator ride up." Rick began poring over magazines and journals, looking for that paradigm shift. One day in 1979 he found it in angioplasty, just then getting approval from the Food and Drug Administration. Rick switched employers, joining U.S. Catheter and Instrument, which brought the angioplasty balloon to market in 1980. Within four years, the procedure took off, and Rick got a sales manager position with U.S. Catheter in Boston. "My job was getting salespeople to go toe-to-toe with cardiologists. It all came together for me: my teaching, the factory job, the ice cream truck. I excelled."

Not excelling was Rick and Janice's marriage. They divorced in 1984. Rick says his ambition-fueled long hours at work and the traffic-snarled commutes of Boston doomed the marriage.

"A year later I got headhunted to American Hospital Supply and I moved to Orange County, in California. I loved California, the lack of hierarchy. In Boston I was hampered by a lack of a Harvard or MIT pedigree. In California, nobody asked where I had gone to college. All that mattered was that doctors liked me." Still, Rick says that moving three thousand miles away from his daughter Tess was the toughest decision he's ever made. Tess was four years old when Janice and Rick divorced. He would not see much of her for the next eight years.

Single and focused, Rick thrived in California at American Hospital Supply and quickly got himself noticed by head-hunters in the medical device industry. In 1989, Rick was recruited for his first CEO job, at Target Therapeutics, which made catheters for minimally invasive liver surgery and later brain surgery. Rick took Target from scratch to $15 million in sales and an IPO in 1992. He was a week short of forty years old and had made his first $5 million. But there was a huge hole in his own heart. Tess. With a shock, Rick realized that he had missed too much of her childhood—the entire grade school years—and no amount of success or money could get it back.

Rick moved back to Boston and learned that a CEO who had taken a company public was welcome anywhere, Harvard degree or not. He took the helm of another start-up in sports medicine, called Innovasive, and took it public in 1996, later selling it to Johnson and Johnson.

AN ANSWER TO BABY BOOMER
BACK PROBLEMS

Rick was now rich enough to retire. But the working-class kid from Buffalo loved to work. He soon joined Vertical Group, a New Jersey hedge fund that invested in medical device companies. There, Rick saw a large gap in the device market. "There is plenty of room for products that do only twenty million a year in sales—single products that meet a surgical need." As Rick described it, big companies just don't know how to get at this market. Venture capitalists are uninterested because of the small size and because start-ups can't afford the long FDA approval process or the distribution and reimbursement costs.

To get at this market, Rick started Incumed in 1998. Its purpose is to incubate single-product start-ups, get the product through FDA approval, and then sell the start-up to a larger medical device company. One of Rick's Incumed start-ups is called TranS1. It makes catheters that permit high-tech spinal surgery done through tiny holes.

"This is a great, great field!" Rick shouts above the din at The Great Adirondack Steak & Seafood Co. "You have large pools of patients with back troubles, yet for whom surgery is still too invasive."

As baby boomers age, and begin to lose their golf swings to stiff backs or their ability to pick up grandchildren from deteriorated disks, they will flock to surgery, Rick believes . . . but only if the surgery is quick and relatively risk free. It can be, says Rick, if the surgical hole is small. Rick describes a small area of the body located between the tailbone and the anus, a perfect place to go in and relieve pressure on a nerve root from a compressed disk. Only the tiniest surgical instruments are capable of doing this.

I listen and order another draft of Wee Heavy Scotch Ale.

What about location . . . not your tailbone-anus thing, but where you chose to live and work? Rick says he and his family spend the school year near Wilmington, North Carolina, in a rambling house on a golf course development. Why Wilmington? "It's a town that is perfectly sized for us. Three hundred thousand population. No long commutes." When Rick remarried, he vowed he never wanted to miss his kids at bedtime. He had originally looked at Charleston, South Carolina, also small, but concluded it was too Old South, too Old Money. The agent told Rick, "If you like Charleston without the pretense, you'll like Wilmington."

"But," I asked Rick, "if you like the piney woods and sea breezes of America's coastal Southeast, wouldn't high-tech Raleigh-Durham seem more logical?"

"Not for me. It feels too much like Orange County or Silicon Valley," Rick says. "Long commutes. Plus, in a funny way, I think these places get parochial. When you work in odd places, as I do in Wilmington and in Lake Placid during the summer, you have more time to think. You can think independently . . . you can listen to your instincts." Rick says that with the Internet, he and his Wilmington colleagues can open up the world as a resource, tapping talent from Boston or Tokyo. "In Wilmington, I have a couple of superb catheter designers I work with. The rest of the work we outsource. What I want is a high revenue-to-head-count business. And I want my family by my side. And I can have both in Wilmington and Lake Placid."

———

Six months later I caught up with Rick by e-mail. He was effusive. Things were humming.

"The new Start-up, TranS1, is cooking. We just returned from our first spine trade show (North American Spine Society) in San Diego and I am happy to report we knocked it out of the park." Indeed. Rick's company was told it had the most novel and innovative procedure and product at the meeting. Between surgeon, corporate, and investment banker interest in the company, Rick says he never had to wander more than thirty feet from the exhibit. "I relish these experiences much more these days than I did in the past. They do not always happen."

I asked Rick about his family.

"Alec is in fifth grade and Hailey is in pre-K at Cape Fear Academy. We love Cape Fear and Wilmington. The schools measure themselves against other schools on a national basis. They understand Wilmington kids will compete globally, not just regionally, a concept that I fear has not yet permeated the rural South in general."

After graduating from Georgetown in 2001, his daughter Tess got a job teaching ~~taught~~ first grade at a private, mostly African-American school in Los Angeles. This September Tess moved to Seattle and is working for a nonprofit adoption agency. Her plan is to return to the University of Washington to secure a master's degree in public policy, Rick says.

The update from Rick inspired me to dig out the notes I had jotted during our dinner at The Great Adirondack Steak & Seafood Co. Alas, some of the notebook pages were blurred and gave off an odor like ale—the pages were unreadable, in other words. So I asked Rick to clarify his back-and-forth life between Lake Placid and Wilmington.

He wrote back:

"You asked about the size of our properties. We have two acres on Mirror Lake, with a 3,500-square-foot main house and 1,300-square-foot guesthouse. Our Wilmington home is 6,000 square feet on 1.5 acres. Together, they cost about the same as one executive home in Boston or Southern California.

"The family still goes to Lake Placid from late June through mid-August. During the summer I work out of Lake Placid on Mondays and Fridays and spend Tuesday through Thursday in Wilmington."

Rick's typical working day in Wilmington affords him at least an hour more per day of private family time than he experienced living in Boston or the Bay Area. His commute is only seven minutes. The extraneous activities associated with day-to-day living are just so much easier to manage. His travel is still extensive—about 30 percent of his working time. New regional jet service to Charlotte, New York, Washington, and Atlanta makes the world readily accessible.

Rick travels the world preaching the TranS1 gospel. The technology meets a huge unmet need for a minimally invasive approach to resolving lower back pain, he says. The current form of surgery is so morbid that when polled, most spine surgeons say that they would not have the surgery performed on themselves. They would rather live with the chronic pain.

Early tests of TranS1 have gone well.

"We have performed lumbar fusion of diseased disks with three patients in Brazil. All three patients had no postoperative sensation of pain in their lower back. They were treated five months ago and continue to live active lives without the chronic back pain they once had. They all had quality-of-life scores well above what you would typically see a couple of months after spine surgery." Rick and his team will be in Brazil to start a more rigorous clinical study of twenty-five patients in two medical centers. U.S. clinical study work began in April 2004. The current lumbar fusion market in the United States represents 200,000 procedures annually, driving about $2 billion in product revenue. Rick wants a large chunk of that. "Three patients do not make a procedure or a company," he says. "But we are thrilled with the early clinical experience."

I remind Rick of his previous observation that living in Wilmington and Lake Placid forces him to "shop the world" for talent.

"We are living it at TranS1," says Rick. "We find ourselves tapping into more paid consultants than I have in the past. The Internet makes this a more viable option. We have acquired specialized laboratory equipment at tremendous savings on eBay. Monster.com has been a source of finding and networking with quality people."

Digital photography, procedure animation, CAD design drawings, literature searches, pre-op CT imaging assessment—all are communicated and manipulated over the Internet. This lets Rick and his TranS1 team work effectively and efficiently from remote destinations. Rick says he doesn't think he could have pulled this off in Wilmington back in the late '80s and early '90s. "Part of the fun of jumping back into the start-up role again is the thrill attached to using technology to gain efficiency while reducing cash burn."

FINDING THAT ELUSIVE WORK-LIFE BALANCE

Finally, I ask Rick if he has at last found that elusive work-life balance. Managing a successful career in balance with being a dad is perhaps the most difficult thing he does, Rick says. There have to be sacrifices; there is no way around it. When employees and shareholders are betting their livelihoods and personal wealth on you, you must be there and accountable. Being there for the family is not just a question of physical presence but of being focused and tuned in to the family members when you are together. This is what Rick says he struggled with in the past. When he lived in California or suburban Boston, the fast pace of the environment combined with long working hours and commutes made it very difficult for him to decompress and connect with the kids. He usually ate dinner after the kids and found himself putting them to bed before he had time to completely unwind from work.

But Wilmington and Lake Placid have been different on two fronts: His commute is a nonissue. He sees his kids off to school and sometimes drives them in a car pool in the morning. Second, the low-key, more laid-back environments make it easier for Rick to shift gears "from work mode to family mode."

"It is hard to explain, but there is a distinct difference in the environmental pace that helps to refocus my mind," he says. "I feel more connected to the community and friends here than I have elsewhere. I still at times struggle with the transition but it is an easier environment in which to do it. Obviously, in Lake Placid it is much easier. I religiously work Mondays and Fridays in my home office on the phone or via e-mail. But by five-thirty I typically dive off the dock into Mirror Lake with the kids, and work is immediately behind me.

"Obviously, maturation has helped as well. Having been through this before, I am somewhat more comfortable with the appropriate management of my time. I am more able to accept that it is okay to have a personal life and devote some time to it. My wife would assert that I am not completely reformed . . . but . . . even she would admit that time, experience, and location have made me a better dad and partner.

"In summary, I think technology allows us to reassess how and where we do things. We do not need to be geographic captives to the industry in which we work. Stay tuned as we continue with the grand experiment."

CHAPTER 9

America's Hometown

Over the glittering copper dome of the Iowa state capitol building, with the Iowa Cubs baseball stadium under my left wing, I sailed into Iowa's largest city, Des Moines. The approach to landing at the Des Moines International Airport was straight out of a Chamber of Commerce brochure—a gentle, curving base turn toward Runway 5, ordered from the control tower by a flat Iowa farm drawl with one plainspoken objective: to bring the pilot safely back home.

I had departed Lake Placid the day before and flown into South Bend, Indiana. By luck (good or bad, depending on where you sit), I'd spent the night in a South Bend hotel that was host to the annual College Football Hall of Fame awards dinner. South Bend is what I would call the American Vatican. It is home to our soil's mother religion. No, not Protestantism or Catholicism. Football! Large, packed men of all ages, some with limps, some with flattened noses, few with any discernible neck, roamed the hotel. They crowded the bar. They talked loudly and slapped each other's backs. They smiled broadly. Some had blonde wives, some were towing their humongous kids. White men and black men greeted one another as brothers.

South Bend may be an American treasure, and Notre Dame one of our great universities, but I can't see South Bend competing for intellectual talent against the likes of New York, Boston, and Silicon Valley, or even against its midwestern peers such as Columbus, Madison, or Lawrence. This has to do with what is valued and honored. Football is honored in South Bend.

Football is holy in South Bend. Electrical engineering takes a backseat. Gene splicing sits in the bleachers. The average South Bender easily can name five Fighting Irish quarterbacks (. . . Johnny Lujack, Paul Hornung, Joe Montana . . .) before he can think of one entrepreneur. That's okay. Thank God for diversity. South Bend is far better pursuing excellence as a top football mecca than as a biotech center.

Sunday morning at the South Bend Regional Airport was not crowded, the footballers being too arthritic or hung over to get an early start. The takeoff into humid, cloudless skies was smooth. The skies over Chicago were gray and thick, but my route took me to the southwest, where it was clear, and then intersected on a pure westward route with that vital American artery, Interstate 80. The west wind pushed hard against my airplane's nose and slowed my ground speed to under 100 knots. I watched traffic on I-80 below, and saw that I was not much faster than cars in the left lane. In two hours I crossed the Mississippi River atop the Quad Cities of Moline and Rock Island, Illinois, and Davenport and Bettendorf, Iowa. Not long after came Iowa City, home to the University of Iowa Hawkeyes, with its superb NCAA wrestling program and writers' workshop.

———

My mental autopilot was snapped off rudely when outside the Skyhawk's windshield I saw more dark clouds rising upward like ghostly Swiss Alps. Oh, damn. More T-storms. How fast they boil up in the Midwest! I say good-bye to Interstate 80 below and bank the airplane north in an attempt to sneak around the brewing storm. Wondering how Des Moines is doing, I check the radio—there are scattered clouds. Perfectly flyable. The GPS moving map shows Des Moines located behind that weather front lurking at my ten o'clock position. Which means I should be able to buttonhook around the storm and land. That is how it works out. The streets in Des Moines are shiny wet, but the storm has passed.

Des Moines is the birthplace of American presidential campaigns every four years. Every August it is home to America's largest state fair, called the Big One by locals and attended by more than a million people each year. It is August now, but I elect to skip the Big One and its Tilt-a-Whirl rides and the Kids' Ugliest Cake Contest in order to see a fellow named Peter Scanlon. Peter had suffered a sharp career defeat in the New York area and was attempting to start anew in a town he'd never even visited before.

PETER SCANLON—
ACTING ON GOD'S GUIDANCE

"In 1999, my family and I moved from Connecticut to Des Moines, Iowa. We have never looked back." Thus began Peter Scanlon's e-mail. Peter, an insurance executive, mentioned that he and wife, Jane, were born, bred, schooled, and married on the East Coast. They never imagined that their journey would take them to Iowa.

"When we considered moving to Des Moines, we had to look on the map to find out where Iowa was located—a mind-set born out of the *New Yorker* cartoon that shows Manhattan on three-quarters of a page and the rest of the United States on the remainder. We no longer have that mind-set."

Peter Scanlon is almost like a modern, white-collar version of Tom Joad, the Oklahoma refugee in John Steinbeck's *The Grapes of Wrath*. Peter's exodus came at the worst time possible—in middle age, in midcareer, with two children at home and one headed to college. It could not have been easy for Peter that his father had been very successful in New York, attaining the chairmanship of Coopers & Lybrand, the accounting firm (now part of PricewaterhouseCoopers).

Young Scanlon desperately wanted to match his father's success. "I had worked at Cigna, in life insurance, for nineteen years, out of the Hartford headquarters," he says, beginning his story. Peter and I are drinking lattes in Zanzibar's, a funky coffee shop on Ingersoll Avenue on the west edge of downtown Des Moines. A table away a ponytailed guy stares intently into the screen of his Apple laptop. We could be anywhere.

Peter continues: "Three years ago, Cigna spun off a start-up, called Benefits Access. We were trying to put a toe in the dot-com market. I was the senior vice president of sales. It was a chance to shine, to catapult my career, to get noticed by senior management at corporate headquarters. We tried to sell single-point-of-contact benefits administration to midsize corporations on the Internet. But the start-up was more work, more stress than I was prepared to handle. I burned out.

"The first day of unemployment was scary as hell. I was panicked for a couple of weeks. Then I began to listen. A friend advised me to trust God first, and only when I was feeling His peace begin to ask questions. I asked:

- What should I do?
- Where should I do it?
- How much money do we really need?"

Peter prayed and "quite quickly I got an answer. I felt a deep need to move to a smaller city. I had never felt this before, but my wife surprised me by being all for it. She had felt it, too.

"I got three job offers, two in New York, one in Des Moines. I came to Des Moines in January 1999, and right away I felt, 'I could be successful here.' I had an intuitively good feel about the people. I called my wife back in Connecticut and said: 'This is a town we could live in. We can live well here.'

"Understand that my wife and I have no roots in Des Moines. This was completely a spiritual intuition."

If his intuition was spiritual, then Peter's action—packing up and moving—was either bold or crazy. It's one thing to move away to college as a young and flexible eighteen-year-old, knowing there is little downside. It's quite another matter to chuck your twenty-year residence when you're middle-aged and unemployed, with mortgages and college bills pressing down. A false start in a strange town would be disastrous.

Was Peter scared?

He looks at me oddly. "No. I had peace in God." Then Peter smiles and says, "One of the things you get to do when you move is reinvent yourself. My wife has come alive, teaching art at the Des Moines Art Center. You can meet people easier here in Des Moines. You have the time to get involved in school and church. We were stuffy Episcopalians in Connecticut. Now we have become high-energy Methodists.

"One daughter was in high school, the other in sixth grade. Emily, the older, pushed against the move. In fact, she hated my guts. Our younger, Nora, loved it. She says, 'Kids are different here. They do stuff in groups.'"

Peter says church is a big deal in Iowa. "No homework on Wednesdays. If the teachers assign homework on Wednesdays, the local pastors let the principals know about it."

I asked Peter if the cultural life in Des Moines ever feels, well, dull, by New York standards. "Funny thing is, when we lived in Hartford, we seldom went into the City. I don't think we realized just how little we did until we left and didn't miss it. We have a world-class museum in Des Moines. In the arts, we have one of two Andy Goldsworthy galleries in the country. The other is in La Jolla, California. We don't lack for much here. The only thing Des Moines misses is good regional theater."

THE NEAR ABSENCE OF
STATUS COMPETITION

One thing the Scanlons are happy to go without is New York status competition. "Immensely wealthy people live in Des Moines—I know that for a fact, being in the insurance business—but they don't show it. There is one Jaguar dealer in the entire state. The wealthy don't drive Jags. I live in the nicest suburb, Clive, but I've learned not to mention it. In New York, people looked for any excuse to mention they lived in Greenwich or Scarsdale or on the Upper East Side. Home prices are so cheap here in Des Moines. My secretary can buy a nice home."

Indeed, Peter and Jane's 3,700-square-foot house in the Country Club section of Clive, fourteen miles from downtown Des Moines, cost only $340,000. Peter's secretary, Kathy, and her husband, Kelly, are building a 2,700-square-foot house with four bedrooms, a full basement, and a large kitchen.

Your secretary?

"Two hardworking people can build the home of their dreams here," says Peter.

How is Peter's professional life in Des Moines? "The biggest thing that has happened to me, as an insurance sales manager at Amerus Life, is that I can get results without driving people into the ground. It took me eighteen months to see that pushiness doesn't work in Iowa. During my first three-sixty [job performance] review, I got good numerical results, but got dinged on culture. There is a midwestern indirectness that I was not used to. I had to learn to read people better, to pick up the signals. Funny thing is, now that I don't push people so hard, I am so much happier in the way I work.

"My work life goes like this. When I am in town, I leave for work about seven-thirty. I run four to seven miles most mornings—I get that in before leaving for work. It takes me twenty-five to thirty minutes at that time to drive into downtown. I leave the office at six-thirty. It takes me twenty minutes to get home at that time. There's no traffic at six-thirty because with a lot of banks, insurance companies, call centers, and the government, Des Moines is a four-thirty to five departure town."

"I WOULDN'T LIVE IN NEW YORK OR L.A. FOR TRIPLE THE PAY"

That's when he's in town. One of Peter's downsides is travel. Although Des Moines is Iowa's state capital, its population of only 199,000 means the city has been designated a spoke, not a hub airport by the nation's major carriers. "I travel one hundred thousand miles a year," Peter admits. "From Des Moines, it means I spend lots of hours at Denver, Dallas, and Chicago hubs. It used to annoy me, but now I turn it into time to think and read. To slow down. It works. People at the United Airlines counter know my name. Sure, it takes a little longer to fly places out of Des Moines, but in the grand calculus, it's not much time, compared to the daily commutes in places like New York and Los Angeles. I watched my father, chairman of Coopers & Lybrand, waste a good part of his life commuting from Connecticut into New York for forty years. Now I wouldn't live in New York or L.A. for triple the pay."

Ah, pay. What is it like for a New York–area guy seeing a smaller Iowa paycheck? "We make less money than we did in Connecticut, but I have a thirty-seven-hundred-square-foot house in Des Moines and we had only a nineteen-hundred-square-foot house in Hartford." Peter pauses and sips his latte. He looks up.

"I am one of the few people who probably feel better off today than four or five years ago. *It's not what you earn, but what you keep.* That includes keeping your emotional and spiritual sanity."

Deteriorating economic conditions drove the Scanlons to Des Moines and the Bartons (of Chapter 7) to central Pennsylvania. They were ahead of the curve. But in 2004, millions of American families remain stuck in high-cost urban and suburban coastal areas. They might do well to consider the example set by the Scanlons and the Bartons.

Here's what interests me. Even though midcareer hiccups pushed the Barton and Scanlon families to cheaper locations within the United States, other, deeper reasons have kept them there. (No, I'm not talking about the fact that both families now live in homes twice the size.) Dave Barton is attempting to build a new high-tech career, implausibly two thousand miles away from his old haunts in Silicon Valley, the so-called tech capital of the world. Peter Scanlon has found spiritual contentment, a closer marriage, and a more congenial management style at work in what might be called America's hometown, Des Moines, Iowa.

Both are finding their best selves in small communities.

Not everyone does, of course.

BAREFOOT AND PREGNANT IN IOWA

Tish (the Dish) Williams's belly is sticking out to Nebraska when I meet her. She also looks a little less confident than her *Upside* magazine gossip babe column photo had depicted. During the Silicon Valley boom of the late 1990s Tish wrote some of the best dish on Silicon Valley billionaires such as Larry Ellison and Scott McNealy, and she shared it daily on one of the most popular technology-business Web sites. She was a sensation.

Now here she is, in Des Moines, seven months pregnant and covering hog farming for the *Des Moines Register* business page, which nobody has ever confused with the *Wall Street Journal* or the *Financial Times*.

We are drinking tea in yet another chichi Des Moines coffee shop. Maybe there are only two such coffee shops in the entire state of Iowa, and this exhausts it. The purple-haired lass with nose rings at the counter looks as if she has been airlifted straight from the Chelsea district in Manhattan.

This is Tish's first pregnancy. Crossing her legs to get comfortable, she talks about the move.

"When you come from the Bay Area, Iowa seems conservative. You can tell they don't have a lot of lawyers around here. The city of Des Moines is fixing its streets, and they just leave the earthmovers and cones lying around."

Sounds like paradise for young boys, I think.

I ask: "What's your job like, Tish?"

"Well, today I just interviewed people at the Iowa State Fair. It's, uh, not the same as interviewing San Francisco investment bankers. During the boom, in Silicon Valley, you had the feeling that people were changing the world. You don't get that feeling here. There are two hundred software companies in Iowa, but none of them have that fever pitch.

"When I filled out the application at the *Register,* I refused to fill out the 'former job salary' line. I didn't want to become the laughingstock around the watercooler."

Why is Tish Williams here in Des Moines? Turns out her husband, Dave Raymond, is the play-by-play announcer for the Triple A baseball team, the Iowa Cubs. Dave and Tish met at Stanford. They are both thirty years old. "We're here because the next step is the major leagues. Dave's dream is to be a major-league baseball announcer. He's so close. We've agreed that we'll spend the next two years in Des Moines to see if he can make his dream come true.

"Also, I was born in Iowa. We moved to Southern California when I was four, so I don't have too many memories of Iowa. My mother was on a school board in Iowa, and when we moved she was flabbergasted at the poor quality of California public schools.

"The San Francisco Bay Area is the world's best place to be if you are single. The cost of living is so high, but you spend most of your time out of the house anyway. You don't want to live in the Bay Area and pay those mortgages and sit at home and rent movies. That would make the movies very expensive movies, when you think about it. You want to get out and enjoy the weather and the restaurants. Once you have kids, though, it's a different story. The Bay Area sucks for kids."

Tish eases around in her chair.

"I'm getting used to the idea that we might live anywhere. If Dave gets a call for a major-league job, we're out of here. Tampa? Chicago? Who knows. Our dedication is to a major-league job."

Tish squints hard: "Do you think Dave will make it?"

Six months after I interviewed Tish, Dave got the call—from the San Francisco Giants—to announce twelve games a year. His "day job" remains in Des Moines, calling games for the Triple A Cubs, but Tish and Dave are on the way up—and out.

GOOD KING MICHAEL OF DES MOINES

My journey to Des Moines, Iowa, ended at the Iowa Cubs' Sec Taylor baseball stadium, to visit team owner Michael Gartner.

Though a Hawkeye native, Michael Gartner had been plenty successful in New York. He rose through the ranks at the *Wall Street Journal*, becoming the *Journal*'s Page One editor for five years. Then he moved into television and there became an even bigger media fish as president of NBC News, a peer of Roone Arledge at ABC. All this by his late forties. Then, suddenly, the job blew up when it was learned that NBC's *Dateline* had rigged a test in which certain trucks exploded on impact. This was too bad—these vehicles did have safety issues—but the journalistic legerdemain was inexcusable and Michael Gartner ended up taking the bullet.

Michael, personally, had nothing to do with the rigged show, and could have rehabilitated his career in New York had he chosen. But he did something else. He moved back home, to Iowa. He bought the *Tribune* (then the *Daily Tribune*) in Ames, with its circulation of thirty thousand. Iowa newspapering was in his genetic code. Michael's maternal grandfather, Dr. John Charles Gay, edited the *Waterloo Morning Tribune*. His father, Carl, was an editor for the *Des Moines Register* for more than forty years. So when Michael Gartner sought to rehabilitate his career after the exploding truck fiasco, he did it by going back to his spiritual roots. He set out to make the *Daily Tribune* the best small-town newspaper in America.

Small-town newspapers once occupied a nobler position in America than they do now. William Allen White's *Emporia* (Kansas) *Gazette* was one of the country's best in the early twentieth century. The *Berkshire Eagle* in western Massachusetts punched above its weight in the post–World War II years and launched the careers of many accomplished journalists. Still, by the time Michael dove in, the gravity was running against small-town papers. National chains had been buying up most of them, beginning in the 1980s, and slashing costs, effectively reducing them to shoppers. Gartner pledged to make the *Daily Tribune* an exemplar of small-town newspapering, a crusader for liberal and good government causes, and he succeeded in making it a lively community newspaper. In 1997 the *Daily Tribune* won the Pulitzer Prize for Michael's editorial writing.

Rehabilitated once more as a journalist, the exploding-truck monkey off his back, Michael was back in Des Moines, spending his time as owner of the Iowa Cubs and a crusader for good government.

I realize how ridiculous the phrase "crusader for good government" must sound to many, but there is a certain Upper Midwest earnestness that is real, and Michael possesses it. You see it in Minnesota and Iowa more than anyplace. People in

these parts like their state and local government. Local government produces parks, hiking trails, bicycle paths, a safety net,
and the best public schools in the country. You pay higher taxes,
but then you look out the window and are satisfied you got your
money's worth. Why this works in Minnesota and Iowa and few
other places is a question I will leave to political scientists, but
the fact is, Minnesota and Iowa are the closest thing in the
Western Hemisphere to that liberal dream of social democracy,
of good government, of Sweden and Denmark.

Now sixty-two, the white-haired Michael could just as well be
Good King Michael of Des Moines, Iowa. I've come to see him
at his palace, Sec Taylor Stadium, which in fact is a palace of a
ballpark, one of those postmodern jewels with old-time baseball
feeling, the intimacy of 10,500 seats and close sight lines. The
Iowa Cubs draw 500,000 in a season.

Michael keeps the prices low so a family can sit in the bleachers (seats: $6 for adults and $4 for kids) and eat hot dogs and not
shell out more cash than they would seeing a movie. It's a great
idea. Michael's full of good ideas, in fact. One of them is to take
state gambling tax money and give it to any town with good
ideas. Iowa took Michael's idea and now has a $211 million fund
offering ten grants. Dubuque won a $25 million grant to refur-
bish its waterfront. Fifty-nine smaller Iowa towns shared a $25
million grant to building community swimming pools, hiking
trails, and windmills.

But I didn't come here to praise Michael Gartner. I came
here to bury the snowy-haired goo-goo liberal. I figured he was
big enough to handle it.

So I blurted out: "What occurs to me, Michael, as I look
around Des Moines, are the words Garrison Keillor uses to sign
off on his Lake Wobegon stories. Everything is above average.
Comfortably above average. But in being comfortably above
average, doesn't Des Moines drive out its most talented and
ambitious people?"

Gartner disputes my "nail that sticks up gets hammered down
or else packs for California" theory. But he doesn't quite refute
it. He cites the thriving insurance and mortgage business in Des

Moines, which really are national class, as examples of Harvard Business School professor Michael Porter's theories on clustering. He mentions Norman Borlaug, who won the Nobel Prize for hybrid corn.

Problem is, the Borlaug story is thirty years old. And insurance is hardly a cutting-edge business, even if Des Moines companies such as the Principal Group are state of the art when it comes to using computers. In fact, insurance seems like a perfect business for the Iowa mentality. It is stable. It is service oriented. It helps people. It is safe and boring.

I bring up the computer company Gateway, a sore subject for some Iowans. Gateway was founded in the early 1980s by Ted Waitt from Sioux City, Iowa, way up there in the northwestern corner of the state. All of Waitt's first hires were from Sioux City. In every possible way, Gateway was a company of Sioux City, Iowa, except for one crucial thing. The company, soon after its founding, had tiptoed across the Big Sioux River into North Sioux City, which is in neighboring South Dakota. Why? South Dakota has no income taxes. So here was an example of Iowa taxes chasing away bragging rights to one of America's brightest entrepreneurial stars of the 1980s and 1990s.

Michael mumbles that he doesn't know the "particulars" of the Gateway story, and doesn't want to argue about it. Iowa niceness. Iowa indirectness. Instead he wants to talk about his latest good government crusade. This one has a snowball's chance in hell of passing, but I applaud Michael for thinking about it. He wants to extend the school year to eleven months.

Doesn't Iowa already have some of the best public schools in the country? Yes, Michael says, but you have to look forward. "Life is crappy for the uneducated. With shrinking farm and skilled-labor jobs, that's not going to change. In fact, it will probably get worse. We have to prepare Iowans at all levels to make a living with their brains.

"I look at Iowa's strengths and I see a heritage of equality, of common interest. It's in our interest and in the interest of equality that we send Iowans out into the world with the best possible start."

Sitting in California or New York, where state government is widely regarded as a joke, where teachers' unions have soaked up money meant for educating children, where budget deficits run into the billions, it's easy to gaze upon Good King Michael of Des Moines with an amused squint. But in fact, he is himself an Iowan gone yonder and come home, he knows his state, and his dreams for Iowa are good things that often come to pass.

After my meeting with Michael, I drove out to the Big One. It is indeed the biggest state fair in America, square miles of beauty queens, homemade ice cream, rides, sack races, and prized hogs. The beauty queens in Iowa, well, they tend to become Big Ones themselves within the first five years of marriage. The homegrown Steve Jobs or Jeff Bezos probably has long ago packed his bags and left. But so has the child molester, con artist, drug lord, and porn king. Des Moines is an idealized version of America's hometown, and for plenty of souls that's a mighty fine place to be.

CHAPTER 10

Gold in Montana's Hills

At 6:30 A.M., the airplane's engine kicked in, and so did the caffeine from my dad's tar-black coffee.

I don't know how or why Dad continues to brew this swill. At age sixty-seven, after suffering yet another bout of midnight heartburn that would bring tears to his eyes, he checked himself into the hospital one morning. The doctor ran an EKG and said: "Call your wife. Tell her to bring your toothbrush. You're staying here." Later that afternoon Dad was put under anesthesia, his chest was cracked open, and a quadruple bypass was performed. Now the old buzzard's seventy-four, works out at the gym six hours a week, walks another three miles a day, eats any damn thing he feels like, including massive bowls of vanilla ice cream and hot fudge sauce, and starts his day with a four-hundred-milligram jolt of caffeine in a large cup.

The sun was just creeping over the horizon and the Skyhawk was ready to go. I had flown in from Des Moines and was lined up on Runway 13 and headed from my parents' home in Bismarck, North Dakota, to Bozeman, Montana, with a stop in Billings.

I was nervous.

Up until now all my solo flying had been over relatively flat land, not over big mountains. The Alleghenies, Appalachians, and Adirondacks are as golf hazards compared to the Rockies. And my plane is not a high-performance machine. It has a service-ceiling limit of 14,000 feet. Even that's an exaggeration. Take the Skyhawk much over 12,000 feet, and its performance becomes very squishy. Also in the mountains one must weigh the possibility of downdrafts, which like the hand of God can slap the little Skyhawk down at the rate of 2,000 feet per minute. Considering that the Skyhawk can climb only about 300 feet a minute in the thin air above 10,000 feet—well, you do the math.

After takeoff I bank right and cross the Missouri River south of Mandan. Directly below is Fort Lincoln. There, in the spring of 1876, General George Armstrong Custer rounded up his troops and embarked on his final, fatal mission, a 350-mile journey into southeastern Montana, to an encampment near the Little Bighorn River. I will roughly follow Custer's route today. The path takes me over little western North Dakota towns such as the improbably named New England, where I once ran a two-mile race in high school—poorly, if memory serves. The air is so clear this morning that I can make out brands of pickup trucks parked around what must be the morning coffee hangout for local farmers and ranchers.

Twenty miles west of New England, the landscape changes abruptly. I'm over the North Dakota Badlands. With its canyons and bluffs and red rocks, it looks like a small-scale version of the Grand Canyon. The Dakota version was carved out by the Little Missouri River a few thousand millennia ago. But as abruptly as the Badlands arrive, they vanish as I depart North Dakota and enter the Big Sky country of Montana.

From here, all I have to do is follow the Yellowstone River straight into Billings. Navigating an airplane by local landmarks is called pilotage, a French word (pronounced *pee-low-taj*). In the early days of flight, pilotage was all pilots had, which is why even today you see the names of small towns printed on water towers. Now we have beautiful color moving maps in our airplanes, electronic marvels that talk to global positioning satellites 22,500 miles above the earth. It's a miracle, GPS navigation, but on this fine morning I'm going to turn the thing off and use nothing but the Yellowstone River and good old-fashioned pilotage to find Billings.

Eastern Montana is parched and dreary, the part of the state you never see in the state's promotion brochures. The exception is the fertile Yellowstone Valley. This green ribbon is no more than about a mile wide on each side of the river. It's one of the prettiest natural creations I've seen from the Skyhawk, a reminder of why I love piloting a small airplane so much. One flies at much lower altitudes than when in a commercial aircraft. One gets to look out the front window, to enjoy a 270-degree view, low enough to really see things. It's wonderful to follow the meandering Yellowstone River valley, this ribbon of green cutting through arid brown land all the way into Billings.

The Billings Logan International Airport is on a bluff. It was hard to know this by looking at the sectional maps. I had correctly reckoned the airport to be on the northeast side of town, near the fairgrounds I now see ahead out the window. But I'll be damned if I can find the airport itself. Suddenly I'm nervous and aware of Dad's coffee pressing on my bladder. On my bowels too, come to think of it, but I put that out of my mind. The Billings tower says, "Do you have the airport in sight?" Uh, not really. "At your two o'clock position, six miles." Oh, Lord—yes! It's up on that monster bluff! Now I will have to land the Skyhawk on what looks like a giant aircraft carrier.

One thing you never want to do on arrival at a bluff airport is land your airplane short. Short goes straight into the side of the bluff. Short is a loud boom, a fireball, and a crying spouse on the other end of the phone.

Approaching Billings I hear myself say: "Land long, idiot!" Do I really need such a reminder? Yes I do. When you learn to fly, you are trained to land on the numbers. The runway numbers are generally painted about 150 feet in from the end of the pavement. You try to land on the numbers so you have plenty of room to roll out without excessive use of the brakes. This is a good habit to get into if you want to fly into small airports with short runways. Well, the Billings airport is built to accommodate commercial airliners. Runway 28 is a whopping two miles long and it runs slightly uphill. I could probably land on the last tenth of this giant runway and stop the airplane before it rolled off the pavement. Therefore it would be the pinnacle of foolishness to try to land short in Billings, especially with that bluff wall. One downdraft could push my little airplane into the side of a bluff and . . . *boom*.

What did I do? I landed short! I got so fixated on not landing short, that I did exactly that—actually landing short of the numbers, about 50 feet in from the edge of the pavement. There is a lesson in here somewhere, about the folly of fixating on the negative. But I have no time to elaborate on this subject, because my bladder is bursting.

I park at Edwards Jet Center, rush in to evacuate Dad's coffee, rehydrate with a bottle of Rocky Mountain spring water, and slide into a leather chair in the pilots' lounge. I pull out the charts and prepare myself for the real mountain flying ahead. To get from Billings to Bozeman, which is only ninety minutes away by Skyhawk, it looks as if I'll have to traverse the Gallatin Pass. This will be my first serious Rocky Mountain flying. Dad's coffee talks to me and I make another dash to the bathroom.

BUG SMASHER GOES THROUGH GALLATIN PASS

The day is rapidly warming and my climb after takeoff out of Billings is sluggish. I want to get up to 10,500 feet, which will allow plenty of margin over the 6,700-foot Gallatin Pass. But the airplane is performing pathetically in the hot and thin Montana air today, and it takes me forever to get up to ten five.

Simplest thing is to follow Interstate 90. On this leg, I'll take no chances and back up pilotage with the trusty GPS moving map, which also depicts Interstate 90. It's comforting to have this high-tech toy as backup, because forty miles ahead are a pair of mountain passes, and I can't tell which is Gallatin. The moving map says it's the one on the left. As I get closer I see that the mountains on both sides of the Gallatin Pass are higher than the Skyhawk's 10,500 cruising altitude. Should I go up to 12,500 feet? The pass seems wide enough, so I stay put. Through the Gallatin Pass I grit myself for the possibility of Venturi-effect funnel winds. I'm nervous as a cat, looking up at the peaks on both sides of the pass. My mouth is dry. My butt squinches. But the wind remains calm. Thank God.

The Bozeman airport is immediately on the other side of the Gallatin Pass, in a valley whose floor is only 4,400 feet. This means I'll have to chop power and drop 6,100 feet of altitude over the next twelve miles. That's a hell of a drop. Montana pilots suffer a higher than normal rate of fatalities during bad weather, due to the act of flying blind through the clouds amid the tall mountains. I can see the airport ahead, but I can also see that I'm still too high, despite having chopped the power to idle. I ask the tower for a 360 descending turn in order to lose more altitude. That plan works, the rollout is perfect, and the landing is sweet.

I taxi up to the Yellowstone Jet Center. The parking lot, or ramp as it is called, is filled with corporate jets glittering on black pavement—Citations, Gulfstreams, Falcons, Global Expresses. The superrich California/New York crowd has arrived for the month of August—David Letterman, Tom Brokaw, numerous Silicon Valley billionaires—all with fabulous spreads in Montana. Credit them for good taste. It's beautiful here in Bozeman, and for the next few minutes I feel like a card-carrying member of the billionaire crowd myself, my very own airplane parked alongside the $20 million jets.

Sweet God, I enjoy feeling rich.

———

The city of Bozeman, Montana, is what writer David Brooks calls a latte town in his achingly funny book *Bobos in Paradise*. It's a place where the rich go to don flannel shirts and Gap jeans, rent a Hummer, and then get back to nature—Kalispell, but with a university. It's a fun town, in a big bowl overlorded by ten-thousand-foot peaks, with great trout fishing and every possible outdoor activity.

Bozeman still has much of the same feel as when it was established in 1864. When gold was discovered sixty miles to the west, many took the new Bozeman Trail, which was established by a transplanted Georgian named John Bozeman. Many who followed this trail for gold returned to the valley to take up farming and business. So began the town of Bozeman in 1864.

Drive twenty-five miles east over the Gallatin Pass in the Absaroka Range and you'll hit Livingston, with a year-round population of 6,581. Livingston is the hardscrabble cousin to Bozeman. Here live forest-fire fighters, construction laborers, and Bozeman's hotel workers, who make their living off the tourists who slide, ski, and shush through the surrounding Gallatin National Forest as well as Yellowstone National Park, just forty miles to the south. These are the folks who can't afford to live in Bozeman. Instead, they man its 7-Eleven stores.

It's beautiful land, varying in topography and climate, from temperate river valleys to snowcapped peaks and open ranch lands. You'll find deer, elk, wolves, and the ancestors of the Shoshone, Nez Percé, Blackfeet, Flathead, and Sioux tribes that once called this land home.

And crazy as this seems, it's also where you'll find one of America's coolest Web entrepreneurs.

ANDREW FIELD— ## A RARE DOT-COM SUCCESS

I first met Livington's Andrew Field in 2002, at dinner in Belgrade, Montana, just outside of Bozeman. Over drinks— Moose Drool Ale for me, Merlot wine for him—Andrew told me about his business, Printingforless.com, and my first thought was, Oh, Lord, here we go. Another goofball who thinks he can rip a section out of the Yellow Pages, run his finger down a page until he finds an old-fart industry—Yo! Printing!—and decide that it can be "dot-commed."

Pardon my boredom, but I'd seen a hundred dreamers like that in Silicon Valley during the Great Boom. They weren't real entrepreneurs at all. They were Business Model Dorks. They'd tried dot-comming just about everything you can imagine . . . toy stores, furniture stores, plumbing supplies, nose rings for teenage girls, battery-operated, remote-control belch machines.

One of these start-ups, Webvan.com, raised a over billion dollars to dot-com grocery stores. What became of all these dot-coms? Most of them failed, of course. Spectacularly so, flushing billions of state pension fund and university-endowment dollars down the toilet.

I listlessly listened to Andrew Field while toying with my steak and swilling the fine local ale. As Andrew talked, I played with my napkin and pondered one of life's grand questions: Should I sample the other brews, such as Pig's Ass Ale and Grizz Whizz? Hmmm.

About five minutes into Andrew's pitch, something he said clicked—it had, as Hemingway said, the ring of truth about it—and I began to take notes. Here is Andrew's story.

In 1997, Andrew and his wife, Victoria, bored with their auto repair shop business—which was profitable but no longer growing—bought the largest print shop in Livingston. *Large* is a relative term in a town of 6,581, as Andrew soon learned. His dilemma was well known to small-town printers everywhere on the planet. In order to print four-color brochures and real-estate flyers, a printer must have access to a Heidelberg press that cost $5 million or more. Debt service on these multimillion-dollar presses is at least $25,000 a month. Andrew quickly discovered that his print shop's entire revenue, during slow weeks, barely topped $25,000.

At first, Andrew tried expanding his sales territory to include not only nearby Bozeman, but Yellowstone Park and Billings, Montana's largest city with a population of 92,000, seventy-five miles east. This strategy stopped the bleeding. It popped revenue to $80,000 per month. But with ten employees to feed, the business still was a break-even proposition at best.

On a crisp fall afternoon in 1998, Field knocked off work early to go fishing. The pure, cold water of the local mountains supports tremendous populations of rainbow, brown, brook, and cutthroat trout and Field was pretty handy with a lure. In the meditative murmur of the Yellowstone River, Field began to think about his business. Specifically, about his big, expensive—and mostly idle—printing press. It was his costliest outlay and it sat quiet more than half that day—from when the shop closed at six until it reopened the next morning at nine.

Surely, thought Andrew, other small-town printers around the country suffered similar wasteful downtime.

They had to.

It was endemic to the business.

Inherent.

Intractable.

But what if (thought Andrew, still hip-deep in the Yellowstone River) . . . what if . . . I could locate and aggregate all that idle time around the country, and list it on the Web for customers needing a last-minute print job?

Field recalled an article he'd read about an early dot-com success called Priceline.com, which allowed online customers to name the price they wanted to pay for anything from an airline ticket to a hotel reservation or car rental. Priceline's search engine would go out and find it. Maybe a similar business model could work for printing. Just maybe, Andrew thought, I could use the Web to create a job-share network to connect printers with customers. Printers would get more business, and customers could get better deals, particularly on last-minute jobs where they are often slammed by rush fees. Better still—the printers would remain anonymous, allowing them to maintain their current pricing structures in their own communities. By day these printers could serve their local townsfolk with their published price. By night they would be participating in this national auction.

Yes!

No—hold on! The idea had merit only if you saw printing as a commodity. Andrew knew it wasn't a commodity. There was a great variance in the outcome of print jobs. Without an experienced color separation expert on hand to look over the incoming layouts and photography, print jobs could turn out awful. Faces on brochures would be green, grass would be blue, and customers would be pissed as hell. Maybe not pay.

But what if . . .

. . . we handled all the prep work and customer service and

just farmed out the printing. In an age of digital files, this would work!

So Andrew Field packed up his lures, tackle, and handful of silvery trout and drove his truck back into Livingston. His launched a Web site, called Printingforless.com, in March 1999. By September orders were up to two a day. Not exactly a great beginning. But then word got around, and by 2002, when I first met Andrew, Printingforless.com had grown to $8 million in annual revenue a year. He began to receive orders from places as far away as New York and Texas and the United Kingdom. "Once you have sufficient bandwidth [provided by high-speed lines], location is no problem," Field said.

———

In July 2003 I landed my Cessna on the narrow, windswept runway on a bluff outside Livingston and visited Andrew again. I wanted to see how things were going—whether his company had hit any potholes. Andrew picked me up at the runway in his GM Yukon and we drove to his office. On the way we stopped for cold, bottled water across the road from the Teslow Grain Elevator, the tallest building in Livingston. A pack of Harley-Davidsons roared by and kicked up dust.

Field has seventy-five employees and six dogs crammed into the old Farmer's Creamery in Livingston. Outside temperatures were pushing 90 degrees the day I visited, and the heat from the Macintosh computers had the Printingforless.com office cooking at 100 degrees. The employees wore shorts and sandals. Service reps sweatily worked the phones, asking customers such questions as: "Are the faces in the Photoshop file you just e-mailed me *supposed* to be green? If not, we would be happy to correct them."

In 2003, Printingforless.com raked in $10 million in sales, up 30 percent from the year before, and eked out an $80,000 profit. Field has added service reps with backgrounds in color processing and printing to make sure the customers always get what they want in their brochures and catalogs: flesh-toned faces, blue skies, and emerald green grass. This service kicker protects Field from any challenger who thinks that Printingforless.com simply brokers excess printing capacity for the cheapest price.

The investment in phone service reps began paying off in 2004. The company's first-quarter profits were $250,000. Andrew projects sales of $17 million for the year—70 percent growth over 2003.

NEVER BEEN TO NEW YORK CITY—"THE NOISE AND STINK"

Here's a shocker. Field is forty-four years old and had never seen New York City until 2003, when a trade show caught his eye. What did Field think about the bright lights of the big city?

"I really enjoyed my visit to New York City this year," he e-mailed me in the fall of 2003. "Seeing the Statue of Liberty for the first time from the Forbes Highlander yacht was pretty special [I had invited Andrew to New York to present at our magazine's annual Up-and-Comer Conference]. A few of us jaded businessmen stood outside and got a bit misty eyed.

"That said, the noise and stink and crowds are not my cup of tea, notwithstanding the stimulating environment and great food. I found New Yorkers to be quite friendly, even if they are still suspicious about making friends. Now that I've tried it both ways—Livingston and New York—I've decided that it is best to visit the city accompanied by (or meeting) friends or family, since the best dinners include great conversation. New York's food and ambiance can enhance, but not replace, the personal connections that enrich our lives. So many people, in such close proximity, with so little real closeness."

Anyway, why leave? Andrew and Victoria own a custom home on twenty-two acres near Gallatin National Forest, halfway between Livingston and Yellowstone Park. Andrew says their home has a gourmet kitchen and plenty of stonework that keeps the place snug in the winter, cool in the summer. The Fields have a view of Pine Creek Peak, a year-round glacier.

"So, Andrew," I ask, "how much do you think your spread would sell for, if you put it on the market?"

"Oh, about two-fifty," he says.

I tried not to gasp.

Andrew urged me to seek validation of that astonishingly cheap price (from an urban coastal perspective) from Mike Pincon, a recruit from Chicago. Mike is the guy at Printingforless.com who recruits other printers around the country to participate in Printingforless.com's reverse auction. Mike had fallen in love with Montana on a trip to the Big Sky ski resort in 1995.

Mike explains: "I happened to stay in Livingston and was enthralled with the quality of life and the genuineness of the people. It was tough to go back to Chicago, to the rat race."

Back in the Windy City, Mike couldn't get the West out of his mind. During the late 1990s Mike started checking employment sites such as Monster.com and learned of a start-up called Printingforless.com, then advertising for entry-level employees. Mike, in his mid-thirties, was an old hand at digital prepress work so he couldn't afford to take an entry-level job. But he called up Andrew Field anyway and liked what he heard. As Andrew's company grew and began to have a need for experienced managers, Mike jumped in.

That was three years ago. Two years ago Mike met another midwestern refugee, from Dayton, Ohio. "I instantly fell in love with Lori. We began dating, had a baby, Megan, and just got married." Mike and Lori recently bought twenty-eight acres near Fleshman Creek ranch and built a new house on the property. The cost for land and house came to less than $200,000. True, the house is small—1,700 square feet—and the basement is unfinished. Mike figures that can always be expanded. Priceless is the twenty-eight acres of land near the Gallatin Pass.

Lord!—twenty-eight acres for $200,000!

Montana's cheap costs make all the difference for the success of Printingforless.com. Here's why. The Printingforless.com model was tried—and failed—in high-cost Silicon Valley during the Great Boom. Collabria, based in San Mateo, California, was launched in 1997, two years before Andrew's Montana epiphany in hip waders. Collabria folded in June 2001, laying off a hundred employees and vaporizing $46 million for venture capital investors like Bessemer Venture Partners, Lightspeed, the Internet Capital Group, ABS Ventures, and Mitsui Comtek Corporation.

Just a few months after Field began pulling in customers from all over the world, Collabria's investors decided the print-auction business model couldn't work. True enough. It can't possibly work if you're an overfunded, bloated Silicon Valley start-up. Maybe it works only when you're an unknown, never been to New York City peckerwood in rural Montana who is fighting for his life.

So maybe Web commerce, except for the odd Amazon or eBay, is meant to grow like the Web itself—organically, from the bottom up, with low cash burn. Maybe the medium is the model.

The success of Montana's Printingforless and the failure of California's Collabria also underlines how broken the current venture capital model is. The problem is in the way the coastal venture capital business process works: hand an entrepreneur $50 million or so to build a business fast, go public in eighteen months, and hope for a $500 million valuation on the first day as a public company.

Home-run baseball is the only game the large Silicon Valley venture capitalists know how to play—or can play. Consider the math. A typical premier VC firm may have ten partners and $1 billion under management; thus each partner manages $100 million. Each partner must parcel out his or her $100 million over five years, or $20 million per partner per year. Under such a structure, it's impossible to make hundreds of $100,000 investments, or even dozens of $1 million investments. Instead, these big-time VCs are forced to make $5 million investments and swing for the fences. Realistically, maybe only two of the ten investments will succeed, but the winners can bring in as much as $100 million or more. In order to hit home runs, the VCs need to invest in start-ups they believe they can take public in a few years. And that excludes almost all organic-growth start-ups in the boonies—such as Printingforless.com.

Like the weight lifter who can lift up the front of a Chevy but can't bend over to tie his shoes, the traditional East and West Coast venture capital communities are too muscle-bound to see smaller opportunities. Collabria failed because it was weighed down with high overhead costs and gaudy expectations. It needed a big payday quickly or, in the petri dish of the Silicon Valley, it looked like a failure. When that payday didn't happen, the VCs folded the tent. Contrast this scenario to that of the peckerwood in rural Montana who has a very low overhead. The peckerwood can take the time to find customers and nurture them and grow organically. The VCs have priced themselves out of organic growth. The peckerwood can make little experiments—he can iterate. The big VCs have priced themselves out of patience and iteration.

Part of me says, screw the coastal VCs for their greed and blindness. The other part of me says, what a fine opportunity for some fresh thinkers with a new vision of small-scale venture capital.

GREG GIANFORTE—BOZEMAN'S VETERAN ENTREPRENEUR

I'm sitting on a dock overlooking the Gallatin River, eating a ham sandwich. Another pair of legs, clad in Lakestream boots and Hodgman booties, dangles above the Gallatin. They belong to Greg Gianforte, founder and CEO of a company called RightNow, an "e-service" that automates call centers. He wears a New York Mets baseball cap. Greg is a New Jersey native and a five-time entrepreneur, battle tested and wise. His experience helped him steer RightNow past the dot-com crash that hit places like Silicon Valley with meteoric force and squashed the CEO careers of so many rookies. RightNow has posted twenty-four quarters of growth and did $28 million in sales in 2003, adding customers such as British Airways and Travelocity. Greg says between bites of ham sandwich that

RightNow is the largest employer in Bozeman after Montana State University, with 240 people.

Why did he pick Bozeman?

"I had an epiphany that the Web would remove the constraint of geography," he says. "My wife and I had been to Montana before. We both love to ski, hunt, fish . . . the whole outdoor thing. We bought a forty-two-hundred-square-foot house on thirteen acres, with a river running through our property."

I interrupt and ask a question whose answer I know will bring pain. How much did you pay, Greg, for a 4,200-square-foot house on thirteen acres, with a river running through your property?

"Hah! Six hundred thousand!"

Sheesh.

Greg continues. "I wanted to start another company. So it had to be in a university town, which in Montana means either the University of Montana in Missoula or Montana State here in Bozeman. In my eyes, Montana State is a better science and engineering school. I started RightNow here in 1998."

Greg is familiar with the coastal skepticism that says you can't build a successful technology company in the boonies. He lists the objections. "One, you can't raise capital in a small town. Bull! I raised thirty-two million in two phone calls [from Boston's Greylock Capital and Summit Ventures]. Yes, it helped that I had been successful before.

"Two, you can't hire enough talent in a small town like Bozeman. Bull again! I created a Web site called www.iloveithere.com. Then I got the alumni list from Montana State and I mailed a postcard with the Web address to all engineers that had gone to Montana State. We did some research. It showed that many of these engineers would want to come back to Bozeman if the employment opportunities were right. This strategy has worked like a charm. I send out postcards to Montana State engineers every six weeks.

"Three, you'll be secluded . . . far removed from any business networking infrastructures. Well, there are eighty-five tech businesses in Bozeman now. Pretty good networking, I'd say."

Greg Gianforte is a fast, brash talker—exactly what you'd expect from a guy wearing a Mets cap. But it's strange to hear that voice anyway, juxtaposed against the burble of the Gallatin River. Golly, it sure is heaven out here. But just as surely Greg's line about Bozeman being a hot place for an Internet company could be, to use his own favorite word, pure East Coast bull. I challenge him again.

"No. I'm dead serious," he says, swinging his legs off the dock. "I'll give you seven upsides for doing business in Bozeman." (As I am to discover, this guy likes his lists.)

"One, the productivity dividend from eliminating long commutes. Employees get more work done at work. That's good for the employees and their families. I try to set an example. I'm home by six and very rarely do I work weekends.

"Two, I can't go to dinner without seeing three or four employees. At first I thought this was a bad thing, life in a fishbowl. Now I understand the benefits. It's made me more patient with people. Just a guess here, but I think that being visible in the community is a force for more ethical corporate governance.

"Three, there's no IPO fever like you find in California or Boston or New York. Bozeman is not a get-rich-quick culture. People here have the quaint belief that something worth doing will be, by necessity, hard work.

"Four, you won't be starved for culture. My wife, Susan, and I participate in more arts and cultural events here in Bozeman than we ever did in the New York area. Dinner and a show in New York runs you five hundred bucks. Not in Bozeman. Here, we leave the house at seven-fifteen for a seven-thirty show.

"Five, employee turnover is lower.

"Six, there's a great work ethic.

"Seven, the quality of life is great. RightNow doesn't pay California wages, but we do pay Seattle rates. The average salary at RightNow is fifty-four thousand. This buys more house in Bozeman than in Seattle."

———

Whether Greg is correct in saying Bozeman is a cheap place to live depends on where you live now . . . the law of geographic/housing relativism. By coastal standards, Bozeman is dirt cheap. By Montana standards, it's getting up there. A typical untenured professor of English literature at Montana State—which is what *Zen and the Art of Motorcycle Maintenance* author Robert Pirsig was before he had his nervous breakdown, recovered, and wrote a bestselling book that eventually made him a millionaire—would find a Bozeman house way beyond reach today.

As I look around at the Gallatin Valley and smell the mix of the mountain-fed river and pine needles, as I feel the warmth of the western sun, as I savor the taste of the delicious ham sandwich and lemonade and lick mayonnaise from my fingers, I want to believe Greg Gianforte with all my heart. Montana! What a neat place. I want to move here myself, and I begin to mentally make up a list of selling points for my wife and kids. I buy the culture argument. A pretty university town could supply all the culture this North Dakota native needs. But a question lingers. For anyone with large entrepreneurial hopes who might be thinking of moving to a paradise like Bozeman, it's vital this question be answered convincingly.

Can you recruit enough engineering, management, marketing, and sales talent if your company takes off?

I press Gianforte on the talent issue. Snobby question: Does a regional university such as Montana State produce talent on the level of a Stanford or MIT?

For the first time today, Greg hesitates a bit. The gears in his head are working. He doesn't want to destroy the credibility of his story on RightNow's success with some inflated answer about Bozeman as the West's Wellspring of Talent. Then again, Bozeman's much too small a place to tick anybody off with a blunt answer. Here comes Gianforte's diplomatic answer:

"For technical talent, I leave that question to Mike Myer, the head of engineering. His attitude is that people who come to work for us have to be brilliant. They must love working on hard problems. Mike has a narrow funnel: one hire per hundred applicants. He thinks that at a public school such as Montana State, which is easier to get into than MIT or Stanford, the talent is equal at the top. You just have to be more rigorous about identifying it and recruiting it. We also concentrate on getting Montana State expats who currently work in Denver or Boise to come back here. That's a different situation, because these are older employees with a track record at Hewlett-Packard or J.D. Edwards or some big company like that.

"So, yes, we have had to go outside of Bozeman more to pull in senior managers. More of late. There is not much management talent here, but that's no fault of Montana State. There just aren't many large employers here. We are now the largest outside of the university."

DAVID BAYLESS—THE MOUNTAIN ENTREPRENEUR'S YENTL

The CEO of Pioneer Entrepreneurs is driving me back to the Bozeman Comfort Inn and attempting to explain why he had walked away from a venture capital job, his name newly engraved on the door, from a firm that had just raised a $150 million fund based on the superlative 34 percent annual return of its previous fund . . . and why he had junked his VC career just prior to the biggest IPO boom the world would ever see.

Dave Bayless!—you could have been rich! Didn't you know that being a venture capitalist was the fastest legal ticket to sudden wealth on the planet?

"Guess I didn't have the passion to be a VC," Dave Bayless tells me, keeping his eyes on Interstate 90. We are rolling past the town of Belgrade in Dave's Audi A4, which is not the car he would be driving had he stuck it out as a Dallas-based VC. More like a Mercedes 500SL coupe, I'm thinking.

Dave is mindful of steering his little Audi, so he fails to detect my sour thoughts about his spectacularly blown career. Staring at the road, Dave tells me his story . . . born to an Air Force family, grew up in Great Falls, a city of sixty thousand, north of Bozeman. Attended Montana State University, earned good grades, picked up an M.B.A. from Northwestern. Stayed in Chicago for a few years, then headed off to Dallas and into the world of big-league finance, where he mastered the debt side of acquisition finance. During the 1980s Dave got into the huddle for some of that decade's major deals, including cable TV loans for John Malone and the employee buyout of United Airlines. Then Dave sidestepped into private equity and cut his venture capital teeth at Citicorp Venture Capital, finally hooking up with a Dallas venture capitalist named Jim Hoak. That was in 1991. Had Dave just stuck it out for ten years, and surfed the IPO boom that followed, well, he probably could buy half of Montana today.

"After I quit Hoak, one of the fund's limited partners called me up. He was a nice guy, a mentor. I thought he would be sympathetic. But he was angry. He said, 'Well, smart guy, what are you going to do now?'"

"So what *did* you do, Dave?"

"I worked just hard enough doing temp CFO work to make the mortgage payments and thought about what I wanted to do. I would get on my mountain bike and ride all day in the trails and along the river and think. My wife was supportive, thankfully. What I determined is that I wanted to work with start-ups. Start-ups in the very early phase. Promising start-ups where the entrepreneur's gut instinct was more important than analysis. Where the most important thing was to go sell something.

"I've learned a lot about bootstrap entrepreneurship. Stuff they don't teach you in business school. I continued with my Rent-a-CFO pitch to keep money coming in, but I worked only with start-ups. In some cases I took stock options instead of cash. I made enough money from that to start Pioneer Entrepreneurs."

SMALL-TOWN ENTREPRENEUR ADVOCATE

Dave Bayless now calls him himself a venture catalyst. Pioneer Ventures is his vehicle to spread the entrepreneur's gospel in

Bozeman and the Rocky Mountain West. Dave is inspired by the YPO—Young Presidents Organization—a global membership of CEOs under the age of forty. YPO enjoys the reputation of a terrific networking group, which is what Dave would like Pioneer to be for technology entrepreneurs who happen to live in sparsely populated areas such as Montana. Pioneer Entrepreneurs currently sports sixty dues-paying members from sixteen states and four countries.

A few months after my visit with Dave, while back on the ground in California—if one can be on the ground in California—I took part in a Pioneer member discussion call. Dave had asked me to share my observations on urban/coastal versus small-town entrepreneurism. I said if the IPO market stayed punk for a decade, the coastal areas would be seen as too expensive to support most start-ups. Speed-to-profit would replace the crazed spendthrift game of speed-to-IPO—thus low overhead would matter greatly. India, China, and the American boonyack would gain at the expense of the American urban coasts. In theory, anyway. But unknowns remained—chiefly capital formation (could it be done from the boonies?) and talent recruitment (ditto).

Dave's Pioneer members weighed in with a barrage of intelligent comments and questions. Everybody worried about capital. We agreed that Bozeman's most successful tech entrepreneur, Greg Gianforte, the founder and CEO of RightNow, was an exception because of his prior successes. All the coastal venture capitalists had heard of Gianforte.

But for unknown entrepreneurs toiling away in small cities, there was very little venture capital to be tapped. A mismatch existed between the billions of dollars available to entrepreneurs in Silicon Valley or Manhattan and the paucity of it for start-ups located in the boonies. "Somebody could get seriously rich serving this unserved market," I said, and I do believe that.

On talent, the Pioneer group had mixed opinions. Talent recruitment in the early stages of a start-up, when you were hustling 24/7 to make a product and sell it, was not terribly hard. But if the start-up somehow caught lightning in a bottle, and was forced to grow fast just to keep pace with demand, well, that could be a problem. Recruiting talent fast enough could be a barrier. One entrepreneur put it this way: "It's easy going from one to twenty employees. It's hard going from twenty to two hundred."

True enough. When RightNow filed with the Securities and Exchange Commission to raise $60 million in a summer 2004 IPO, "it listed an unusual risk factor to its business: its hometown, located in southwest Montana," reported the *Wall Street Journal*. This, according to RightNow's filing, "could result in difficulty attracting qualified personnel."

Bottom line: It's difficult to raise money and recruit talent in outposts like Montana. But that's exactly why Dave Bayless has the right idea with Pioneer Entrepreneurs. He is filling a need. Despite walking away from certain millionaire status in Dallas, Dave loves running his organization in Montana, loves the start-ups and people he meets. It's evident he's found what he wants to do. He's working where he wants to—at home, in Bozeman.

Most of all, he's happy.

I decided to start my own company five years ago and moved from a large city (Portland, Oregon) to a more desirable, recreational environment simply because of the quality of life. What Boise has to offer was something I feel more and more employers will hope to find when they, too, decide that the bigger city isn't making the cut anymore.

In addition to a diverse and strong economy, low crime rates, strong real estate market, healthy educational programs, and a thriving downtown, Boise is a recreationalist's heaven. I can be out my door and into some of the country's best mountain biking in five minutes (and I live eight blocks from downtown). I am thirty minutes away from a skiing resort that set the national trend for affordable season passes ($200). I can fly-fish two blocks from the downtown core or drive an hour to a variety of world-class fishing rivers. Tee times are easy to come by and the green fees are very reasonable for such challenging, well-kept courses. Sun Valley, one of the nation's top resort communities, is only 2.5 hours away and Idaho in general offers more cubic water per square inch than any other state, ideal for those interested in kayaking, rafting, and fishing.

Don't get me wrong. I work my butt off. My business did over $4 million in sales last year and has experienced positive growth from the day I moved here five years ago. I spend a good ten hours a day working and another four hours a day recreating. You do the math.

I'm young, motivated, and hardworking. I also value my free time greatly. I chose a city that would allow me to work hard, grow my business, and still find the happiness I look for outside of work through recreation. I travel back to a bigger first-tier city once every other month to get my cultural fill. If I lived in a big city, I wouldn't be able to afford to travel, own real estate, or live the life that brings me such balance.

DAVID HALE
Boise, Idaho

CHAPTER 11

Toni and Mike's Permanent Island Getaway

If you carry around a full tank of envy in your life, please do not read this chapter. Your latent jealously is likely to erupt and consume you. This might be my favorite story in the book, because it's so fantasy filled and yet true—I've come down to verify it with my own eyes and ears.

Thumbnail sketch: California couple, Toni and Mike Sottak, thirties, no children yet, ditch their public relations jobs in 1998 and devote a few months to their passion: scuba diving.

Months turn into a year.

The money starts to run out.

Now what?

Move back to the San Francisco Bay Area?

No! The technology economy is overheated.

Stay in the islands?

Perfect! Except for one niggling detail: How to make a living?

Oh, that.

Hmmm—buy a dive shop?

They don't know anything about it.

The only career thing Toni and Mike do know is public relations. So why not, they figure, start a PR firm right down here in the balmy Caribbean? And that is precisely what they do . . . but let's not rush the rest of their story.

Seriously, let's not. We're on island time now. Let's eeeeeeeease back. The story of Toni and Mike Sottak must unfold at balmy island speed and be savored like a Tiki Temptation, which, I learned one morning from watching the

Bahamian channel on the telly during my visit, is made by shaking together the following (enough for two twelve-ounce drinks):

- 1 ounce Mount Gay Gold Barbados rum
- 1 ounce Mount Gay Silver
- 1$\frac{1}{2}$ ounces crushed raspberries
- 1$\frac{1}{2}$ ounces mashed banana
- 1 ounce orange juice
- 1 ounce pineapple juice

Sip your Tiki Temptation around sunset while slouched in a wooden beach chair on the white sands of the Grace Bay Club. Wiggle your toes in the warm sand.

Relaxed yet?

Okay. Let's start at the beginning. Mike Sottak grew up in working-class Worcester, Massachusetts, located about forty-five miles west of Boston. His friends, neighbors, and families spent their days and earned their money working with their hands. (Even today, the Caribbean island dweller and businessman seems uncomfortable using self-descriptive phrases like white-collar that remove him from his roots.) He attended Boston University and majored in journalism, intending to be the next man-on-the-street columnist for the *Boston Globe*.

Instead, Mike Sottak landed in Boston Celtics clover, in a public relations job. It's a break he came to appreciate much later. It was the mid-1980s and Mike didn't realize it, but he had courtside seats to one of the great NBA teams. With the legendary K. C. Jones as coach, the Celtics started Larry Bird, Kevin McHale, Robert Parish, Dennis Johnson, and Danny Ainge—with Bill Walton coming off the bench—and played astonishing basketball. Mike was there in sweat-drenched Boston Garden on the hot June night in 1986 when Boston beat the Houston Rockets for the world championship. It was the perfect job if you were male, young, and single. But since about a million young and single males would have killed to have a job like that, it didn't pay much, and so young Mike eventually moved into corporate PR.

It was another step away from his journalism dreams. Corporate public relations jobs have the reputation among journalists as being soul killers, among the most servile jobs an educated person can do. That can be true. Much depends on the corporation and its executives. The jobs in technology tend to be good ones. There is a lot of change and action, and the companies are generally run as enlightened meritocracies. Here again, the Irishman from Worcester lucked out. Mike joined a small company soon acquired by Cadence Design of Silicon Valley. Cadence sells software used for semiconductor chip design. Better yet, Cadence was led by one of the most dynamic and zany CEOs in the business, a tall, lantern-jawed dead ringer for the motivational expert Tony Robbins named Joe Costello. After Mike moved to Silicon Valley, he worked directly for Joe. It was like going to work and inhaling cocaine and laughing gas at the same time.

Mike and his new bride, Toni, a fellow PR professional who worked the agency side, settled down in Sunnyvale, a middle-class redoubt of three-bedroom houses, strip malls, and boring architecture. Mike recalled his fun days with the Celtics, and Toni was an urbane Philadelphian. They decided Sunnyvale wasn't cutting it, so they moved to San Francisco and bought a condo on Potrero Hill.

This was life the way it ought to be for a young, ambitious, childless married couple! Two professional jobs, good income, nights out dining, and no worries in a world-class city. Only one problem: As Silicon Valley boomed in the mid-1990s, so did the crush. Traffic along Highway 101, the area's central artery, became nightmarish. By 1997, Mike's commute from San Francisco down Highways 101 and 237. . . past the old Agnews state mental hospital to finding a parking spot at Cadence . . . well, that sorry fandango took sixty to ninety minutes, one way, requiring Mike to leave Potrero in the dark. "Some days I spent four hours in the car," says Mike.

Another thing happened in 1997. Joe Costello, the ebullient inspirer, quit his CEO job in an apparent burnout. Mike knew it would never be as fun again, that the odds of clicking with a new

CEO as he had with Joe were negligible. So Mike quit, too, and began working at home. Using Cadence contacts, he picked up work easily. No longer did he waste three to four hours each day in a car blankly zoning out on the river of brake lights ahead. For the first time, he had the time to enjoy his Giants season ticket.

Now he had a different problem, however. He was bored.

"SCREW IT. LET'S BUY LAND HERE"

Here Mike got lucky again. He and Toni shared a passion—scuba diving. How many golfers or pilots or fishermen or hunters can say their spouse shares their passion? Lucky dog! As newlyweds, Mike and Toni spent nearly all their vacation days and dollars puttering around the West Indies, the Virgin Islands, and the Gulf Coast of Mexico. Now was the time, Mike and Toni decided in the fall of 1997, to go for it—to take an entire year off and devote it to island living and scuba diving. They had enough money, thanks to Cadence stock.

Three months into their vacation, Mike and Toni found themselves in Bonaire, an island off Venezuela. Over dinner they ran into an engineer from Boston who had repatriated to Bonaire and opened a restaurant. From nowhere, Mike suddenly got the idea to ask this Boston engineer a life-changing question. Mike sucked in his breath and just blurted it out: "How did you *know* it was the right time to move to Bonaire?"

The ex-Bostonian looked Mike in the eye and said: "You'll never know, boy. You just do it."

Flying back to San Francisco, Mike and Toni pulled out the airline magazine map and decided that if they were to pull off their big move, they'd want to live on an English-speaking island. An hour's flight to the United States, tops. They looked closer at all the little islands in the Bahamas and Caymans. Oh yes, the dog. They'd have to be allowed to bring Duke without a long quarantine.

An even bigger question: How to earn a living when the money runs out? Mike and Toni took another trip to the Caribbean in early 1998. They brought their checkbooks, ready to buy a dive shop on Harbour Island in the Bahamas. They went so far as to hire a local attorney and accountant to examine the dive shop's books. But they soon figured out they'd have to work seven days a week to make it go. Forget that. Maybe forget this dream. Anyway, what kind of couple in their peak career years just picks up and moves to the islands? These flights of fancy were fun while they lasted, but it was time to get real.

Toni and Mike had almost locked their dream away in a pick-proof file cabinet when Mike got a tragic wake-up call. His younger brother, sick with liver disease, succumbed at age thirty-seven. That was the whack on the head Mike needed.

Life is short, Mike concluded. "You hear that all the time. But now I could see that," he says.

Again Mike jumped on an airplane to the Caribbean, this time leaving Toni behind in San Francisco. When he wound up on Providenciales, Turks and Caicos, no big bells went off. But time was passing, his brother was gone, and he was tired of dithering. Mike called Toni and told her to rent the Potrero Hill condo and get herself down here.

Some money remained in the bank from their Cadence stock, but not so much they could quit working. So Toni and Mike kept up their PR freelancing from Turks and Caicos, with no more than a personal computer and a slow dial-up connection, thinking it would tide them over until something else turned up. At first it was slow going. Mike filled the idle hours buying and selling stocks over the Internet. Keep your envy in the holster, readers, because you may not like what happens next. The Irish American from Worcester gets lucky again! Mike's big stock investment was . . . eBay, which quickly turned a fat profit, all of it free of capital gains taxes in Turks and Caicos. Now the pressure was off.

More months went by, and pretty soon clients like Xilinx of Milpitas, California, and Chartered Semiconductor, of Singapore, started coming. Somewhat to Toni's surprise, their clients gave the Sottaks little trouble about their island lifestyle. Feeling luck on their shoulders, Toni and Mike looked at each other, shrugged, smiled, and said once more: "Screw it. Let's buy land and build a home right here."

Mike elaborates: "We made so many decisions that now look incredibly risky. Leaving our jobs, thinking we could service clients with a dial-up modem. But at the time, it didn't seem risky at all. Once we said 'screw it' and decided to move, a calm came over us. The only regret we had is that we didn't leverage ourselves more and buy land right on the beach. We didn't think we could afford it. Turns out we could have."

Mike and Toni built a 2,800-square-foot home with three bedrooms. They also rented an office that was a five-minute drive away. Why move half a world away, only to get an office? "I knew I would succumb to the island torpor if I worked at home," says Mike. "It has worked out great. No meetings. No corporate bullshit. We're both more productive."

DROPPING IN FOR ISLAND GOSSIP

The Sottaks' typical working day? They usually arrive in the office off the Leeward Highway near Thompson Cove by 9 A.M. (Toni tries to get in a beach walk before she arrives) and have a fairly normal office setup, except for their clothes. Instead of shirts and ties, Toni and Mike wear shorts and flip-flops. Their dog putters around the office. Notes Toni: "She only barks when we're on an important phone call." They also have a fair share of distractions, mainly a regular flow of islanders who stop in for a visit—everyone from the local resident looking for some work or asking for a church donation to their new set of friends: scuba-dive instructors, fishing-boat captains, restaurant owners.

"They like to drop in for the island gossip," says Toni.

"And the air-conditioning," notes Mike.

Then there are the incredulous visitors from the States, probably wondering what island soul-selling black magic Toni and Mike must have performed to enjoy life this well. When I visited the Sottaks in July 2003, Mike's sister, brother-in-law, and their two boys had arrived from New Hampshire and managed to get badly sunburned on the first day.

Island life has its upsides—on many days the Sottaks go for a scuba dive in the morning and get into the office at around one o'clock—as well as its downsides: In heavy storms they sometimes lose their telecom connection.

They keep up with industry gossip through a variety of e-mail newsletters and Web sites: *EE Times, Woodstock Wire, Semiconductor Reporter,* the *New York Times,* the *Wall Street Journal,* Forbes.com. Many of the pubs offer a free "push" service where they automatically send e-mail alerts and news on key topics. The Sottaks have magazine subscriptions, too, but many arrive so late that they can't rely on them for news.

As for gossip, they use Instant Messaging with friends, colleagues, and clients. "We chat every day with someone 'on the ground' in Silicon Valley," says Toni. They also attend key semiconductor industry events—two or three per year.

During their first year living on Provo the Sottaks had fourteen sets of visitors—all of them staying at the Sottak house. At the time, Toni and Mike worked from their house. This encouraged them to get a real office away from their home so they could get some work done.

When word of Mike and Toni's incredible lifestyle began leaking out, others, including Toni's sister, followed them to Turks and Caicos. Back in the States, the boom was on, and business poured in. There was plenty of work for everyone in Turks and Caicos. Toni and Mike decided to formalize their freelance business and incorporated it as Wired Island PR. They now manage twelve freelancers around the world who do corporate writing of all kinds: direct mail, presentations, articles for trade publications, some annual reports. Most of Wired Island's clients, such as Chartered Semiconductor of Singapore and Broadcom and Xilinx of California, are in the semiconductor or semiconductor design field. Wired Island lost only 15 percent of its business from the boom peak of 2000, and by 2003 was back up and growing.

TURKS & CAICOS + VERMONT SKI CHALET = SAN FRANCISCO CONDO

What's missing? Nothing. Toni and Mike even started a family in Turks and Caicos. Their daughter Savannah, four, goes to a

British preschool called the Ashcroft School. A second daughter, Lindsey, arrived in late 2003. And the Sottaks are saving a ton of money, since their first $150,000 of income is not taxed, either by Turks and Caicos or the United States.

To escape the summer heat as well as to have a place to spend a real snowy Christmas, the Sottaks bought a ski lodge in Vermont. They moved up there for a few weeks in the fall of 2003, so that Toni could have their baby Lindsey in an American hospital. Aside from Vermont's cool mountain air— their lodge is on Stratton Mountain, an hour over the Massachusetts border—it is just close enough (without being too close) to Mike's parents in Worcester and Toni's in Philadelphia.

Are you envious? Don't read the next paragraph.

The ski chalet in Vermont and the island home in Turks and Caicos cost the Sottaks about the same as their smallish Potrero Hill condo in San Francisco.

Incredible.

Back on Turks and Caicos, Toni and Mike are becoming regular "Belongers"—a title granted only to the native born and a few special immigrants. In 2002, Mike and a partner even built an Irish bar on the island, called Danny Buoys. "We are the first bar on the island to serve Guinness draft," boasts Mike. Although Turks and Caicos is English speaking, there are few American expats. Most are English or Canadians. "So we're getting in some Molson ale," says Mike. "We also televise live English football during the season."

During my visit, the Sottaks rather thoughtfully put me up a walkable quarter mile away from Danny Buoys, in a luxury condo development called Renaissance on the Beach near (appropriately) Forbes Point. I would rise with the sun and walk for an hour barefoot on white sand past the Turks and Caicos Club, Treasure Beach, the Grace Bay Club, and Club Med. Non-Belonger that I am, I would be sweating like a pig by the time I returned, and I was only walking. The air in Turks and Caicos is surprisingly dry and light, the humidity being a full twenty percentage points lower than the Caribbean average. Or so the local real estate brochures bragged. I believe it. Noathing's eempossible, as native pronunciation would have it.

I flip on the television and hear island calypso gospel music, a slower and more liquid version of reggae. Evangelical churches flourish on the island. Right now I am fascinated to watch, against the backdrop of calypso gospel music, funeral announcements, of all things. The names of these deceased islanders are so melodic! Margaret Tawana Lawanda Swain-Meeres, age forty-three. Stefan Cyril Alexander Grant, age thirty-five. Elder Dr. Callender Shaddrack Roberts, age ninety-three. Way to go, Shad!

These death announcements go on and on, to the tune of a warm wave calypso beat:

> *"I'm dancing . . .*
> *with an angel*
> *with an angel*
> *with an angel . . ."*

Me, I'm still sweating like a pig. This is not due to the island heat but the endless Bushmill and Guinness boilermakers I drank last night at Danny Buoys. The delicious pineapple chicken dinner I had did an inadequate job of soaking up the booze, a flaw I must speak to Mike about. I help myself to four Advils, another glass of ice water, and switch channels.

The local news is that a U.S. Air Force C-17 jet made an unscheduled landing at Provo the week before, and islanders are still yacking about it. The green high-wing military transport was used to support President Bush's trip to Africa, and normally the jet would refuel in the air. But something went awry and it had to land on Provo, where there happens to be during the summer of 2003 a simmering anti-Americanism. Hard to tell how deep this resentment goes. A local election is going on, and there on the telly is a candidate named Emmanuel Rigby, properly indignant. I switch channels again, to sports. The next Monday, after I leave, a woman diver named Tanya Streeter will attempt to break her world's free-dive record at nearby Beaches Resort.

Streeter has already gone past 500 feet. She is the only woman to hold a world's record in a sporting event contested by both men and women. On land, she can hold her breath a stunning eight and a half minutes.

"Some jugs that lady has," said a customer at Danny Buoys that evening.

———

Since the Sottaks' great escape, costs in Provo, with a population of ten thousand, have gone up "to almost Bay Area levels," says Mike, but a glance at the real estate brochures says Mike's been smoking island ganja. Land and houses are still a heck of a lot cheaper down here. I figure Toni and Mike's Provo house, plus their ski chalet on Stratton Mountain in Vermont, cost about the same as an average dollhouse with shag green carpets in Silicon Valley. Am I repeating myself? Sorry, I just can't get these prices out of my head.

Not everything is cheap down here. Telecom costs are obscene, as Cable and Wireless, the island's provider, has no competition. "Our telephone and fax costs come to $6,000 a month. We do everything we can by e-mail," says Mike.

Adds Toni, "Telecom is our single biggest cost. Since we chose to live here knowing that telecom costs were high, we don't feel it is fair to pass all of this expense on to our clients, so we end up eating a lot of the cost. We've been working on ways to cut costs like using Instant Messaging more and trying to do a lot via e-mail. But there is no way around the basic need to talk on the phone and participate in conference calls. The really frustrating thing about our telecom costs is not how expensive they are but how unreliable they can be. We pay three to four times more for telecom than we would in the United States but consistently have issues with our Internet connection speed and our ability to get an active outside line to make a call to the States at ninety cents a minute!"

"We recently moved our office two miles down the road and just found out that this half of the island is wired in copper instead of fiber. So our three-hundred-and-fifty-dollar-a-month

DSL connection performs fifty percent slower than it did in our old location! And, this being an island, it is sometimes difficult to find an operator to connect you when you need to make a call. We try to keep things like this in perspective, but it is difficult sometimes as we know what service is like in the United States."

Toni says everyone on the island thinks the Sottaks are worka- holics because they often work till 7 or 8 P.M. and they sometimes see Mike on his cell phone talking to a client while they're at a restaurant or out for the evening. "But," says Toni, "we know that compared to our lives in Silicon Valley, we are far more bal- anced in terms of the work/life equation."

Indeed they are. Noathing's eempossible.

PART 2

CHAPTER 12

The Turbulent 2000s—
the Decade of Cheap

E conomic forces sweeping the planet favor a small-city migration and revival. If you were intrigued by the stories of relocation and reinvention in Part 1, and you feel inspired to set out on this great adventure yourself, your timing is good.

Okay, just what are the economic forces driving the Turbulent 2000 economy today? The answer lies in a riddle.

Question: What do these have in common—the search site Google, the television show *Blind Date*, China and India, Wi-Fi, $29 DVD players, and Max Oshman, a teenage Web designer from Summit, New Jersey?

Answer: They are actors in a play called the Cheap Revolution, a phrase I began using in my *Forbes* column in 2003. Still confused? Read on.

Google

This red-hot company handles 750 million page views a day and has become the fourth-most-visited Web site in the world. Google performs its Web-search miracle with a backroom technology plant consisting of about 100,000 cheap servers— basically, mail-order PCs without monitors—that cost about $2,000 apiece. When one of these cheap crunchers goes on the blink, Google junks it, just like an old razor blade, and slips in a replacement. Pay attention to the money Google does *not* spend. No fat service contracts. No bloated in-house "fix-it" departments. Google's cheap ways save 90 cents on the typical information technology dollar, according to Mike Nevens, former head of McKinsey & Company's technology practice.

Blind Date

With children ages seven and eleven, my wife and I decided last year to unplug our TV during weekdays. On weekends we allow the kids only approved DVD movies. So it is with some sense of guilt that I admit to being a closet fan of *Blind Date*—the raunchy show on the WB Network featuring men and women on a first date. Hilarious are those pop-up cartoon bubbles that spell out what the men and women are really thinking. Shows like these are popular with viewers. They're extremely popular with studio executives, because they can be produced at a tiny fraction of the cost of *The Sopranos* or *24*. Credit this TV trend to (or blame it on) technology, which has shrunk $500,000 worth of film/video production equipment down to a cheap camcorder and a PC. Sure, the technical-quality gap is noticeable—today. But the quality gap will disappear in five years.

China and India

"How about those Mavs!" says Roger, the perky help-desk guy, to my Dallas friend on the phone. My friend is attempting to straighten out a credit card problem. On the other end of the line is Roger, apparently an educated Brit who speaks with a high-toned Oxford accent. My Dallas friend has just returned from England, so the two get to talking. But something strikes my friend as odd, out of place. Why would this educated Roger be doing lowly call-center work? So my Dallas friend asks, "Where are you, Roger?" It turns out Roger is calling from India, and his real name is Rogesh. He is working for $300 a month. When Rogesh completes his engineering degree, assuming he stays in India, he can expect to earn $1,000 a month. In China, as well, very sharp young men and women aspire to make $1,000 a month. In go-go Shanghai this feat requires an advanced engineering degree, but jobs for the qualified in China are plentiful. Global companies such as Taiwan's TSMC, America's Cisco and General Motors, and Germany's BMW are currently building plants in China, hoping to tap this abundant, affordable talent.

Wi-Fi

France Telecom lost $23 billion in 2002. How? Like many other European state-owned telecoms, it had foolishly forked over billions for so-called 3G ("third generation") wireless spectrum a few years ago. Whoops. Then came dirt-cheap Wi-Fi and a host of other off-the-rack wireless wonders. To the established telecom giants, Wi-Fi looked like a nerd hobby at first. Not so now.

$29 DVD Players

Buy 'em at your grocery store. That's what the Karlgaard family did over Christmas, when our regular DVD player died and we looked into the abyss of a holiday without *How the Grinch Stole Christmas* and Chevy Chase's *Christmas Vacation*.

Max Oshman (aka Flash Kid)

Max and his global team of Web designers—average age twenty-three—have signed up clients such as Stevie Wonder, Bad Boy Records, and Microsoft. The team charges about one-tenth of what a typical Madison Avenue or Hollywood Web designer might. Max's team has no office. They work virtually, from their homes in Russia, India, Hong Kong, and Ohio; even Max is not quite sure. All any team member needs is a fast PC, cheap Macromedia software, and a high bandwidth connection. Now, were I a Madison Avenue executive competing with teenagers working out of bedrooms, I think I might head out for a three-martini lunch and never return.

What I've described in the last several pages are the first few drops of a storm that will sweep over most industries and professions during the next ten years. Are you ready for the Cheap Revolution?

NOT YOUR FATHER'S OUTSOURCING

The development to watch now—and it's a shocker—is how far and fast the Cheap Revolution can go. In 2003, Massachusetts General Hospital began e-mailing MRIs to India, where the scans are read by $20,000-a-year radiologists. By contrast, the annual income of an American radiologist is $350,000, on average. Why does Mass. General do this, and why are smaller regional American hospitals expected to join in? Short answer: They can, with the click of a mouse.

In late 2003, IBM announced that it would outsource almost five thousand software jobs to India. It seems as if we read a story like this once a week. Recall the report from my *Forbes* colleague Robyn Meredith, in Chapter 3: "General Electric already has twenty thousand employees in India—most at the Jack Welch Center. American Express has ten thousand and counting. General Motors is doing computerized engineering models of crash-testing there. Every big American and European company is already in India or expanding—the tech jobs first and everything else on its way, at one-tenth to one-fifth the cost."

Engineers with Ph.D.s in China start out making $12,000 a year. Most are as good as ours. There sure are a lot more of them. China graduates four times as many scientists and engineers per year as does the United States—600,000 versus 150,000. Consequently, China has upgraded itself from making cheap goods only to having its bottomless supply of engineers research and design products, too. The country is expected to become the world's largest manufacturer of sophisticated semiconductor chips by 2005.

In Malaysia, DHL Worldwide Express has built a huge, high-tech room full of computers tracking packages and cargo shipments around the world. Electronic Data Systems and HSBC Bank and others are building human relations back offices and credit-card processing units there.

"Some experts estimate 30 percent of all American white-collar work could be moved offshore at lower cost and equal quality," Robyn wrote me.

CAN WE COMPETE?

Will the Cheap Revolution hand America its head?

That's the political hot potato of our day. The question is very much unsettled. Amidst the dramatic recovery in U.S. stock prices and GDP percentage growth rates that occurred during 2003 and early 2004, job growth, well . . . job growth showed up rather late in the cycle.

True, job growth typically lags stock prices and GDP percentage growth rates at the beginning of any recovery. But by the early months of 2004, the *New York Times* was noting: "Both the White House and the Fed are confronted by a recovery unlike any in modern history. Economic growth has been soaring for months, corporate profits have shot up, and the stock market has regained much of its old ebullience. Yet job creation has been slower than in almost any previous recovery, and wage growth has slowed to a crawl." Why? The *Times* took a stab: "That appears to reflect another big new element that lies entirely outside the president's control: the enormous increases in productivity, which have made it possible for companies to squeeze more output from each worker."

The *Times* story quoted John Makin, a senior economist at the American Enterprise Institute: "The evidence is powerful that we can have 4 to 5 percent growth without hiring much."

You could argue that the liberal *Times* has its own agenda and is inclined to put a negative spin on any Bush administration economic figures. You might be right. But John Makin and the American Enterprise Institute tilt in the other direction. They want to give the Bush administration the benefit of the doubt. When Makin is worried about jobs, we should be, too.

For the first time in forty years, Okun's Law is being challenged. Arthur Okun was an economist who posited in the 1960s that rising GDP percentage growth rates would always reduce unemployment. For every point above 3 percent that GDP growth rises, the unemployment rate falls by half a percentage point, said Okun. The next forty years would prove Okun right. When the economy grew, jobs followed.

But now it would seem Okun's Law needs an amendment to account for the Cheap Revolution's offspring: rampant technology-led automation and equally rampant outsourcing. Call it Okun's *Alice in Wonderland Asterisk*. It works like this. As productivity rises on the twin jets of technology and outsourcing, the GDP percentage growth rate *has* to keep rising, too ("faster and faster"), just to keep employment levels running in the same place.

BIG WINNERS, BIG LOSERS

The Cheap Revolution will benefit both America and the world—in the aggregate. But down at the street level, where we live, expect to see big winners and big losers.

American people, companies, cities, and regions located on the right side of the Cheap Revolution will do just fine. Two companies perfectly positioned to thrive in the Cheap Revolution are Wal-Mart and Dell. Both are extremely effective users of information technology; both operate some of the best supply chains in the world. Both outsource routine work when they can (Dell to Malaysia, Wal-Mart to China). Both are headquartered in low-cost heartland cities, Wal-Mart in Bentonville, Arkansas, and Dell in Round Rock, Texas, a suburb of Austin. It would be very hard for any cheap attacker, even one located in Bangalore or Shanghai, to get underneath the cost and efficiency structure of either Dell or Wal-Mart.

By contrast, look at Sun Microsystems, a legendary Silicon Valley company. Alas, Sun has got its nipples caught on the wrong side of the Cheap Revolution. Whereas Dell sells "blade" cheap servers that cost a few thousand dollars apiece (like a razor blade, you dispose of them when they are outdated), Sun earns its keep by selling servers that cost $30,000 to $200,000. Sun is headquartered in California's Silicon Valley, where the company pays real estate costs easily five times, on a square footage basis, that paid by Dell.

It doesn't stop there.

A sizable chunk of Sun's thirty thousand employees work in Silicon Valley. The residential community nearest to Sun's headquarters is Menlo Park, where a 2,200-square-foot, three-bedroom, two-bath house on a typical suburban lot (only a quarter acre in Menlo Park), cost $1,400,000 in 2004, according to Coldwell Banker. An equivalent house would cost $242,000 in Austin and $202,000 in Bentonville. Sun thus is forced to pay its employees significantly higher salaries to live within a reasonable driving distance to work, a "tax" that inflates Sun's operating expenses to levels incompatible with the Cheap Revolution.

In the era of the Cheap Revolution, American employers will be under tremendous pressure to cut costs and keep cutting. Even a dose of monetary inflation, should it come (it probably will, but more on that later), will not do much to relieve this pressure. *Once and forever, the Internet has let the cost versus comparative advantage genie out of the bottle!* Customers can easily shop the globe for prices. Vendors must respond by slashing their own cost of goods and operation. Again, the Web makes this dynamic mercilessly unavoidable. Because we all can shop the world for a better price, we do. Good luck to any CEO who ignores these pressures and tries to pass along rising costs to the customer. That won't work.

Suffice to say it's a rough environment, and America's employers, when they are not striving to automate jobs or off-shore them to Asia, will begin to look at the cost advantages of relocating out of pricey urban coastal regions and into America's heartland. They will because . . .

. . . the cost differences between urban coastal America and heartland America are staggering! Consider this example of 2004 house prices across America. (House prices matter, because they affect salaries.)

Average Price for a 2,200-Square-Foot-House on ¼-Acre Lot

PRICEY COASTAL SUBURBS

Palo Alto, California	$1.5 million
Greenwich, Connecticut	$1.5 million
Santa Monica, California	$1.2 million
Georgetown, D.C.	$900,000

FASHIONABLE UNIVERSITY CITIES

Boulder, Colorado	$539,000
Eugene, Oregon	$312,000
Charlottesville, Virginia	$295,000
Madison, Wisconsin	$268,000

HEARTLAND RISING STARS

Tampa, Florida	$284,000
Charlotte, North Carolina	$247,000
Boise, Idaho	$235,000
Mobile, Alabama	$227,000

CHEAP HEARTLAND CITIES

Memphis, Tennessee	$207,000
Fort Wayne, Indiana	$199,000
Tulsa, Oklahoma	$174,000
Binghamton, New York	$154,000

A house in Palo Alto or Greenwich costs ten times more than a similar house in Binghamton. Certainly, the price gap between urban coastal areas and the heartland has always existed. But today the gap is the largest since the Great Depression, when people were abandoning farms.

The gap isn't normally this large. When I left my hometown of Bismarck, North Dakota, during the mid-1970s to attend college at Stanford University, in Palo Alto, the price gap between Palo Alto and Bismarck was about two to one. (Remarkably, the first house to sell for $100,000 in Palo Alto didn't occur until 1972!) During the late 1970s, thanks to the electronics boom and California's population growth, Palo Alto began to pull away. By the end of the 1970s, the price gap was four to one. For a while during the early 1980s, Bismarck kept the gap locked, thanks to an oil-drilling miniboom in western North Dakota. But from 1984 on, it's been all Palo Alto. Today the gap is eight to one.

Because of the way global competition exerts downward pressure on business operating costs, I think more American businesses will pull up stakes and relocate to the heartland. Therefore the urban-heartland real estate gap in 2004 may be at its widest. (Rising mortgage interest rates, certain to occur by 2005, will shrink the gap, too.) Which means, if you currently live in a high-price urban coastal area, you might consider cashing out and moving to an equally nice (or better) house in a much cheaper location. Now is the time to do it, to arbitrage that historically large price gap.

We're equity bandits who took the cash out of our Katonah, New York, house and got a much nicer property up here and a far smaller mortgage. Besides, all the math in the world is almost irrelevant when one sees their eight-year-old daughter jump in the air exclaiming "I love Maine!" upon hearing Dad now has the time to be a chaperone at her upcoming class trip to watch the minor-league Portland Sea Dogs.

JOHN GATES
Cumberland, Maine

YOU'LL GET MORE THAN MORTGAGE RELIEF

What will you leave behind? Crushing status competition, for one. The May 28, 2003, *New York Times* wrote about a woman named Amanda Uhry, founder of Manhattan Private School

Advisers, who counsels worried Upper East Side parents, at $1,000 a visit, on how to get their children into private school. Uhry attracts clients with newspaper ads that say: "Private School is a 14-year, $300,000 commitment, *if* your kid is lucky enough to get in. You need us now."

Yes, you do. And if you want to continue playing in the coastal executive-class leagues—rich anywhere else—you won't just pay through the nose in real estate. You will continue paying the "urban-executive surcharge" again and again: in private schooling, private club memberships, status cars, and the variety of wardrobes you will need for business, business casual, the sailing club, the golf club, the opera, and so on.

Why do parents on New York's Upper East Side worry so much about private schools? There is immense pressure among the executive class to ensure that their children don't fall out of the executive class. One way to do this is to get Johnny and Katie into an Ivy League college, which pretty much guarantees a professional career trajectory. Well and good, but consider the chain of events needed to get Johnny and Katie into Harvard. It starts with the right prep school . . . which itself starts with the right day school . . . which must begin with the correct kindergarten . . . which starts with the proper preschool! Mania for an Ivy League education has reached a point of absurdity. It causes a Wall Street rascal like Jack Grubman to squeeze a million-dollar donation from his employer, Citibank, for a Manhattan preschool, just to gain his twins' acceptance.

The blood sport over grades, SAT scores, and admission into the right college has gone nuclear in America over the last generation. It has become the most high stake, hard fought of status competitions among the professional middle class and executive class in urban coastal areas. It has fed a $1.3 billion-a-year industry in consultants who specialize in boosting SAT scores and counseling on college applications.

Funny thing is, college admissions officers discount most of that effort anyway. In fact, the very worst place to be from when trying to gain entrance into Harvard may be such executive-class enclaves as the Upper East Side of Manhattan, Georgetown,

Summit, New Jersey, or Marin County, California. Fred Hargadon, the dean of admissions of Princeton, once told the *Stanford Observer* (when he held a similar post at Stanford) that the children of the executive-class suburbs, with their Stanley Kaplan–enhanced 1,500 SATs, with their "traveled extensively in South America" résumés, with their varsity letters in lacrosse or field hockey or any sport uncontested by the masses of American youth, all look the same to him. Hargadon said he had no way of distinguishing them. The boy from rural Georgia with a passion for drawing comic books stands out every time.

Three years ago, while returning back to Silicon Valley from snowboarding in Tahoe (normally a five- to six-hour drive!), I stopped for coffee at Starbucks in Rocklin (in the suburbs east of Sacramento). A quick stop for coffee turned into a house-hunting trip. . . . We thought, here is a great place to live, just over an hour from the slopes. So after a few weeks scoping things out and talking it over with my wife, I gave notice to my CEO that I was heading for the foothills.

The gains? A brand-new house in a great neighborhood a few blocks from a great golf course, which cost one-third less than the house I sold in Silicon Valley. A great church, friends, an outdoors lifestyle; even the restaurants and shopping ain't too bad.

BYRREN YATES
Rocklin, California

NEW TAX TARGETS—
THE COASTAL URBAN MIDDLE CLASS

Writes Daniel Henninger in his terrific "Wonderland" column in the *Wall Street Journal:* "A salary of $30,000 in Los Angeles has the same buying power that a salary of $13,448 has in Tuscon. For Las Vegas, the figure is $13,241. New Yorkers' third-favorite refugee camp is North Carolina. Easy to see why. You've got to earn $45,000 in the Big Apple to buy what $7,191 gets in Durham."

For the executive class, the ratios are larger than even this. Thank the progressive tax code (or not). The last dollar of a $75,000 Des Moines income is taxed at about 18 percent, toting up federal and typical state and local taxes but figuring in deductions for mortgages, et cetera. The last dollar of a $300,000 income in a high-tax jurisdiction like New York or California is taxed in the 40 percent to 50 percent range. And that's with the Bush tax cuts, which sliced the top income rates from 39.6 percent to 35 percent.

Thus, all things being equal (which they never are, of course) it takes a family income of $300,000 in Manhattan or Palo Alto, a $250,000 income in Washington or Boston or Los Angeles, and a $150,000 income in Seattle or Atlanta, to enjoy a lifestyle comparable to a $75,000 family income in Des Moines—in other words, the beginnings of an executive-class lifestyle.

It's almost a sure bet that the tax burden imposed on the urban executive class will get worse in the coming years. It will get immediately worse if Bush is not reelected and John Kerry lets the Bush tax cuts on income, dividends, and capital gains expire, beginning in 2006.

And it will get immediately worse if Bush is reelected, too! Likely targets, in a Bush or Kerry administration: tax deductions for expensive homes and salaries (e.g., raising the $80,000 limit on wages subject to Social Security taxes).

Republican or Democrat in charge, here are more reasons why the overall tax burden will get worse for the urban middle and executive classes. Start with state taxes. American states with the largest budget deficits are those, like California ($38 billion in 2003) and New York ($13 billion in 2003), whose economies did the best during the Great Boom. Easy to explain why. New York is home to the financial industry. California is home to technology. Salaries and bonuses of employees in these states skyrocketed and the taxes paid on them filled state coffers. Stock market returns during the Great Boom, in particular, flooded states like New York and California with tax income from capital gains revenue. In the banner stock year of 2000, more than a third of California's revenues came from capital gains taxes!

These states now have a monstrous problem: big deficits, but no clear way to pay for them. Politicians being politicians, the easy answer (at least to them) is to hike taxes even more. New York City mayor Michael Bloomberg decided in 2003 to raise city income taxes by 10 percent on incomes over $100,000 for single people. Former California governor Gray Davis vowed to balance the state's budget—with a $38 billion deficit, he would have had a long way to go—on the backs of high-income earners. The executive class, in other words. Will California's new governor, Arnold Schwarzenegger, be able to resist?

The prognosis stinks at the federal level, too, thanks to a developing nightmare called the Alternative Minimum Tax.

Writes *Forbes* in its April 1, 2002 issue: "By 2005 the AMT will claim 13.4 million victims—including 79% of taxpayers grossing $200,000 to $500,000; 46% of those earning $100,000 to $200,000; and 23% of those with incomes of $75,000 to $100,000—projects a study by Jerry Tempalski, an economist working at the Treasury Department."

Who will the AMT hit hardest?

"If you make north of $100,000 and live in the coastal states with high taxes and high costs (and thus lots of deductions), you are in the group that stands an excruciatingly high chance of getting hit by the AMT over the next few years," writes *Fortune* magazine in its June 23, 2003, issue. The magazine says 95 percent of taxpayers in the $100,000 to $500,000 income range will be hit. "Here's the bill. You'll be paying an extra $10,000 a year in taxes, on average."

GET READY FOR A LONG, FLAT STOCK MARKET

Ah, but won't the stock market bail you out over time and fund your dream retirement? Sorry. Don't expect the stock market to bail you out. History speaks loudly on this matter, and what it tells us is:

- America is in the early years of a financial Great Bust that began in 2000. The stock market's revival between late 2002 and early 2004 is only a halfhearted "catch-up" to the highs of 1999–2000. It is likely the stock market will level off or retract after the 2004 election—maybe before.
- The Great Bust could take ten or fifteen years to resolve.
- This Bust will fall hardest on the beneficiaries of the Great Boom—America's urban coastal regions.

No, I don't like writing these words. Readers of my *Forbes* column know that I am a bull by nature. But I am a bull who was mugged by the reality of the 2000–2002 bust, which I failed to anticipate and during which I lost about $200,000, half of it in private equity (er, dot-com start-ups that went belly-up). As a result, I have become a bull of a fair-weather sort. When federal fund rates are below the rate of inflation, when inflation itself is low, when taxes are being cut and regulatory burdens are being lightened, and when equity prices are reasonable, sure, I'm a bull. As a circumstantial bull, I predicted the impressive stock recovery in late 2002 to early 2004. But now I have changed my mind.

After my $200,000 walloping during the 2000 to 2002 bust, I became a more respectful student of market history. Here is what I learned.

The stock market's long bull run of 1982 to 2000 was unprecedented. It began in August 1982 (when the Dow was 777) and ended in January 2000 (when the Dow was 11,723). History is clear: This kind of sustained performance is unlikely to repeat in our lifetimes. Putting the Great Boom into an historical context, we see that American stocks returned, on average, 15 percent a year, counting dividends but net of inflation, during this wonderful period. How good was this? Good enough to double your money every four-and-a-half years!

Thus, between 1982 and 2000, if your returns were only market average, your stock portfolio still would have grown sixteen-fold. Put another way, your grubstake of $100,000, invested at the market's bottom in 1982 and simply left untouched in a broad S&P index fund, would have been worth $1.6 million at the market's peak in 2000.

Stock market returns during the Great Boom were more than twice as good as historical averages.

Let's compare the Great Boom to the much longer period of 1900 to 1981. During these eighty-one years, stocks returned an average of 7 percent per year counting dividends but net of inflation. Now, 7 percent is not bad—it doubles your money every ten years. Had the years of 1982 to 2000 been marked by historically average market returns of 7 percent, your $100,000 grubstake invested in an S&P index in 1982 would have been worth $360,000 by 2000.

Check out the dramatic difference: $1.6 million (Great Boom returns) versus $360,000 (historically average returns).

THE QUESTION IS . . .

What rate of stock returns can we expect between now and 2015?

- Average returns of 7 percent?
- Great Boom returns of 15 percent?
- Somewhere in the middle?

Sorry. The answer is, probably average or slightly worse. Warren Buffett, the chairman of Berkshire Hathaway and investor par excellence, says American stock markets, in an attempt to correct for the 1982–2000 Great Boom, will under-perform until the year 2015 or so. During this 2000–2015 period, Buffett thinks stocks will return only 4 percent a year, counting dividends and net of inflation.

There is a bit of a silver lining here (but only a bit). Since most of the Great Bust stock carnage occurred between early 2000 and late 2002, Buffett is willing to say that between 2004 and 2015, the markets could return 6 percent to 7 percent a year, or slightly less than the historical average.

Buffett's sober realism is echoed by a Who's Who of American investors, including John Bogle, the founder of the giant mutual fund Vanguard; Bruce Johnstone, former manager of Fidelity's giant Equity-Income Fund; and Bill Gross, the chief investor for the giant bond fund, PIMCO.

Just so you won't think I'm reaching for the most obvious name—Warren Buffett—and basing my forecast on him alone, let's look at the range of other stock market forecasts in circulation. They are breathtaking in scope. You will find plenty of smart seers who think the stock market can do far better than return 6 percent to 7 percent a year between now and 2015. One of them is Art Laffer, the supply-side economist and inventor of the Laffer Curve, which posited (accurately, as it turned out) that lower taxes usually yield higher tax receipts, thanks to a flurry of economic activity that always responds to reduced taxes. Laffer told *Barron's* in early 2004 that he thinks American stock markets are the most undervalued they've been in forty years! Perhaps a quarter of what they're really worth! Hello, Dow 40,000! Other supply-side economists of repute tend to agree with Laffer, if more cautiously and only directionally. They include Brian Wesbury, chief economist for Chicago's Griffin, Kubik, Stephens & Thompson and the forecaster I most often quote in my *Forbes* "Digital Rules" column; Abby Joseph Cohen, the perpetually bullish (and often right) analyst with Goldman Sachs; Ed Yardeni, chief strategist of Prudential Equity Group; Larry Kudlow of MSNBC's Kudlow & Cramer fame; my boss Steve Forbes, a forecaster of uncanny accuracy; and my mentor, George Gilder, author of *Wealth and Poverty* and numerous other sage books and articles. These bulls believe that the Bush tax cuts have ignited a multiyear economic recovery and stock market rally that will easily surmount any historical gravity.

That said, you can spin 180 degrees on your heels and find equally smart forecasters who are convinced that stocks will perform much worse between now and 2015—worse than even the moderately bearish Buffett and Bogle crowd say. A sampling of these really bad news bears includes Bill Baldwin, the lethally bright editor of *Forbes* and a valuation fundamentalist who told me he thinks the Dow and NASDAQ are worth no more than 6,000 and 800, respectively; and Marc Faber, a Hong Kong hedge-fund manager who says Europe and the United States are in a long-term eclipse to rising Asia. What about the market's 2003 rally? It didn't impress Jeremy Grantham one whit. Grantham is the founder of the Boston investment bank Grantham, Mayo, Van Otterloo & Company, which manages $48 billion, presumably none of it dumb money. Grantham told *Barron's* in late 2003: "The simple story is that the market is over-priced and will go to a trendline P/E, which we now believe is 16. Currently the market is around 24. This is just not a bear market rally but the greatest sucker rally in history."

Which camp should you believe? Were this a football game, I would cheer my socks off for the bulls, and not just because I, like any good American, want a bullish outcome. During the last twenty-five years, optimists such as Art Laffer, George Gilder, and Steve Forbes have proven to be more accurate in their fore-casts of the American economy, by far, than the other two camps. (Buffett, for all his stock-investing prowess, often gets the macrotrends wrong, believing the world is in worse shape than it is. Perhaps Buffett, a political liberal, gets too easily derailed by his dislike of the tax-cutting conservative administrations. Hey, it happens. Many political conservatives grew grumpy dur-ing the Clinton years and failed to see the 1990s boom.)

Still, if I had to wager my own retirement fund, I would bet on the Buffett and Bogle prediction of 6 percent to 7 percent stock market returns between now and 2015. Here's why. As the U.S. economy entered 2004, the stock markets had already rebounded, the dollar was softening badly, gold prices were soar-ing, and the federal government was spending like nothing seen since the LBJ administration—adding 27 percent in discre-tionary spending in the previous two years.

These trends spell one thing: monetary inflation. And stock markets hate monetary inflation (because it artificially taxes long-term capital gains).

So let us suppose that Buffett and Bogle are most likely to be correct in their forecast of slightly below-average portfolio returns occurring between now and 2015. If they're right—and I hope like hell they're wrong, though I doubt it—the lifestyle implications for millions of families, particularly those clinging to their cushy middle-class status in pricey cities and suburbs, are not good.

Let's say you are forty-two years old, hoping to semiretire to a life of professional consulting, hobbies, and charitable good works at age sixty. That's a goal shared by many white-collar professionals. I hope you make it. But do realize that the difference to your portfolio between a 7 percent return (versus a 14 percent return) during these critical next eighteen years of your life, from age forty-two to sixty, is not 2×, as suggested by the percentage difference. It is 4×, as impelled by the laws of compounding over eighteen years! It is the difference between a retirement stash of $250,000 versus one of $1 million. If your dream is to semiretire to a life of consulting, hobbies, and charitable good works at age sixty, and you think you'll live to age eighty, would you want to launch your great autumnal adventure with only $250,000 stashed away?

GOOD-BYE TO THE GOOD LIFE?

If the stock market won't fund your dream of a perfect retirement, what else might? Stock options at your company? Better think twice about that.

Consider a typical employee in a high-cost Boston suburb. She works at a tech company, has two kids, and is forty years old. She holds a director-level job in marketing communications and makes $120,000. Incredibly, it probably takes every last nickel she and her husband earn—he's a freelance software programmer who made $100,000 a year during the Great Boom but is lucky to scrape together $60,000 a year now—to pay the mortgage on their $800,000 house in the Boston suburb of Sudbury, Massachusetts.

You may be mystified, even outraged, to think that a couple making $180,000 a year struggles. Let's not mince words. We are not talking about deprivation. We are talking about a couple who has every right, by education, hard work, and career achievement, to expect an executive lifestyle (which some might call upper middle class). The most important trapping of this lifestyle is a nice house (at least 3,000 square feet, with four bedrooms and three or more baths) in a nice neighborhood. If it's a suburb, the lots are a quarter acre or more, the setbacks from the street to the house give a feeling of spaciousness, the neighbors are educated and interesting, and the public schools rank in the ninetieth percentile or above in the state and do not pinch on special-needs cases or extracurricular activities such as orchestra and hockey. Driveways in the neighborhood are lined with late-model foreign sedans, Chevy Suburbans, and copies of the *Wall Street Journal*. If it's a city co-op, there is a doorman. If it's a town house, there are multiple floors and tall ceilings.

Beyond housing, the executive-class family has enough discretionary cash to enjoy some, if not all, of the following:

- Private schools.
- European or tropical vacations.
- Private club membership.
- A housekeeper who comes at least twice a week.
- A lawn crew that comes once a week.
- Wardrobes that are contemporary, come from nice stores, and are plentiful enough to fit any occasion. Put another way, the executive-class man has plenty of suits for serious business meetings, sport coats and golf shirts for business casual outings, and weekend garb for boating or fly-fishing.

THE NEW CLASS DIVIDE— ANXIOUS VERSUS NONANXIOUS

You get the picture. I realize that attempting to define "executive class" by income and possessions is arbitrary and perhaps even shallow. It is certainly annoying if you work hard yet are not there yourself, and even more annoying if you had attained that perch for a few years during the Great Boom but since have fallen out. It may not even be, in a technical sense, accurate. Executive class by urban American standards is ninety-ninth percentile rich by world standards. All I'm trying to do here is portray a lifestyle that transcends day-to-day worries about money—that is, orthodontia payments that can keep you up at night. Some might call this upper middle class. I prefer to call it executive class. It's what many of us with education and ambition want.

But let us suppose you march to a different drummer. Let's say you've done as many noble souls have done throughout America's history: You've chosen to forego a high income for the satisfactions of a more artistic or service-oriented life, say a musician, a painter, a competition amateur athlete, a coach, a pastor, or a schoolteacher. Congratulations. But wouldn't you still prefer, if you could, to live without anxiety about money?

In the Turbulent 2000s, maybe the income divide that ultimately matters to us and bears upon our happiness is not executive versus middle. It's anxious versus nonanxious. We all aspire to be nonanxious about money.

Here's the dilemma millions on the urban coasts face. If we have executive-class aspirations, we may find ourselves like the couple making "only" $180,000 in Boston, New York, Washington, D.C., Los Angeles, or San Francisco. We know that nobody should feel sorry for us, because we could easily attain nonanxious middle-class status if we wanted to. Just trade down in housing, give up the Lexus, and put the kids back in public school. We could live like very comfortable schoolteachers. But how many of us are really prepared to do that? By education and ambition, we always had thought of ourselves as executive-classers. It isn't easy giving up the dream. During the Boom we probably sailed into executive-class ports with ease and grace and put down like we belonged there, for the long haul, without a worry in our head. Now in 2004, we still live among the executive class, but the margin for error is thin, and we worry.

If we've chosen the different drummer path—we're trying to live on the urban coasts on a $75,000 family income—we find ourselves getting priced out of the most basic amenities: a short commute to work, good health care, leisure activities that used to cost much less. Much as we might have chosen our different drummer path to avoid anxiety about money, we find ourselves ever more anxious about it.

I have been a broker at a major wire house for twenty-four years. Although it has been a personally rewarding career, my city, Los Angeles, has become more congested, expensive, and rude. I have craved a return to basics for a long time and have seriously thought of relocating to the country for the past couple of years. September 11 provided the catalyst and telecommuting provided the means.

My manager has been supportive of my move to upstate New York, my friends envious. I think there are many, like me, searching for Mayberry. And it couldn't have come at a better time.

NAME WITHHELD BY REQUEST
Schoharie County, New York

GONE IS THE ASSUMPTION OF RISING INCOME

Ah, remember the Great Boom? Lots of us, particularly those pursuing executive-class lifestyles, enjoyed rising incomes in many forms. During the Great Boom our aspiring executive-class marketing communications director didn't just make a salary. She made a bonus that could run easily to 50 percent of her salary. Better yet, she might have made a boatload of money on stock options if she were lucky enough to have worked at a high-flier such as computer storage giant EMC during the 1990s. Many such high-fliers existed in the 1990s. They were clustered in places like Silicon Valley, Boston, New York, Washington, D.C., Los Angeles, and Seattle, and to a lesser degree in Atlanta and Dallas.

How life has changed! For the past three years there have been few stock-option gains for our mythical marketing communications director and few for anybody else. In July 2003, America's exemplar of stock-option riches, Microsoft, home to some ten thousand millionaires, decided it would no longer grant options to its employees. From now on, Microsoft intends to grant only a trickle of shares. Appropriately, given the new penury, these few shares granted will be called *restricted shares*.

During the Great Bust, raises and bonuses mostly disappeared, too. Will they return when good times return? Yes, but in a more modest fashion. Salary competition from white-collar workers in India, China, and the emerging eastern European nations such as the Ukraine and Croatia, will keep a lid on American salaries and bonuses for some time. As mentioned in Chapter 3, Marc Benioff, the founder and CEO of Salesforce. com, told me in June 2003 that he thinks 25 million American white-collar jobs will vanish into software or flee overseas during the next decade. If Benioff is even a smidgen correct (the U.S. Labor Department pegs the number at a more modest 3 million), ponder the implications.

Question: Will you have the guts to ask for a big raise given the global oversupply of talented labor? The tough-case scenario—one you'd better prepare for—is that most white-collar employees in America may be forced to live on flattish salaries and smallish bonuses for many, many years.

(The best-case scenario is that a booming economy and impending waves of baby boomer retirement will create huge demands for skilled labor in the near future and thus offset any salary pressures from China or India. History supports this optimistic view. After all, one hundred years ago America needed 40 percent of its adult labor force to grow its food. Now it takes less than 1.5 percent, but nobody complains about it, because we have absorbed the descendants of all those farmworkers into higher-paying, less-backbreaking jobs. Still, what may be different this time is (1) the sheer size of the Chinese, Indian, and Eastern European labor forces; and (2) the utter ease with which white-collar jobs can be globally shopped via the Internet. "From a technical and productivity standpoint, the engineer sitting six thousand miles away might as well be in the next cubicle and on the local area network," said Intel chairman Andy Grove at a software conference in October 2003.)

Now, we must acknowledge another unpleasant possibility.

LONG IPO WINTER

Please God. Just one more bubble before I die!
—Bumper sticker seen in Silicon Valley in 2003

When stocks began climbing out of the pits after the Iraq War during the spring of 2003, hopes rose for the return of the Great Boom. The search company Google symbolized this hope, becoming the most openly talked-about IPO candidate in years. The idea was, when Google went public, it would break open the logjam and stock-option riches would flow once more. That hope is misplaced.

The IPO phenomenon, or probable lack thereof during the next several years, is worth examining. IPOs were the prime mover, the cornerstone of the stock-option economy that propelled a few million American families into financial comfort during the Great Boom.

Initial public offerings in 2002 numbered seventy-nine, the lowest level since 1979. Worse were the paltry nineteen IPOs of venture-capital-backed companies. This latter market is almost binary—it's either on or off. When NASDAQ booms, the switch is turned on and venture-backed IPOs become a near daily occurrence. But when NASDAQ falls or moves only modestly, these speculative technology IPOs tend to dry up. Entire quarters can go by with no IPOs at all. In 2003, the once-hot IPO factory known as Silicon Valley saw only two dozen IPOs—this during a year when the NASDAQ rose 43 percent. Best guess for venture-backed IPOs in 2004 is forty to fifty.

Contrast these droughtlike numbers to those of the Great Boom. IPOs of venture-backed companies numbered 242 in

1999 and 264 in 2000, according to the research firm Venture One. We can say without exaggeration that the technology IPO market has collapsed.

Why do IPOs matter in our calculus? Because when all those IPOs were hatching during the Great Boom, offering cool jobs and overnight millionaire status to employees, the talented white-collar worker in coastal hothouses such as Boston or New York or Seattle suddenly had . . . leverage! Don't like your job? Join a dot-com. Get rich. Gun your Ferrari past your old boss and flip him the bird.

That was the idea, anyway.

Big employers, not just in Silicon Valley and Manhattan but in every urban coastal region, were forced to respond to the suddenly widespread poaching of their best and brightest workers. Across America, large public companies began handing out stock options to their employees in an effort to keep them. During the 1990s, America went crazy for stock options. Options became the hottest topic at any urban coastal cocktail party during the last half of the Great Boom. And all because rampant IPOs forced the hands of big companies and made it so.

IPOs are fragile flowers. They blossom only when the soil and sun are just so. For the next ten years, the forecast doesn't look so good.

If Warren Buffett is correct about modest stock market returns until 2015, then Silicon Valley, Boston, Washington, D.C., New York, Seattle, Los Angeles, Atlanta, and Dallas had better get used to a trickle in IPOs for many years—the occasional Google aside. Sure, there might be a bumper crop of IPOs every now and then (2004 could be one of those minibumper years) just as there will be a year or two when the broad markets, and particularly tech-rich NASDAQ, grow in double-digit percentages, as they did in 2003. But we will come to define a "bumper IPO year" by the standards of 1986, not 1995–2000. A few dozen IPOs a year, at best. Not several hundred. Not even close.

WHITE-COLLAR WORKERS
LOSE LEVERAGE

You may hate this idea. I hate this idea. But let me tell you who loves the idea of far fewer IPOs. America's large companies! They hate IPOs, because rampant IPOs have a way of poaching their most talented people. When it's raining IPOs, the folks who run large companies are forced to (a) pay higher salaries, (b) pay higher bonuses, or (c) throw stock options around like Halloween candy. The rational folks who run large companies don't like doing any of these things. They are perfectly happy not to have any outside competitive pressure.

So a dearth of IPOs in Silicon Valley means a dearth of stock options for everybody else. This trend only becomes certain in the persnickety post-Sarbanes-Oxley world. Shareholders and regulators want companies to treat option grants as a direct expense that hits the profit-and-loss statement. Bottom line: fewer options. Microsoft is a trendsetter.

We are back to a world where the majority of white-collar knowledge workers in America will have to live, save, and plan for their future salary, what bonuses they may receive, and very little, if any, stock options. That is the probability, anyway, whether we like it or not.

If you find that you are executive class or middle class, and you feel anxious about your economic future even during a burst of high-GDP growth rates and rising stock prices, you might open up the *where* of your happiness for consideration. There may be no better time to move on and begin a new life than now.

But what place is best for you?

CHAPTER 13

America's Renewed Search for Meaning

Yes, smaller cities and towns remain vastly cheaper from a housing standpoint. Most of them—except for a few resort towns such as Aspen and Jackson Hole—are freer of "status competitions" (the social pressure to drive a fancy car, enroll the children in private schools, and take European vacations) that add costs to a typical professional middle-class lifestyle in big cities and suburbs.

Yet economics is not the only force driving people to seek larger lives in smaller places. I detected something quite different while talking to hundreds of urban/suburban refugees for this book. Call it a longing for life's intangible rewards, for things such as serenity and a sense of purpose. America has entered what I and many observers think is a religious or spiritual Great Awakening, triggered by millennial change, a turbulent global economy, post-9/11 fears, and, lastly, an aging population (baby boomers in particular) that feels life's calendar winding down. Whatever is driving America's search for meaning, I believe it will beckon Americans out of pricey, status-competitive, time-robbing urban and suburban centers toward a more pastoral lifestyle.

"ALL THE TOOLS OF ECONOMIC COMPENSATION ARE SHOT"

The annual Oshkosh air show is nirvana for flying buffs. For a week in late July and early August, every imaginable form of flying contraption, from colorfully painted homebuilts, to pristine antique warbirds, ultralights, rotorcraft, and gliders, flies into the Wittman Regional Airport for an orgasmic revelry of all things airborne. If it flies, the owner tries to make it to Oshkosh in midsummer. The show, formally known as the EAA AirVenture Oshkosh, is startling in its expanse. Nearly three thousand planes are spread across the 1,500-acre site. Anything can wind up here, from a *Spirit of St. Louis* replica to a Stealth fighter. Each afternoon is highlighted by the finest air show you'll see anywhere.

Waiting there was another flying buff, headhunter David Pasahow. David is a partner with the international executive recruiting firm Heidrick & Struggles, which has offices in all of the world's major cities. David operates out of Dallas. His specialty is relocating high-powered corporate executives to smaller towns and communities. David is a longtime pilot on the board of the Experimental Aircraft Association, a sponsor of the Oshkosh. He's there every summer.

We met at the Oshkosh Hilton Garden Court, on the grounds of the airport. After a few moments of chitchat, David and I talked about the people who were leaving the big cities and my belief that there was a new exodus afoot.

David piped in with agreement before my last sentence had ended. He wasn't talking about family heads who were desperately scraping to pay the mortgage or who were one step ahead of the tax collector. There were no Tom Joads in this bunch. His clients are people who had tasted the good life but recognized how fragile their situation was. They had powerful executive jobs in big cities, but they also had whopping mortgages, payments on the BMW 745i, country club dues, and private school tuitions. As long as they kept jobs that paid in the mid-six figures or better, they were okay. But those jobs were disappearing during the Great Bust. Even survivors were worried like hell.

"All the economic tools of compensation are shot," David said.

Above us, World War II–era Mustang fighters danced in the sky and made a lot of noise. "For the first time in twenty years high-powered executives are able to admit to recruiters that work and pay aren't everything in life," David shouted. Imagine that. Career suicide is the phrase that usually comes to mind when an executive starts to blab about the meaning of life, particularly in front of a recruiter. Not so anymore.

Also, for the first time in twenty years, David says CEO candidates are willing to move, or at least consider moving, to places like Des Moines or smaller. He mentioned one CEO that he moved from Chicago to little Muscatine, Iowa, to run a manufacturing business. The CEO's answer to the question "What about culture in Muscatine, Iowa?" could be the theme of this book: *"Because of the money I'm saving in Muscatine, I take my family to Paris when we want culture."*

David Pasahow says that the top achievers in any industry—young, childless, adrenaline junkies, especially—probably will always want to live in New York, Washington, Silicon Valley, Los Angeles, et cetera. But he said that the Midwest is coming back in some areas. In particular, David thinks there is a renaissance going on in manufacturing. The productivity benefits of information technology are only now beginning to reach manufacturing, from Web-based sale of tool parts to real-time supply chains.

Funny thing. Inspired by the stories of life reinvention that he helped facilitate, David himself pulled the trigger in 2004. He left Heidrick & Struggles in 2004 and hung out his shingle as Blue Line Advisors. It's basically just David and his e-mail contact list. Much like Rick Randall, the spinal catheter entrepreneur in Chapter 8 who works from both Lake Placid, New York, and the Carolina coast, David similarly splits his time between two home offices—one in Dallas and another in his favorite small town, Iron Mountain, Michigan.

I left Oshkosh the next day and while airborne in my Skyhawk over Iowa I recalled the words of Hal Wagher, who sent me a note from Rolla, Missouri: "I recently moved from the Atlanta sprawl to a small college town in Missouri after an epiphany in my car. As I sat in bumper-to-bumper traffic on

I-285, I calculated in my head that my one-hour commute to work (and one hour back) each day cost me 26 days of my life per year that I was never getting back. I now enjoy the extra one month of free time per year in daily increments romping with my children on the living room floor."

So simple, yet so prophetic.

In L.A. two years ago I had a Wilshire Boulevard radio-ad sales job paying in the mid to high $100s with a 1.5 hour commute to my $500K home. My wife and I sought a way out. . . . In Tucson there was nothing to do; in Sedona, we couldn't afford a cathedral-ceiling view of the red spires. Palm Springs is too crowded now; it looks like Orange County. But thanks to a Web search, bingo, we found Cathey's Valley, forty-five minutes from Yosemite, a thirty-minute drive past cattle ranches up from Merced (population 60,000), population 320.

We're living on boulder-strewn oak savannahs in a Tuscany-style four-bedroom, two-bath villa on four rolling acres, three hundred steps from bass-filled lake. It cost $285K. This is Mariposa County, noted for not a single stoplight for its mini-population of about seventeen thousand.

GARRETT BERGMARK
Mariposa County, California

The search for meaning permeates our literature. It's Sal Paradise in *On the Road*. It's Phaedrus in *Zen and the Art of Motorcycle Maintenance* traveling cross-country with his son. It's John Steinbeck and his venerable standard poodle in *Travels with Charley*. It's Hunter S. Thompson and his attorney traveling to Las Vegas to cover the Mint 400 in *Fear and Loathing in Las Vegas*. Journeys, whether serious or comic or exhausting, are what life is all about.

The journeys can be imaginary. When I was a child I loved to open books and look at maps. I would run my fingers over the towns, the states, the rivers. The best were those bumpy wall-hanging maps where you could actually feel the mountains.

Percolating inside us—at least for me—is this love of American geography, and of travel. Maybe that's where this started. On those afternoons on the living room floor as a kid, the sun striping the carpet and my fingers tracing the rivers and finding the towns. Now, as publisher of *Forbes*, I get to travel the country trying to find businesspeople who are doing great things in unusual places.

BABY BOOMERS DOWNSHIFT

Between 1946 and 1964, some 77 million people were born, the largest population bulge to ever hit America. The baby boomers are now firmly ensconced in middle age and are beginning to downshift into more manageable life expectations. This is more than just predictable life-cycle change. Much of it has to do with the Executive-Class Dropout phenomenon you see in every urban coastal area in the United States. College-educated boomers who once dreamed of attaining a comfortable middle-class lifestyle or better are reconciling themselves to the likelihood that the hot economy of the late 1990s, and especially the white-hot stock market, will not return during their productive years. Again, Warren Buffett's prediction of fifteen lean years makes any subsequent asset boom an event that will occur too late for most boomers to exploit.

How are boomers adapting to the twin pressures of aging and a Cheap Revolution economy? The question almost answers itself. If you were a business, you would, as quickly as possible, try to reduce your operating costs to offset a maturing product line and a bad economy. Likewise, downshifting baby boomers will seek to reduce their personal and family "burn rates" as they began to downshift and adjust to lower incomes and asset returns.

And—let's be honest. Do aging boomers really want to compete with twenty-somethings?

What drove the worker of the mid-1990s was energy. High energy. Nonstop high energy. The fuel propelling such forward motion was a combination of things. Entrepreneurship, certainly. Money, no question. Snapping up a special moment in history as well. But as the Great Boom '90s toppled into the Great Bust '00s, the energy level came crashing down. Some of that mojo has returned, of course, with the economic recovery. Perhaps it will never return for those of us past a certain age.

Many of us who were at the white-hot core of the market simply don't have the physical stamina to rev up our engine all over again, at least to the same degree. In addition, we've grown older and our priorities have changed. The 24/7 lifestyle is no longer acceptable. Writing a grocery list is preferable to writing a business plan. Ask Louis Rosetto, the founder of *Wired*, what he's doing these days, and it's simple: "Playing with my kids," he says. No publishing ventures? "No." Nothing in the hopper? "Not really." Louis can do that because he did well in the sale of *Wired* to Condé Nast, but the foundation is the same. Work is simply not the be-all/end-all it was when there were quick and vast fortunes to be made.

For those of us in our late thirties to late fifties this has enormous consequences. We're probably married, and we have children, a house, and a mortgage—maybe aging parents to look after, too. Our ability, or even desire, to keep pace with the twenty-something up-and-comer who works eighty hours a week is diminished. We can't do it. We don't even want to do it, because the psychological cost is awfully high. The 24/7 schedule puts your own personal and mental health at risk. It can be disastrous for marriages.

I live in Galesville (population 1,450). That has not stopped me from working my way up from truck driver to president and CEO of a regional auto parts store chain (with 112 locations) in La Crosse, Wisconsin (population 52,000). I have traveled all over the United States in the course of my work, and visits to New York City, Boston, Philadelphia, Washington, D.C., Dallas, L.A., and San Francisco have all been interesting, but my conclusion is that there is no place like home.

I am typing this letter on my Mac iBook hooked to broadband cable via Wi-Fi installed in my ninety-year-old Victorian home, which cost $50,000 a few years ago. I enjoy the knowledge that I know the name of every neighbor in a two-square-block area and can leave my windows open at night to draw the clean night air. I also know that I can sleep well because most of our sleepy town starts shutting the lights down before midnight and I won't likely hear sirens in the night.

RICHARD BEIRNE
Galesville, Wisconsin

For the millions of stressed American families living in high-cost areas, the anxiety of the Turbulent 2000s has a potential upside. It can launch a change of thinking, as it did for Jonathan Weber.

A WEB MEDIA MOGUL STARTS OVER IN MISSOULA

One fine day in July 2003 I flew from Seattle to Missoula, Montana. I chose a route direct to Spokane, but from there swapped strategies and kept Interstate 90 under the wing. Flying over mountains in a single-propeller plane is safe if you adhere to a few rules. One, always clear the mountains by at least 2,000 feet, lest a sudden downdraft push you into granite. Two, go early in the day to avoid bone-rattling turbulence, or worse, thunderstorms. Three, follow a highway in case you have engine troubles and transform into a glider.

The land between Spokane and Missoula is heartbreaking in its beauty. Under the left wing lay the resort town of Coeur d'Alene, Idaho, which graces the northern shore of the lake by the same name. The air was so clear that visibility out the window must have been a hundred miles. Below I saw the Coeur d'Alene Resort golf course, famous for its floating green—is that natural grass or rubber? I couldn't linger. Crossing the Bitterroot Range into Montana, I eased back on the power, began a descent from 11,500 feet, and presently landed in the college town of Missoula.

Meeting me at the airport in his battered Nissan convertible was a living example of the Silicon Valley boom and bust— Jonathan Weber, founding editor of the *Industry Standard*. During the late 1990s Weber's magazine was a must-read if you followed the tech IPO market. Credit in large part goes to Jonathan, who left a good tech-beat editor's job at the *L.A. Times* to grab the entrepreneurial brass ring and a chance at magazine top editorship and glory. Under Jonathan's guidance the *Industry Standard* became a publishing sensation, selling 7,558 ad pages, more than any other magazine in America in 2000. The next year an odd thing happened— the *Industry Standard* went out of business, a spectacular flameout.

Jonathan was exhausted from seventy-hour workweeks, in no shape to stick around and wait for a tech recovery. He also needed to lower his cost of living. So in 2002 he moved from pricey San Francisco to Missoula, his girlfriend's hometown. Jonathan got a job as a visiting professor at the University of Montana's journalism school. Today he lectures at the university part-time and reports full-time for *Off the Record Research*, an independent stock tracker based in San Francisco. The beauty of living in the twenty-first century is that Jonathan can write about European wireless companies for a San Francisco research outfit from a western university town. He hops a Northwest Airlines jet to Europe every six weeks or so. Most days he rises at 5:30 A.M., grabs a strong cup of coffee, toddles to his home office, fires up the computer with its 1.5-megabit-per-second wireless Internet connection, and opens up the world.

Jonathan told me about his typical day in Missoula during lunch at an outdoor patio overlooking the Clark Fork River. The day was western picture book—big blue skies, a dry 85 degrees. We ate salads and drank iced tea. Jonathan wore Ray-Ban shades, surfer shorts, and flip-flops—his typical workday getup.

Nice life. Maybe if you think creatively and put the where of your Life 2.0 into play, shaky economic times can be a splendid opportunity for rebirth.

A CALIFORNIAN RECOVERS
IN COLUMBUS

Remember Rick Randall in Chapter 8? He made his first $5 million in the medical device industry by age forty, but lost his marriage. Now Rick's figured out how to have work *and* family success by putting geography into play. His life is a model for those seeking a balance without compromise.

Rick's story got me thinking about an old friend, Jim Ward. Jim was a Stanford track star in the 1960s. He set the freshman record in the 440-yard dash and later ran on a mile relay team ranked fourth in the country. After college Jim became a millionaire by age thirty, lending money to home builders. Then, as a hobby, he began to pursue his love of racing cars. He got as far as the Atlantic car division, one step short of the Indy 500.

I first met Jim back in the 1970s. He was a go-getter, all right, but so competitive and tense I once saw him bang his head against a pillar at a bank, over and over, when the line was too long. His philosophy applying to all endeavors, work and play, was Pedal to the metal! Not surprisingly, Jim succeeded in everything he touched. With one exception. Marriage. His first failed. So did the second. Number three was headed for disaster, brought on by Jim's off-the-charts type A behavior and by the birth of a son suffering from severe dwarfism. A control freak, Jim learned he could control neither his son's medical prognosis nor the outcome of his marriage. Nearing a breakdown one day, Jim had a revelation. If he didn't change gears, he would lose his marriage, and maybe his sanity. He temporarily shut down his construction-loan business, quit racing cars, and moved his family out of California to Columbus, Ohio.

Jim e-mailed me the rest of his story.

"Julie and I decided to move to Columbus in late 1996. We decided to try Columbus for three years, to see if we liked the winters. Julie liked it here—and it was much more of a change for her than me. We slowly concluded that it was best to stay in Ohio and raise our children with Midwest values. I knew I had to get out of the stress of long business days. I have always loved what my career is—construction lending—but during the old days in California I was working so many hours that I suspect even the quality of my business decisions was at risk. In the end, I just ran out of energy for the art of the deal. Financial rewards and power seemed a nuisance rather than a reward. I started resenting the ring of the telephone. The three years I took off relocating to Ohio were the best of my life. Not one day goes by when I don't feel truly blessed and happy. Along the way I simply have lost my ego and desire for being in power. I enjoy and respect others' success and skills. I was poor at this when younger—I felt threatened by talented people.

"Also, I have gone back and worked hard at retrieving some of the neat people I met and lost track of during the hectic journey—I have maybe twenty old friends back again. It is awesome."

In 1999 Jim restarted his construction-loan business and found he had not missed a beat—he now has $35 million under management. He travels to California a week a month. For the most part he is content to let others run the business while he attends to his marriage and boys and produces a book on the history of Stanford track and field.

A SPIRITUAL GREAT AWAKENING?

The other day my college alumni magazine arrived and I read two items in it that seemed a trifle bizarre, yet were part of a piece. A woman from the class of 1991 wrote that she had experienced a "spiritual awakening, stopped practicing law and become a shamanic healer." She founded the San Diego Circle Shamanic Healing Arts Center, which hosts classes and workshops on many Native American traditions and shamanic practices. She adds: "I love it. I have my own shamanic healing practice where I see people in my home office, which my kids call 'the goddess room.'" She says she finds it "an amazing experience to be a conduit for healing miracles," especially since she is healing herself as a "part of the bargain."

Elsewhere in the magazine I learned of a communal house in Palo Alto called Magic.

"As a group," the article goes on, "the 'Magicians' value cooperation, healthy living, protecting the environment and, ultimately, the betterment of mankind. The [six adults and two children] spend, collectively, only about $30,000 per year (about half of which goes to property tax), eschew cars and television, wear secondhand clothes and eat too-old-to-sell organic food provided by local markets.

"Some of Magic's rules may seem rigid (a note taped to the house's sole toilet reads, 'Gentlemen, please sit to pee or ask someone where to pee outside.'), but after more than two decades of trial and error, the Magicians believe they know what it takes to maintain an effective community."

Personally, I would choose the stand-up-and-pee-outside option. But here I need to holster my sarcasm, because what drives the Magicians to live frugally and ecologically is a genuine impulse to transcend the stresses and soul-sacrifices of competing and living in one of the most technology- and money-crazed cities in the United States. One can sympathize with that.

Closer to the American mainstream, one of the bestselling books of the young twenty-first century is Rick Warren's *Purpose-Driven Life*, which has sold more than 20 million copies. Warren, founder of the fifteen-thousand-member Saddleback Church in Lake Forest, California, urges a forty-day program of reading and prayer in order to discern God's purpose for your life. Warren's message is gentle yet uncompromising: God, not you, is in charge. Your only responsibilities are to figure out what He wants and live accordingly. Evangelical churches, especially those with a strong therapeutic touch, such as Saddleback in suburban Los Angeles and Willow Creek in suburban Chicago, are the country's fastest growing. These megachurches do a fabulous job (among other things) of nurturing stressed-out people, who are stressed out in large part from the physical wear and tear of trying to live upstanding middle-class lives in harried, expensive parts of the country.

I belong to a megachurch myself, Menlo Park Presbyterian, in northern California. Though I am a much-flawed apostle (as will be apparent to any reader of this book), I nevertheless need to state here that faith has become a vital part of my life. (I am happy to carry on this conversation at greater length with readers at my Web site, www.life2where.com.) A few weeks after I finished writing this book, I had lunch with Greg Gianforte, the Bozeman, Montana, entrepreneur featured in Chapter 10. He told me of his committed Christian walk, and how the megachurch phenomena had hit Bozeman with force. This made me recall my conversation with Peter Scanlon in Chapter 9: "We were stuffy Episcopalians in Connecticut. Now [in Des Moines, Iowa] we have become high-energy Methodists."

In his book *The Paradox of Progress,* Gregg Easterbrook wrote: "Ever larger numbers of people enjoy reasonable standards of living, but may feel an inner pang on the question of whether their lives have purpose. Predicting transition from 'material want' is not to say that people will cease caring about material things; it is a prediction that millions will expect both pleasant living standards and a broad sense that their lives have purpose. This is a conundrum as the sense of meaning is much more difficult to acquire than material possessions."

A conundrum, yes.

But plenty of people have solved it, by putting the where of their happiness and purpose into play.

THE 9/11 FACTOR

Graham Allison, an expert on nuclear proliferation issues at the Kennedy School of Government at Harvard, told *The New York Times Magazine* in early 2004 that he thinks it "more likely than not" a terrorist will detonate a nuclear bomb in Manhattan or some large American city.

Several of my contacts for this book cited this fear as reason to ditch large urban areas for smaller communities. Tom Giovanetti wrote to me: "I live near Denton, Texas, forty miles north of Dallas. It's got two universities in it, yet it's far enough from Dallas that we would survive a nuclear blast in Dallas. I said that on purpose, because I think since 9/11, people don't want to live in target zones. I know a ton of people in Washington who have decided that being CFOs of small companies is better than working for Capitol Hill trade associations and lobbying firms."

Lou Barberini was pondering a move out of his home in San Francisco when he wrote me: "Small towns seem less vulnerable to terrorist attacks."

A woman from suburban New York, who asked that I not use her name, wrote: "After September 11, our perspective changed, like many others. We reexamined our priorities and came to the conclusion that although life in the East Coast is fantastic, it is not the center of the universe. What you say about low cost of living, good schools, affordable country clubs, restaurants is absolutely hitting the bull's-eye. Once you get over the idea of having to live in the center of the action, you see a different side of life. My home in Greenwich is worth approximately $650,000 to $700,000, which in Greenwich is at the low end. The same home in Terre Haute, Indiana, would cost no more than $110,000. The biggest home in Terre Haute, which would probably be around 7,000 square feet, would go for about $400,000 with a couple of acres."

Rebecca Kenary of Palm Springs, California, wrote: "I lived in Chicago, New York, Paris, and London for my career and absolutely loved each place. But if I'm not working and getting paid a lot of money, I have no interest in putting up with the hassles of living in a big city. I was fortunate enough to enjoy eight years in Manhattan when the city was safe, prosperous, and booming. September 11 showed how very vulnerable large cities really are."

Here is what I hope. I hope that the campaigns against terrorism and nuclear proliferation succeed. I hope our children grow up and giggle at our post-9/11 fears the way we used to laugh at *Duck and Cover* movies—from the safety of later decades, of course. Let's pray that the unthinkable, of a bomb going off in a big American city, never comes to pass.

Still, you might want to hedge your bets.

PARENTAL BACKLASH
TO SUBURBAN KIDDIE LIFE

Today, average working parents shoulder big burdens—particularly on the urban coast. Alarmingly in this decade, 75 percent of American bankruptcies hit two-parent households with children. Trying to keep up, parents typically feel rushed and perpetually tired. They're burned out from all of the hassles of living in urban America, from the commute to the high mortgage payments to the fact that kids today seemingly have to be driven everywhere. (When did that happen?)

Time magazine spies a growing parental backlash to the overorganized suburban kiddie life. In an article called "Ready Set Relax" (October 27, 2003), *Time* reports that a Ridgewood, New Jersey, mother named Donna Olsen has started a "citywide initiative that encouraged frazzled families to put down some speed bumps in their fast-paced lives." Olsen says she is trying to empower parents to skip soccer practice.

How did it come to this?

Across urban and suburban America, playdates have superseded the days when it was still possible for kids to leave their house on a Saturday afternoon and not return until dinnertime, without causing their parents heart attacks. Sadly, that seems to be gone in urban/suburban America. The reason, of course, is fear. Kids seem to be more threatened today than ever before. Whether this is actually true is open to debate. Has there really been an explosion of child molesters lurking about, or has this story just been overhyped? It's enough that the widespread belief in escalating dangers for kids has taken hold with the consequence of a regimented life for kids and a frazzled life for parents. And it's not only psychopaths in the shadows we worry about. Visit suburban America today and you don't see too many sidewalks. Do you want your kids walking on the curb when teenagers are hot-rodding back and forth?

Every suburban house has a fence today. When I grew up in the 1960s in a small city, kids like me walked through people's back-

yards to get to school. The "kid route" was always through back-
yards. Occasionally we'd pick out an especially cranky neighbor's
yard, then run by and pitch a rotten tomato at his or her window.
Our parents set us little angels loose starting at around age six.

Who in suburban America feels comfortable letting their six-
year-old child walk a mile from the house today? Let's just forget about that if you live in a city or suburb. It's not hard to
conclude that urban and suburban America are not kid friendly.
One more burden for burned-out parents.

"I HAVE A FULL AND BUSY LIFE, SEÑOR"

This story was sent to me the other day on e-mail. The author
is anonymous.

An American businessman was at the pier of a small coastal
Mexican village when a small boat with just one fisherman
docked. Inside the small boat were several large yellowfin tuna.
The American complimented the Mexican on the quality of his
fish and asked how long it took to catch them.

The Mexican replied that it took only a little while. The
American then asked why he hadn't stayed out longer and
caught more fish? The Mexican said he had enough to support
his family's immediate needs. The American then asked, "But
what do you do with the rest of your time?" The Mexican fisherman said, "I sleep late, fish a little, play with my children, take
siesta with my wife, Maria, stroll into the village each evening
where I sip wine and play guitar with my amigos. I have a full
and busy life, señor."

The American scoffed, "I am a Harvard M.B.A. and could
help you. You should spend more time fishing and with the proceeds, buy a bigger boat; with the proceeds from the bigger boat
you could buy several boats; eventually you would have a fleet
of fishing boats. Instead of selling your catch to a middleman
you would sell directly to the processor, eventually opening your
own cannery. You would control the product, processing, and
distribution. You would need to leave this small coastal fishing

village and move to Mexico City, then L.A. and eventually New York City, where you will run your expanding enterprise."

The Mexican fisherman asked, "But señor, how long will this all take?" The American replied, "Fifteen to twenty years."

"But what then, señor?" asked the Mexican.

The American laughed and said, "That's the best part. When the time is right, you would announce an IPO, sell your company stock to the public, and become very rich. You would make millions."

"Millions, señor? Then what?"

The American said, "Then you would retire. Move to a small coastal fishing village where you would sleep late, fish a little, play with your kids, take siesta with your wife, stroll to the village in the evenings where you could sip wine and play your guitar with your amigos."

CHAPTER 14

What Makes a Great Place?

G ay people are the magic key to economic vitality! says Richard Florida—the John Heinz III Professor of Public Policy at Carnegie Mellon University in Pittsburgh. Why, look at Manhattan, San Francisco, and Miami's South Beach. A lively civic gay life is a marker for creativity and is proof of a willingness to flout convention. Both qualities are needed to grow a thriving entrepreneurial environment.

No, no, no, says another expert in regional economic development, Ross DeVol of Santa Monica's Milken Institute. It's capital that counts. Intellectual capital, which you can measure by toting up the number of Ph.D.s and patents held in the community, and good old-fashioned money capital, particularly R&D money and venture capital. Put these two forms of capital together within *breeding* distance, Dr. Florida, and you'll soon get the next Google or eBay.

Aw, you both have your heads in the clouds, gruffs Walter Plosila, a meat-and-potatoes guy who runs the Battelle Memorial Institute's Center for Regional Economic Development in a five-story building near Cleveland Hopkins International Airport. Plosila earns his keep counseling cities such as Peoria and Indianapolis—"blue-collar" cities trying to shake off their gritty manufacturing pasts. Forget the fancy-pants stuff, Plosila says. What's needed is hard realism and civic leadership.

Well, now!

The war of economic-development theories begins to sound comical after you've heard all sides speak with the convincing fervor of religious fanatics. The stakes, however, are not trivial. There are 531 cities in the United States with a population greater than 50,000, and 2,426 others with populations between 10,000 and 50,000. All of the former and most of the latter employ full-time economic development administrators. Their job is to bring business into town.

Add to these city efforts the heftier fifty state development agencies (some of which, like California's, employ thousands) and scores of oddball regional groups, such as the one promoting the Quad Cities that join into a single economic player: Moline and Rock Island (twin cities in Illinois) and Bettendorf and Davenport (twin cities across the Mississippi River in Iowa). Some of these alliances would form new U.S. states, if so permitted, if the boundaries were drawn today to accurately reflect natural regional interests. Eastern Washington State has more in common with the panhandle of northern Idaho than it does with its snooty coastal cousins in Seattle and Bellevue. The Greater Spokane Chamber of Commerce, in fact, sometimes includes Moscow, Idaho, in its promotions—a city more than seventy miles away.

Toss in such twenty-first-century players linked around university research parks (there is an Association for American University Parks, as a matter of fact) and the enviro-friendly, high-value industries they hope to attract, such as software and biotech. Thus you will find acting in concert an archipelago of high-IQ cities such as Davis, California, Madison, Wisconsin, and Raleigh-Durham, North Carolina.

Put it all together and pretty soon you have . . . a $20 billion U.S. industry of regional economic development!

City competing against city.

State against state.

Region against region.

One of the great strengths of the United States is its allowance for, even countenance of, such competition. If one U.S. state wants to launch a low-tax war against its neighbor, as South Dakota did against Iowa in the 1980s, capturing the flag of computer maker Gateway 2000 in the skirmish, that's fine.

Normandy and Provence do not claw at each other's throats in this way. Neither do Saxony and Westphalia. Were I Alexis de Tocqueville traveling around the United States today with my quill pen and a leather bag full of academic journals warning about the homogenization of American culture, I might (being the clear thinker de Tocqueville was) scratch my head. I would see that the United States is still marked by fierce regional pride that carries itself into the arena of economic competition by way of regional economic development. Spokane, Washington, runs ads for itself in Los Angeles comparing crime statistics. Michigan enjoys a good laugh about Silicon Valley's absurd cost of living. South Dakota pokes fun at Iowa. And our Lone Star State neighbors stand arms akimbo and boast: Don't Mess with Texas.

Regional trash talk is big business in the United States.

OLD CLEVELAND VERSUS NEW CLEVELAND

I am attracted to elderly grumps—must be a first-child thing—so while in Cleveland to see Jonathan Murray (see Chapter 6), I decided to go see Walt Plosila at the Cleveland office of the Battelle Memorial Institute. Battelle's main office is 120 miles away in Columbus and is a busy place. Battelle is one of the world's largest, private, independent R&D organizations. With a staff of 7,500 scientists, engineers, and support specialists, the organization develops new products—and more than $1 billion in business—for thousands of companies and government agencies. Typically, this work results in between fifty and one hundred patented inventions each year.

The Cleveland office where I met Plosila, however, is one floor in a five-story building near Hopkins International Airport.

Plosila is a blunt guy in his early sixties who favors that dorky midwestern combo of a short-sleeve dress shirt and a rep tie. At Battelle, Plosila consults to cities such as Cleveland, Indianapolis, St. Louis, and other "distressed" communities that, like his outfit, have seen better days. Plosila has no romantic view of the region. "The problem," he barks, "is that the Midwest has a complacency problem. People are so used to working for someone else that they just don't have that entrepreneurial role model."

Too often, Plosila says, business leaders in rusted-out midwestern cities ask the wrong questions. "They come to me and say 'How can we get to be a part of the information revolution? How can we be a part of the biotech revolution?' They don't see the whole picture. They just want to pour money on a problem to make it go away."

As Plosila talks, I think of Champaign, Illinois. It was there, during the fall of 1992, that a young man named Marc Andreessen developed Mosaic, the first Web browser to employ a graphical user interface. Thanks to Andreessen, for the first time words, pictures, video, and sounds could all be presented on a browser. Andreessen happened to be an undergraduate student at the University of Illinois. For pizza and beer money, he worked for $6.50 an hour at the university's National Center for Supercomputing Applications (NCSA), where he invented the browser. Bizarrely, neither the University of Illinois nor the NCSA capitalized on this world-changing invention. In April 1994, Marc Andreessen and a partner founded Netscape Communications and headed to the Silicon Valley to change the world. There was simply no infrastructure for tech start-ups and no role models of successful entrepreneurs in Champaign.

"Yep—that says it all," says Plosila.

Still, Plosila has hopes for a Midwest revival. The region just has be more realistic about where it can play in a global economy. When measuring the business acumen of a town, Plosila begins by performing an inventory of city assets:

What are the R&D drivers in industry and higher education?

How does the city stack up against not only the best places in the world, but against competitors in the region?

When you begin considering your competition, Plosila says, narrow your scope. Too many cities err by wanting to take on the world. Consider Cleveland. Its competition isn't Silicon

Valley or Boston. That's ridiculous, he barks. Cleveland's competition is Indianapolis or Columbus. "Many cities have a hard time getting realistic about their chances," he says.

One of Plosila's clients is St. Louis. He says St. Louis can't seem to get over the fact that it's no longer 1904, when the city hosted the World's Fair and Olympics and rivaled Chicago for midwestern eminence. Today, St. Louis's peer, according to Plosila, is not Chicago so much as it is Des Moines, Omaha, or that up-and-comer Kansas City, the new kid on the block. Cities like St. Louis tend to look to the past—and with its rich history of automobile manufacturing (General Motors), aviation (McDonnell Douglas), baseball (the storied Cardinals), and popular music (Scott Joplin, Chuck Berry, Tina Turner), who can blame it? But Plosila has labored hard to get St. Louis looking to a future. An inventory of assets showed that St. Louis can be a regional and maybe even, with luck, a national contender in the twenty-first-century field of plant sciences. Plosila points to St. Louis intellectual capital assets that include Washington University's Danforth Science Center and the Monsanto Corporation.

Plosila identifies nine steps that are essential to economic revival.

1. Start with a core competency analysis.
2. Focus particularly on R&D assets in industry, defense, and higher education.
3. Do an economic analysis and ask, "Where does our city have its best chance for breakout success?"
4. After you've determined that, do a benchmark analysis . . . versus the best in the world and versus regional peers.
5. Do a gap analysis. Figure out what the city lacks, particularly in the area of seed capital for entrepreneurs. Do you need more federal R&D money? Have you explored all possible partnerships with the local universities?
6. Do a SWOT analysis: Strengths, Weaknesses, Opportunities, and Threats.

7. Develop an action plan . . . short-term, midterm, and long-term. Ask what the implementing organizations are.
8. Get buy-in to the action plan from city leaders in government, industry, and education.
9. Develop champions! Ask city heroes to step up and become a public face for action and change.

Plosila makes valid points about industrial-city comebacks, but I wonder just how much a city like St. Louis can leapfrog its way into the twenty-first century. Plosila is the expert. Still, I tend to believe that regional dynamism is the net effect of individual talent and ambition, not central planning.

My own view is closer to that of Milken's Ross DeVol, who says the game is mostly about access to capital: both intellectual capital and the kind you can rub between your fingers and dish out as venture capital to entrepreneurs.

Richard Florida's "gay theory"—that is, a robust gay population is a proxy for creative types, therefore cities should do whatever it takes to attract gays—has earned for Florida the attention you would expect. The theory may explain the vitality of San Francisco and Miami's South Beach, but it misses the mark for such "nerdistans" (Joel Kotkin's word) as Silicon Valley (credit goes to Stanford's engineering department) or Salt Lake City (thank the Mormon work ethic). Professor Florida's gay theory is so single-minded, in fact (check it out at www.creativeclass.org), one wonders what agenda may lie behind it. He is quick to disparage any competing philosophy, the sign of an ideologue. He writes that tax cuts are "so vacuous and out of touch it's alarming." Plainly false, that one. Somehow I doubt the great city observer Jane Jacobs (author of *The Life and Death of Great Cities,* among other books), whom Florida calls his intellectual godmother, would have been as close-minded.

Still, one must hand it to Florida for correctly observing that smart, talented people are drivers of economic growth. Some hidebound cities, such as Cincinnati, could use a dose of

Florida's medicine—Cincy desperately needs to hold on to its young, creative types, straight or gay. The density of young entrepreneurial talent (nerds and creatives) is why I think university towns such as Madison and Columbus will be tomorrow's stars.

WHERE TO GET RICH IN AMERICA

If this is your goal, you might be surprised at where America's richest people made their fortunes.

What do these towns have in common: Albuquerque, Austin, Bentonville, Dayton, Denver, Omaha, Racine, and Tacoma? They are the birthplaces of firms that created seventeen of the top twenty-five personal fortunes in the 2003 Forbes 400 annual "Richest Americans" list.

Microsoft started life as Micro-Soft in Albuquerque, New Mexico, in 1975. Michael Dell's side business overran his dorm room at the University of Texas, but he stayed in Austin. The world knows about tiny Bentonville, Arkansas, and mighty Wal-Mart. Everybody also knows that Warren Buffett's hometown, Omaha, Nebraska, is the place he returned to in 1956 (from New York) to start his first investment fund out of a spare bedroom. You probably didn't know that Cox Communications began life in Dayton, Ohio, in 1922. Or that Charlie Ergen started EchoStar in a Denver, Colorado, suburb. Or that Racine, Wisconsin, boasts SC Johnson and that Tacoma, Washington, is where, in 1911, Frank and Ethel Mars began making buttercream candy and chocolate out of their kitchen.

There is a funny American myth that you have to go to big places such as New York or California to make your fame and fortune. Maybe fame. But fortune, as any year's Forbes 400 shows, is more often found off the beaten track.

Best place to make a future Forbes 400 fortune? Start with this proposition: The most valuable natural resource in the twenty-first century is brains. Smart people tend to be mobile. Watch where they go! Because where they go, robust economic activity will follow.

If you agree, then put your chips on cities that (a) attract smart people and (b) are low-cost enough to incubate a business so it won't need much outside capital, which is dilutive to wealth building. In other words, look for cities with these attributes.

Universities, especially those with strong science and engineering departments. As a political science major, it wounds my pride to say the nerds won, but it's true. Cool innovation and new industries spring from a deep understanding of physics, electronics, math, chemistry, and biology, not Gibbon. Business schools and law schools are nice, too, but are of ancillary importance. There is an interesting twist to this. In the old days, a state's flagship university, with its law schools and liberal arts and alumni networks, carried a higher prestige than the ag or tech school. A degree from the University of Iowa hoisted you further up Des Moines business and social ladders than a degree from Iowa State. But this pecking order could reverse in the twenty-first century. The Iowa States of the world are more adept at creating scientists, engineers, patents, and R&D grants.

Stellar K–12 education. There's a very simple proposition at work here. Smart people want smart kids. They demand a strong education for their children. One way or another (public school or private), they will seek it out.

Capital for experimentation. Milken's Ross DeVol is right: Local funds for research and development is a distinct advantage. It doesn't seem to matter if the R&D money is corporate, government, or military. R&D attracts smart people and out-of-box thinkers.

Capital for business risk. The presence of local venture capital or angel investors (rich people who dabble in start-ups) is crucial. So are local bankers willing to look beyond the balance sheet in assessing credit-worthiness. Doug Burgum, who grew Great Plains Software of Fargo, North Dakota, into a $300 million a year business before selling it to Microsoft for $1.1 billion in 2001, likes to tell a story. Great Plains always struggled with local banks to get loans and credit lines. The Fargo print shop whose sole client was Great Plains had no such struggle. The bankers figured they could always repossess the printer if the print shop defaulted. But what do you repossess in a software company?

Celebration of human diversity. Richard Florida makes his point provocatively with gay populations. You could make the same point about immigrant populations, particularly new arrivals from Asia and India, who are more likely to arrive in the United States with an education and a plan for success. Even here, numbers don't tell the whole story. Minneapolis has a low immigrant population compared to other cities of its size, yet it enjoys an international reputation for racial tolerance and harmony. That's the key. As America's cities compete for intellectual talent, such a reputation will count as a real advantage.

Lower taxes and regulation. These things matter, especially in border situations. The classic story of the 1980s is that of Gateway 2000. It was founded in 1983 by a twenty-four-year-old from Sioux City, Iowa, named Ted Waitt, who had the idea of selling personal computers by mail. Waitt staffed his company with family and friends from Sioux City. The company, along with Dell Computer of Austin, Texas, convinced Americans that buying PCs through the mail or over the phone, and later on the Internet, was a good idea. Gateway grew to be a multibillion dollar business. Gateway was as much of an Iowa success story as any true Hawkeye could hope for, with one itty-bitty problem. Two years after its founding, Gateway sneaked across the Big Sioux River into North Sioux City, South Dakota, which has no corporate or personal income taxes. America came to think of Gateway as a South Dakota company. South Dakota is not shy about taking the bow. Iowa gets little credit.

The right kind of civic leadership. I call this the St. Louis Paradox. Every two years I give a speech in St. Louis to the local boosters. These locals are the nicest people you'd ever want to meet, but they always seem a bit too eager to catapult St. Louis from the early twentieth century straight into the twenty-first. During the late 1990s they were all hot for St. Louis to scrap its airplane- and automobile-manufacturing past and morph into the Silicon Valley of the Midwest. This was back when every city in America wanted a piece of the Internet boom. Fat chance. Where was the St. Louis local venture capital? Where were its world-class electrical engineering and computer science departments to match those of Stanford and the University of California? Where were the Indian and Asian immigrants?

More recently the kindly civic leaders were hot to tell me that St. Louis was going to become the next biotech capital, with an emphasis in plant sciences. Well, this made more sense than the previous season's push to displace Silicon Valley. St. Louis does in fact have a rich heritage of plant science knowledge, beginning at Washington University, a university of rising reputation, and extending to Monsanto (and even, arguably, to the happy malt-and-yeast artisans at Anheuser Busch). But I'm wary of these grand civic plans. They tend to squander money and energy. You can't will these kinds of moonshot successes to happen. What cities can do is create the conditions for success. I always advise cities to forget million-dollar bets on a single industry, and instead make a thousand $1,000 bets on bright entrepreneurs who need cheap rent. Why not Wi-Fi up the downtown so that entrepreneurs can sit in coffee shops and surf the Net? Why not lighten the regulatory load for start-ups? Why not run business plan contests, open to everybody in town, regardless of age or pedigree, with $5,000 prizes?

You see, Silicon Valley didn't *plan* to become Silicon Valley. What happened is that in the 1930s Stanford University's president Fred Terman had an idea to build an industrial park on Stanford land in the hopes that this might persuade bright grads like David Packard and Bill Hewlett to stick around and tinker locally. Terman didn't say: "Let's take on Detroit!"

The ability to pass the Entrepreneurial Cocktail Party Test. Here's how it works. You gather two hundred friends and acquaintances in a room—the sort of people who attended your wedding or might attend your funeral—and you clink a glass. The room goes silent. You announce: "I've just quit my job! I'm starting a company!" Watch the immediate reaction. In some communities, people will burst into applause. In others, people will stare at their shoelaces, check their watch, and go home. Thriving communities applaud the bold risk taker.

APPLY YOUR OWN PREFERENCES

As you contemplate your move out of a crushing urban coastal area into a smaller community, you will want to apply your own preferences, ranging from weather to culture to restaurants to health care. Whether a city is poised to grow indeed may be quite low on your list of concerns if you intend only to telecommute or to settle back into a life of quiet semiretirement. Generally, people moving out of large urban areas will be happiest in small cities with a thriving intellectual life—university towns and capital cities. To a transplanted New Yorker who loves movie houses that specialize in obscure black-and-white documentaries, ethnic food, and independent bookstores, Ann Arbor and Madison may be more congenial than Detroit or Milwaukee.

Once you consider the where of your happiness, you'll have to dive deep into yourself (or pray for divine insight as Peter Scanlon did in Chapter 9). Because finding the right place for you and your family will demand you answer honestly questions about your likes and dislikes, your skills and work habits, your willingness for adventure, and your age and your economic status. The following resource section is full of ideas and tools to help you discover your own best *where*.

PART 3

150 Cheap Places to Live

Reasonably priced U.S. cities and towns you might consider as you set out to find the *where* of your happiness.

For more information, visit us at WWW.LIFE2WHERE.COM.

Below we list 150 small towns, medium-sized cities, and larger metro regions in the United States where you can live well and where your dollar will go far.

Of course, the "live well" half of our claim is shot through with subjectivity. It will be highly dependent on who *you* are, and what *you* want out of life. There are plenty of folks who will steadfastly refuse to suffer even one more day of subfreezing temperatures—period, end of story. Others may be bored to the point of madness by living in a small town. They crave big-city stimulation. Their hope is to find such a lifestyle devoid of Manhattan-like expenses and pressures.

One of the great pleasures of living in the United States is its sheer diversity. As I pointed out in the book's introduction, America offers by far the richest selection of location choices in which to work and live—to pursue your American Dream by your own definition. You can choose cities by size, by weather, by political tenor (Portland, Oregon, is screechingly liberal while a city of equal size, Cincinnati, Ohio, is deeply conservative), by industry, by tax and regulatory scheme, by schools, by the arts and music scene, by acceptance of racial and sexual minorities, or by cost of living. You can dwell in the mountains, put down on the beach, reside on a farm, or repair to the high desert.

In other words, you don't have to "settle" when you settle.

Now, some words on how we organized our list of 150 cities. One, respecting America's vast size and diversity, we broke the 150 locations into six categories.

- Porch-Swing Communities (best family-friendly cities)
- Happy Hootervilles (best small towns)
- IQ Campuses (emerging centers of biotech and infotech)
- Steroid Cities (fast-growing, business-friendly metro areas)
- Bohemian Bargains (lively inner cities)
- Telecommuting Heavens (where to work in your underwear)

Two, we purposely excluded from our list the most expensive cities (which include Seattle, cities in coastal California, Boston, New York, and Washington, D.C.); high-priced resorts (Aspen, Jackson Hole, Palm Beach, the Hamptons, Kennebunkport, etc.); and cities such as Chicago and Houston, reasonably priced but too huge.

Our price cutoff was $500,000 for a median professional-class home. Just what is a "median professional-class home"? We considered it to be a 2,500-square-foot house on a quarter-acre lot, with new amenities such as kitchen, bathroom, flooring, windows, and paint—located in a nice neighborhood. In La Jolla, California, a suburb of San Diego, that house would fetch $1,800,000. Happily, most of our "150 Cheap Places to Live" offer such houses in the $200,000 to $350,000 range.

Three, our list was never meant to pass academic muster. My researcher, Adrienne Sanders, and I relied on our own judgments, prejudices, and gut feelings and the help of a rich and eclectic body of published sources.

On house prices, we found the city-to-city comparison chart on www.coldwellbanker.com to be the most accurate and up-to-date. This is an incredible site! Go to the main page and click on "home price index" and see for yourself. I've spent many hours there.

For Porch-Swing Communities, we think demographer Bert Sperling has the right idea incorporating data on crime, unemployment, and stress levels (www.bestplaces.net).

For the Happy Hooterville section, we gave special weight to the findings of Jack Schultz, author of *Boomtown USA: The 7¹/₂ Keys to Big Success in Small Towns*. We trust Schultz because he earns his keep studying and consulting to small American towns (www.agracel.com).

Forbes magazine has the best stuff on fast-growth Steroid Cities (www.forbes.com); while the Milken Institute, a think tank endowed by former bond-trader Michael Milken, is generally dead-on when measuring attributes for IQ Campuses (www.milkeninstitute.org).

A former Milken fellow and writer, Joel Kotkin, has long studied regional U.S. economics. His work is some of the best available (www.joelkotkin.com). Richard Florida, the Carnegie Mellon professor we criticized in Chapter 14 for overweighing rave culture and gay populations as success markers, nevertheless has his pulse on inner-city revivals, and we referred to his work while assembling the Bohemian Bargains list (www.creativeclass. org). Harry Dent's *Roaring 2000s* (www.harrydent.com) and Jack Lessinger's *Penturbia* (no Web listing for Lessinger, but you may be able to find *Penturbia* at www.amazon.com) gave us good ideas for cheap Telecommuting Heavens.

Other sources we used included ACCRA (www.accra.org), AARP (www.aarp.org), Center for Digital Government (www. centerdigitalgov.com), *Frommer's* (palm.frommers.com), *Golf Digest* (www.golfdigest.com), *Fast Company* (www.fastcompany.com), Lonely Planet regional guides (www.lonelyplanet.com), *Money* magazine (www.money.com), *Outside* magazine (www.outside. away.com), *The Wall Street Journal Guide to Property* (www.wsj.com), the U.S. Census (www.census.gov), and various college and university Web sites.

Peruse, enjoy, and learn. Visit us at www.life2where.com for updates. Above all, be discerning (or even skeptical), as you should be of all such "Best Places" lists you may run across, here or elsewhere. In the final analysis, what matters is not what this book or anybody else says. It only counts when *you* find the perfect match to your needs—the *where* of *your* happiness.

PORCH-SWING COMMUNITIES

This category is designed for families and others in search of that Norman Rockwell hometown feeling—vintage Americana suffused by parades, country fairs, and summer evenings playing kick-the-can. Schools are a high priority to many folks considering this category, and the best American K–12 public schools tend to be found in the Upper Midwest—the Dakotas, Minnesota, Wisconsin, and Iowa. The southern United States has a poorer record here, but don't be deterred if you prefer NASCAR to snowmobiling. Good private schools of varying stripes have sprung up everywhere during the last ten years, even in Arkansas. (All those rich Wal-Mart executives living in Fayetteville have insisted on it.) Outside the Upper Midwest, college towns usually are the best bet for public K–12 schools. Family activities are another top consideration in this category. Some families will enjoy the stimulation of college sports, which can be found in places like Columbia, Fayetteville, and Lincoln, while others may prefer the hiking and skiing available in Boise or Spokane. Then there's always just lazing back with your son or daughter to watch the sun set over the gulf waters in Punta Gorda.

ASHLAND, OREGON

City Population: 22,000
House Price: $320,000

Much ado about Ashland. House prices here are 40 percent higher than the national average—blame the proximity to California for that—but Ashland is worth it. It offers an enviable quality of life, lots of recreation, and cultural attractions that rival those of the big cities. That's a good thing because the nearest metropolis, Portland, is four hours away.

Unwind in one of downtown's funky bistros or duck into an old-fashioned specialty store. Even comic-book collectors have their own shop here. Undisturbed by congestion, tourists, or crime, it's hard to be stressed in Ashland.

A local college, Southern Oregon University, has 5,500 students and specializes in the arts, which helps sustain the town's cultural interest. Top of the list: the year-round Shakespeare festival. Bring your picnic basket and catch a live performance of *Othello* or *Hamlet* anytime in one of the three theaters in the center of town, which include a replica of the famous Globe Theatre.

Tired of the Bard? Alpine lakes and several rivers slice through the region, where you can kayak, whitewater raft, or hike along the banks.

BISMARCK, NORTH DAKOTA

City Population: 56,000
Metro Population: 95,000
House Price: $210,000

Sure, it's cheating to list my own hometown, but if you can tolerate the Upper Great Plains weather—a huge *if*—you'll discover that Bismarck is almost a perfect place to raise a family.

The public schools are among the best in the country. Crime is at the bottom of the charts. You may not like the temperature extremes—Bismarck's high and low records are 114° and −61° respectively—or the constant wind, but with three hundred sunny days per year it's unlikely you'll turn suicidal over it. In fact, Bismarck was named the least stressful small city in the United States by demographer Bert Sperling. (North Dakota's largest city, Fargo, was named the second least stressful.)

As the state capital, Bismarck is more cosmopolitan than most cities of its size. It boasts one of the largest medical facilities in a line between Spokane and Minneapolis. The people are exceedingly friendly, which can make a nice cover for the occasional shady businessman.

On the banks of the Missouri River, Bismarck leads the state in outdoor recreational activities: boating, fishing, hunting, bicycling, snowmobiling, and surprisingly good golfing. The area is steeped in history, from Lewis and Clark to Sitting Bull. The

University of Mary, a Catholic college, is an emerging small-college athletic powerhouse.

BOISE, IDAHO

City Population: 186,000
Metro Population: 432,000
House Price: $260,000

One hot potato. You don't have to search far in Boise to see evidence of this city's economic health. Just look around you. Microchip plants, commercial strips, and even a few high-rises have squeezed their way into Boise's otherwise leafy landscape. Canopies of green still arc over rooftops in this "City of Trees," but industry is humming.

The capital and largest city in Idaho, Boise has a growing economy, with a forecast of continued job expansion. You'll find good medical services, relatively cheap housing (remember that America's West is always going to be higher), and a low crime rate. *Forbes* crowned it the second-best place in the country for business and careers.*

Thanks to its low cost of business, Boise has been able to attract and keep tech titans Micron Technology and the highly profitable printer division of Hewlett-Packard. With an average home price of $260,000, an engineer or software jockey can live well here. Museums, ballet, opera, and a philharmonic orchestra in town will keep your highbrow membership valid.

In town, miles of greenbelt trail and acres of parkland rim the Boise River on both sides, drawing everyone from in-line skaters to fly-fishing anglers. An hour outside the City of Trees lies the Boise National Forest, with 2.6 million acres of beautiful wilderness. Ski, fish, hike, or go whitewater rafting on the rivers. Afterward, soak away your sore muscles in the nearby hot spring pools.

**Forbes Best Places for Business and Careers (2003).*

FORBES BEST PLACES FOR BUSINESS AND CAREERS (2003)

RANK	METRO AREA	COST OF DOING BUSINESS RANK	JOB GROWTH RANK	EDUCATIONAL ATTAINMENT RANK	POPULATION (THOUSANDS)
1	Austin, Tex.	48	11	9	1,313
2	Boise, Idaho	5	10	57	452
3	Raleigh-Durham, N.C.	37	38	6	1,232
4	Atlanta, Ga.	73	36	16	4,263
5	Madison, Wis.	70	39	3	433
6	Provo, Utah	42	27	19	377
7	Omaha, Neb.	2	50	43	723
8	Des Moines, Iowa	12	79	36	463
9	Dallas, Tex.	52	44	25	3,646
10	Washington, D.C. Northern Va.	115	24	2	5,054
11	Huntsville, Ala.	17	68	22	349
12	Richmond, Va.	55	52	31	1,010
13	Colorado Springs, Colo.	43	41	17	533
14	Lexington, Ky.	4	112	35	484
15	Houston, Tex.	45	33	49	4,290
16	Fort Worth, Tex.	35	35	64	1,755
17	Columbia, S.C.	26	125	32	544
18	Oklahoma City, Okla.	3	55	77	1,092
19	Ann Arbor, Mich.	112	48	8	591
20	Minneapolis- St. Paul, Minn.	103	73	14	3,016
21	Little Rock, Ark.	24	90	70	590
22	Knoxville, Tenn.	34	56	85	698
23	Santa Rosa, Cal.	90	22	38	464
24	Columbus, Ohio	78	58	33	1,560
25	Nashville, Tenn.	51	66	52	1,252

BOWLING GREEN, OHIO

City Population: 30,000
House Price: $211,000

A smile is likely to greet you upon arrival in Bowling Green. This rural Ohio town is a downright friendly place with low-key charm and exciting educational opportunities.

Bowling Green State University—larger than you may have thought, with twenty thousand students—is the town's largest employer, and drives the town's economic prosperity, community stability, and cultural diversity. Wood County Government and Cooper Engineered Products are also leading employers. The economy has a diverse retail and industrial base.

Townsfolk and coeds come together on campus for Falcons hockey, football, and basketball. They skate together at BGSU's ice arena and pray together in the area's forty churches.

Downtown Bowling Green is wooded and quaint. Much of the town was built during the boom following the discovery of oil in 1886 nearby. A large clock tower gives an historic feel to Bowling Green.

When Bowling Green gets too quiet (and it will), escape is easy on I-75 or I-80. Detroit, Ann Arbor, and Toledo are a short drive away.

COLUMBIA, MISSOURI

City Population: 85,000
Metro Population: 135,000
House Price: $255,000

The University of Missouri (aka Mizzou) infuses this town of eighty-five thousand with life and smarts; it employs half of the town's residents. Brainy students—there are twenty-seven thousand of them—and professors fill Columbia's concert halls, pubs, and cafés. Teenagers in the three public high schools graduate at an impressive rate, and many stay right in town to start college.

In any given month, you can catch one or more festivals—Heritage, Twilight, and (this being a trendy lefty university town) Earth Day. Take the kids downtown on New Year's Eve, where seven thousand of your neighbors will be whooping it up at First Night Columbia, which features a five-kilometer run, fireworks, and other non-booze-related fun.

Live a bit longer by moving to Columbia. Pollution and traffic are minimal and you can buy plenty of fresh organic veggies at the local farmers markets. Pick up an extra zucchini or two. Groceries are about 20 percent cheaper here than in San Francisco.

DES MOINES, IOWA

City Population: 199,000
Metro Population: 456,000
House Price: $251,000

While other big-city employers slash benefits and perks such as flex-time and telecommuting options, Des Moines companies have beefed up their family-friendly programs, making life in Iowa's capital city today feel secure. That may be necessary, because according to *Fast Company* magazine, 68 percent of children under six years old here have no stay-at-home parent, way more than most cities in the United States. But public schools are good, commute times are short, and real estate is cheap.

Des Moines is the *world's* third-largest insurance center, with sixty insurance companies, led by the Principal Group, headquartered here. The financial-services industry is growing, with Wells Fargo's mortgage banking division and ING bringing in thousands of new jobs.

The Des Moines Metro Opera is world class. And for family adventure, visit the Iowa State Fair (nicknamed the Big One—and stifle your jokes about the girth of Iowans, please), the National Balloon Classic, or Blank Park Zoo. View the outstanding collection of works at the Des Moines Art Center or take a hands-on approach at the Science Center of Iowa.

(For the author's extended take on Des Moines, read Chapter 9, "America's Hometown.")

FAYETTEVILLE, ARKANSAS

City Population: 58,000
Metro Population: 311,100
House Price: $239,000

As Wal-Mart goes, so goes Fayetteville. And things couldn't be better for Wal-Mart, the world's largest retailer. So Fayetteville (just a shopping cart ride away from Bentonville, Wal-Mart's actual hometown) is booming.

Professionals of all levels and their families are clustering around the retail giant, making Fayetteville the sixth-fastest-growing metro area in the country between 1990 and 2000, when it grew 48 percent, to 311,000, according to the U.S. census.

Fayetteville beat out all other small cities to reach the top of the Milken Institute's Best Performing Cities Index in 2003. *Forbes* ranked it the third-best small place for business and careers, giving it high points for job and income growth.

Fayetteville enjoys a reciprocal relationship with another large institution, the University of Arkansas—seventeen thousand students—whose main campus is located here. Get your annual checkup at the university's medical sciences facility or catch a Razorback basketball game on campus. If you live within Fayetteville's city limits, you are welcome to dive into the university's indoor swimming pool or smack some balls on the racquetball courts. If you have teenagers, you're in luck. Town residents receive large discounts on undergraduate tuition there. And Wal-Mart donates millions of dollars of scholarship money to the university.

The town itself is charming, with all the coffeehouses, bookstores, and eateries you'd expect in a university town. Adding to its aesthetic charm are the rugged Ozark Mountains, carved through by trails, streams, and lakes. AARP ranked Fayetteville one of the best places in the country to reinvent your life.

Thanks, Sam Walton.

One more thing: A salary of $150,000 in San Francisco, California, has the same buying power that a salary of $39,663 has in Fayetteville, Arkansas, according to a *BusinessWeek* survey.

LINCOLN, NEBRASKA

City Population: 226,000
Metro Population: 250,000
House Price: $245,000

Lincoln has quietly climbed its way to the top rungs of many national rankings in recent years. It is one of America's most digital-savvy cities (according to a 2003 Microsoft study) and the sixth-best entrepreneurial hot spot (says the Milken Institute). Lincoln is among the twenty least-stressful places for children, according to Zero Population Growth. (In my opinion, ZPG is a dubious source on most subjects, but believe this one.) *Forbes* magazine rated Lincoln number four on its "Best Small Places for Business and Careers in 2003," highlighting its low cost of doing business.

Unemployment is low and industry is diversified among manufacturing, printing, insurance, and technology. Lincoln is one of America's fastest-growing cities outside the Sunbelt—and believe us, you'll never confuse Lincoln's location with the Sunbelt.

Lincoln has excellent public schools and if you have to get sick or suffer from frostbite, here is the place. The city's health care costs are among the lowest in the nation, according to a study by Milliman & Robertson, a New York actuarial and insurance consulting firm.

When you've had enough kiddie time (possible, thanks to short commutes here), hire one of the University of Nebraska's twenty-five thousand students to watch your little ones. Plenty of grown-up restaurants await you in town.

FORBES BEST SMALL PLACES FOR BUSINESS AND CAREERS (2003)

RANK	METRO AREA	COST OF DOING BUSINESS RANK	JOB GROWTH RANK	EDUCATIONAL ATTAINMENT RANK	POPULATION (THOUSANDS)
1	Sioux Falls, S.D.	3	15	42	177
2	Iowa City, Iowa	9	19	2	111
3	Fayetteville, Ark.	35	2	68	322
4	Lincoln, Neb.	6	45	24	252
5	Fargo, N.D.	49	48	27	176
6	Rochester, Minn.	97	5	17	126
7	Lawrence, Kans.	56	33	4	100
8	Rapid City, S.D.	4	41	47	90
9	Santa Fe, N.M.	26	47	7	149
10	Cedar Rapids, Iowa	19	81	33	193
11	Missoula, Mont.	40	36	23	96
12	Cheyenne, Wyo.	2	68	58	82
13	State College, Penn.	83	59	15	136
14	Casper, Wyo.	1	29	87	67
15	Bryan, Tex.	45	12	13	152
16	Waterloo, Iowa	8	115	61	126
17	Charlottesville, Va.	110	63	6	162
18	Hattiesburg, Miss.	11	92	52	113
19	Pocatello, Idaho	18	34	48	75
20	Las Cruces, N.M.	34	9	70	177
21	Bloomington, Ill.	137	6	16	152
22	La Crosse, Wis.	106	71	49	128
23	Billings, Mont.	15	79	39	130
24	Brazoria, Tex.	86	66	90	250
25	Bismarck, N.D.	82	61	44	95

PUNTA GORDA, FLORIDA

City Population: 14,000
House Price: $310,000

Once the domain of blue-haired ladies and early bird specials, Punta Gorda is sizzling among young families. A ninety-minute drive south of Tampa, Punta Gorda offers a Gulf Coast lifestyle without the inflated resort price tag.

Forget Florida's reputation for tacky tourists and drug runners. In Punta Gorda, churches outnumber nightclubs eleven to one. Stroll along the marina in the evening with your kids. The greater Punta Gorda region has the lowest crime rate in the state. (Okay, that's a bit of a one-eyed-man-in-the-kingdom-of-the-blind rank when you remember the state is Florida.)

Demographer Bert Sperling counted Punta Gorda as one of the top places to live in the United States. Among its best features: low unemployment—3.3 percent at the end of 2003—and healthy job growth. In Florida, you won't pay personal income tax and your house will be exempt from bankruptcy judgments. So take a chance on the start-up! If you're moderately successful, you can buy a duplex with an ocean view. House prices are low and appreciate quickly.

In this casual haven, you'll see more sandals than loafers strolling the brick streets. Punta Gorda is revamping its downtown and restoring an Old Florida atmosphere to central district streets by adding brick lanes, street lamps, and shade trees.

Your children can study in one of three public elementary schools, a middle school, or a high school with a performing arts theater under construction. After school, they can play Little League, watch the Texas Rangers in spring training, or head out to the Gulf waters for marlin fishing.

SPOKANE, WASHINGTON

City Population: 196,000
Metro Population: 418,000
House Price: $227,000

Spokane has accomplished what too many cities only dream about. It has come back from disaster. After hosting the World's Fair in 1974, Spokane entered a fifteen-year death spiral as the local mining industries shut down. Unemployment reached 13 percent in 1982. But Spokane has bounced back and grown steadily for years (10 percent since 1990). It has attracted professional families and developed businesses to serve them. Yet it's still one of the most affordable places to live in the nation. In many tree-lined neighborhoods you can find an attractive two-bedroom starter home for not much more than $100,000.

As the county seat, Spokane serves as a hub for business, retail, and financial services. The city is the major health care provider for a thirty-six-county region encompassing parts of Montana, Oregon, Idaho, British Columbia, Alberta, as well as Washington.

And it's easy to stay healthy here. Jog or cycle along rolling wheat fields. Raise your heart rate among forests and pristine lakes. To the west lies the gradually sloping Columbia River Basin; to the east the precipitous Rocky Mountains rise above the region.

Fifteen More (Reasonably Priced) Porch-Swing Communities to Consider

Appleton, Wisconsin
Billings, Montana
Bloomington, Illinois
Bloomington, Indiana
Cheyenne, Wyoming
Corvallis, Oregon
Dubuque, Iowa

Enid, Oklahoma
Fort Walton Beach, Florida
Grand Forks, North Dakota
Lafayette, Indiana
Rochester, Minnesota
Sioux Falls, South Dakota
St. Cloud, Minnesota
Yarmouth, Massachusetts

HAPPY HOOTERVILLES

Happy Hootervilles are pocket-size versions of Porch-Swing Communities. They are towns with populations under twenty-five thousand and with reasonable house prices (i.e., reasonable for white-collar professionals fleeing America's pricey urban coast). By the way, Happy Hootervilles present a big challenge in calculating house prices. Most of these small towns have housing stocks that skew toward older glorified shacks with septic tanks out back. Thus Hendersonville, North Carolina, to take one example, boasts that its median house price is only $110,000. Maybe so. But a professional-class family fleeing suburbia wouldn't want to live in that house. The prices listed below are the best estimate for a 2,500-square-foot house with new bathrooms, a modern kitchen, and other up-to-date amenities. That's why the prices listed in this section will appear higher than in other published sources.

BISBEE, ARIZONA

City Population: 6,700
House Price: $255,000

Once a copper-mining boomtown, Bisbee is buzzing again. It's nearly as picturesque as Tucson but much smaller . . . and cooler. Nearly a mile up the Mule Mountains and just a few miles from the Mexican border, temperatures here are 10 degrees cooler than Tucson, which lies ninety minutes northwest of town.

Azurite mineral deposits paint the local hills a shadowy turquoise. Victorian homes speckle them with white. Downtown, brick buildings house galleries, restaurants, and artisan shops, including one that sells handmade Panama hats. Bisbee's twisting streets and narrow paths evoke its pioneering past. Nearly fifty saloons once served up moonshine to mineral miners in the Brewery Gulch area of town.

Housing here is cheap for the West and there's plenty of land. Bisbee's raw charm has attracted artists for years, according to Harry Dent, author of *The Roaring 2000s*. The artists, in turn, are attracting moneyed folk. Sally's Diner now shares town with cappuccino cafés and Chinese restaurants. The number of households grew about 11 percent between 1995 and 2000.

In 1999 Dent considered Bisbee an "early stage boomtown" with the potential to become an upscale or midscale boomtown. Housing is likely to appreciate, but once here, you're more likely to focus on stunning views of the Huachuca and Chiricahua Mountains than on mortgage rates.

DOUGLAS, GEORGIA

City Population: 10,639
House Price: $206,000

Douglas, a sleepy town in southeastern Georgia—midway between Lumber City and Homerville—has been piling up trophies in the last few years. Author Jack Schultz lists it among the best small towns in the country. Georgia's Alliance of Community Hospitals voted Douglas's medical center "Hospital of the Year" in 2002. And the state crowned Douglas a City of Excellence in 2001.

So what's all the fuss about?

Douglas is among the most forward-looking communities in Georgia. Its historic homes, Main Street shopping area, and outstanding medical, recreational, and educational facilities make Douglas a choice place to live, work, and study.

Newcomers are inundating Douglas, the county seat of

Coffee County (population 34,000). Ten years ago, about six thousand students attended local schools. Today, there are nearly eight thousand.

Want smart kids? You're in the right place. Coffee County raised the money to build a new high school and eight elementary schools as well as to renovate older learning centers through its one-cent sales tax from 1997 to 2000, which generated over $14 million. Here's a case where taxes actually buy something.

When your kids are finished studying, take them to John Coffee State Park's living history museum or to the alley for some extreme bowling. Better yet, leave them with a sitter and head to one of the local golf courses. No gophers will shred up the greens here. They're too frightened to come to Douglas, which has its very own Gopher Plantation, which hosts seasonal gopher-hunting expeditions.

EAST STROUDSBURG, PENNSYLVANIA

City Population: 9,888
House Price: $259,000

This Pocono town is much more than mini ski resorts and heart-shaped bathtubs.

It's smart: East Stroudsburg University, a teachers' college, attracts four thousand students from around the country. Roughly a third of the East Stroudsburg community works in education, health, and social services.

It's fun: ski, swim, golf, hike, or picnic near rushing waterfalls. Swing a five-iron with locals and tourists alike at the Great Bear Golf and Country Club, an eighteen-hole golf course sculpted through thick forests.

It's enriching: enjoy wandering through museums, galleries, and concerts throughout the year here. And if you need some big-city juice, Philly is ninety minutes away by car, and Manhattan less than two hours.

Despite the area's fast growth and the busloads of tourists

who visit the town, East Stroudsburg and its Pocono neighbors retain a strong sense of community.

Lehigh Valley International and Wilkes-Barre/Scranton International airports are both within forty-five miles.

FAIRHOPE, ALABAMA

City Population: 12,480
House Price: $245,000

Tuck a napkin under your chin and sit back. You'll find nothing but the freshest crabs, oysters, and shrimp in this Mobile Bay town. Restaurants here are affordable, friendly, and full of fresh veggies from the surrounding farmlands.

Fairhope sits on the eastern banks of Mobile Bay. Rent a sailboat at a local marina or watch others waft by from the town pier, a favorite date spot for locals. At night you can see Mobile's twinkling lights across the bay.

Slow down and breathe deeply. Fresh pungent flowers peek out from every corner in this romantic village. Roses bloom around the main fountain in the summer and trash cans double as planters. Stroll among moss-draped oak trees in the park or window shop in Fairhope's picturesque galleries and boutiques. Sporty folk won't be disappointed. You'll find plenty of biking, golfing, tennis, and fishing.

You won't be in town long before neighbors welcome you. Leather-faced fishermen will wave good morning and the grocery store cashier will soon know your name. Fairhope residents have the time and inclination to chat—in cafés, at the corner store, at the office watercooler. This may be one of the best or worst parts of southern small-town living, depending on your taste.

FRENCH LICK, INDIANA

City Population: 1,941
House Price: $214,000

Tiny at 1.6 square miles, this is no hick town.

French Lick, Indiana, is more than the birthplace of famous hoopster Larry Bird. It's a charming resort town nestled in the foothills of the Cumberland Mountains, about an hour's drive from Bloomington and the University of Indiana.

Thousands of tourists come here annually for the healing waters of the Pluto Mineral Spring. Visitors have been coming for a healthy dunk for more than two hundred years. These days you can soak in luxury at The Spa at French Lick Springs Resort.

The town has more than water. The locally produced wine is said to be drinkable. The French Lick Winery & Coffee Company makes its home in an historic mansion in town. Fresh-air fanatics can also get their fill on the 8,800-acre Patoka Lake area, just a few miles from town.

Compared to America's larger resort towns, French Lick is a bargain. A big-city equity bandit could buy a house here and treat himself to green fees and spa treatments for decades.

GRANTS PASS, OREGON

City Population: 24,470
House Price: $320,000

If careening through white rapids and eating "bubble sandwiches" are your idea of fun, you may want to consider a move to Grants Pass.

The Rogue River shoots through town, carrying with it rafters, kayak riders, and boating enthusiasts. Dozens of companies offer rafting adventures in Grants Pass and escort visitors through Hellgate Canyon and beyond.

Grants Pass is more than an adrenaline rush, however. Tranquil folk come for the affordable housing (compared to

Seattle or San Francisco), green parks, and surprisingly warm weather. Two hours from the Pacific Ocean, Grants Pass sits along the sunbelt of southern Oregon. Two inches of snow fall annually, if that.

Community-owned hospitals and scores of churches will care for your heart and soul.

For your belly, buy your produce at southern Oregon's largest outdoor "growers market," where locals sell the region's gladiola bulbs, fruits, nuts, and dairy products. Industries include meat processing and wood products. In spring and fall, Grants Pass ignites with the color of new blooms or autumnal trees.

Seek indoor inspiration at the Rogue Music Theatre, where the Barnstormers Little Theater Group puts on plays and concerts.

HENDERSONVILLE, NORTH CAROLINA

City Population: 10,420
House Price: $217,000

Two thousand feet above sea level, Hendersonville enjoys Carolina warmth without the suffocating summer humidity of coastal regions.

Henderson County has been the fastest-growing county in western North Carolina for more than a decade, thanks to a diversified economic base of industry, agriculture, retirement, and tourism. Unemployment is low and the school system is among the best in the state. No wonder *Boomtown USA* author Jack Schultz rated Hendersonville among the top small towns in America.

Bargain for a walking stick or pincushion doll at the Henderson County Curb Market. Sellers are local residents peddling only handmade or locally grown goods. Henderson County is one of the largest apple-producing counties in the United States.

Two respected hospitals serve this small town, whose residents (new and veteran) live in humanely priced homes. You'll enjoy Hendersonville's four distinct seasons, with brilliant foliage and mild winters.

Hendersonville Airport has connecting flights to major cities including Newark, Atlanta, Cincinnati, and Houston.

McCALL, IDAHO

City Population: 2,084
House Price: $265,000

If you like Lake Tahoe but hate its larcenous cost of housing (and skiing), you might consider McCall, about a hundred miles north of Boise on Highway 55.

The Salmon River Mountains encase Payette Lake, a high alpine water body with a Lake Tahoe feel. No casinos or cheesy lounge acts here. Once a sleepy lumber town, McCall's exceptional outdoor recreation is transforming the area into a family-friendly resort spot.

Neighbors will invite you for a spin around the lake in their motorboats or Jet Skis. Lake condos, cabins, and resort spas host tourists who use McCall as a launch pad to Idaho's great outdoors. There are more than one hundred mountain lakes within twenty miles of town, a ski and summer resort minutes away, world-class golf courses, hiking, cycling, river rafting, and festivals. Don't be surprised if a deer, elk, or moose keeps you company for a while.

The fun here isn't just for visitors. Locals enjoy the quiet beauty, clean air, and reasonably priced housing all year round. Local government welcomes business and is committed to continued growth.

OXFORD, MISSISSIPPI

City Population: 11,756
House Price: $235,000

What do William Faulkner, John Grisham, Willie Morris, and Barry Hannah have in common—aside from being writers?

They're all from (or spent many years in) Oxford, Mississippi. Not a bad collection of talent for a town of twelve thousand full-time residents.

The University of Mississippi—with fourteen thousand students—has a lot to do with it. Known as Ole Miss, the university helps make this town a cultural oasis of artists and thinkers.

Ole Miss also lures thousands of athletes and fans for ball games of all sorts. Spark up your grill and unfurl your plastic tablecloth. Tailgating is a popular pastime for students and residents alike. To burn off your lunch, amble among downtown's azaleas and dogwood trees.

Oxford is the manufacturing, medical, educational, governmental, and trading hub of northern Mississippi. The Lafayette County region and the state offer tax incentives and finance programs for new businesses.

Young professionals and academics aren't the only ones making Oxford their stomping grounds. Retirees relish the mild climate, convenient amenities, and excellent health care: The town recently remodeled and enlarged Baptist Memorial Hospital. *Money* magazine has counted Oxford among its top retirement communities. And *Men's Journal*, *Modern Maturity*, and *Time* have all featured Oxford's ideal retirement offerings.

TRAVERSE CITY, MICHIGAN

City Population: 14,532
House Price: $234,000

Traverse City nestles on a small inlet on Lake Michigan directly across the great lake from Green Bay, Wisconsin. It boasts sunset views among the best in the country, respectable ski resorts (for the Midwest, anyway), Michigan's best indoor water park, and a huge outlet mall.

Before the growth of its local airport, the town was just too inconvenient for most outsiders to reach. But increased air service to Cherry Capital Airport, three miles from downtown Traverse, is changing that. Four airlines now provide more than

1,800 seats arriving each day from the hub cities of Detroit, Chicago, Minneapolis, and Milwaukee.

There is good reason to fly to Traverse City these days. In *Boomtown USA*, Jack Schultz lists Traverse City among the best small towns in America—based mostly on locals' can-do attitude; good use of local resources; entrepreneurial encouragement; the high quality of health care, education, recreation, and culture; the low crime rate; and access to transportation.

Move fast. Recent growth has pushed Traverse City prices ahead of other small Michigan towns. A median professional-class home will cost you about $234,000 in Traverse City. That's still cheaper than those in college town Ann Arbor, where the same spread runs about $330,000.

Fifteen More (Reasonably Priced) Happy Hootervilles to Consider

Baraboo, Wisconsin
Bardstown, Kentucky
Durant, Oklahoma
Eufaula, Alabama
Gillette, Wyoming
Greencastle, Indiana
Hammond, Louisiana
Lebanon, New Hampshire
Liberal, Kansas
Marble Falls, Texas
Moorefield, West Virginia
Moses Lake, Washington
Nevada City, California
Philadelphia, Mississippi
Spring Hill, Tennessee

IQ CAMPUSES

If your goal is to start a company or buy property that will rise in value, we recommend university towns, especially those with colleges rich in science and engineering departments. Sorry, English majors, but most new American wealth will be created out of gold mines such as nanotechnology, information technology, and life sciences—and, perhaps even more important, from the *application* of these cutting-edge technologies to familiar businesses of all kinds: nanotechnology on manufacturing materials; information technology on finance, shipping, and retail; life sciences on pharmaceuticals and agriculture.

ALBANY, NEW YORK

Metro Population (includes Schenectady and Troy): 876,000
House Price: $328,000

Surprise! The Milken Institute listed Albany near the top of its most-improved cities, based mostly on job and technology growth.

In 2003 the State University of New York at Albany burst into the nanotechnology scene, attracting computer chip consortium International Sematech and toolmaker Tokyo Electron, both building research centers there.

Expect a growing crop of scientists, engineers, and more university R&D grants—all indicators of future wealth and real estate appreciation. A veteran Silicon Valley entrepreneur told me in early 2004 that he thinks Albany is one of the country's up-and-coming tech start-up environments.

Albany's "cool factor" may be low, but Richard Florida's 2002 creativity index reveals that may be changing. The city ranked 17 out of 266 based on its diverse, well-educated, and innovative residents. Frankly, we prefer heat to coolness. The region scores here, too. Rensselaer Polytechnic in Troy turns out students whose IQ can boil water.

In autumn, fiery foliage lights the landscape. But bring plenty of sweaters; this state capital is only for the hardy. One hundred and forty miles north of New York City, winters here are frigid. Luckily, a local airport and easy access to New York City make for quick escape.

ANN ARBOR, MICHIGAN

Metro Population: 579,000
House Price: $377,000

Ann Arbor, home to the University of Michigan, is small enough to be friendly but cosmopolitan enough to satisfy most intellectual snobs.

Families love it for the safe, leafy neighborhoods, rock-solid schools, clean air and water, and reputable doctors. If that's not enough, you have a healthy local economy, more than a hundred parks inside the city limits, and the University of Michigan's stock of Big Ten athletics.

If you don't work at the U of M, you may punch your card at Borders and Domino's Pizza, both headquartered here; Parke-Davis pharmaceuticals and Pall Gelman Sciences (medical equipment) are also employers of note.

For art and live theater, visit Jeff Daniels's Purple Rose Theater Company in nearby Chelsea. For the kids, there's the Hands-On Museum, the Ann Arbor Art Center, and many child-friendly farms and orchards. Warm up at the Matthaei Botanical Gardens during the long Michigan winters.

Running is a popular pastime in the city. If you're willing to travel thirty minutes or so, the Pinckney and Brighton Recreation Areas offer lakes and trails for hiking and cycling.

Like many heartland university towns, Ann Arbor is family friendly. *Outside* magazine rated Ann Arbor among the top places to raise children in the country in 1999 but noted there was a price for paradise: "Positively Dantean Saturday afternoons in fall, when one of the 100,000 well-oiled Wolverines fans is likely to mistake your hubcap for a urinal cake."

ATHENS, GEORGIA

Metro Population: 153,000
House Price: $239,000

When I visited with regional economic development authority Walter Plosila (see Chapter 14), he told me, "Watch Athens." The University of Georgia spurs much of Athens's success. More than thirty-three thousand students attend the university, which blankets 605 acres amid the region's rolling red-clay hills. It is ranked among the nation's top research institutions and boasts America's nineteenth largest library.

Athens's music scene zapped onto the national radar screen in recent years with such homegrown bands as R.E.M., the Indigo Girls, and the B-52s. The famous natives occasionally return to Athens to play local clubs and help out at soup kitchens and schools. Michael Stipe–wannabes still rock downtown clubs with live performances.

House prices are cheap.

BOULDER, COLORADO

Metro Population: 291,000
House Price: $539,000

Boulder is not cheap. Its house prices will seem reasonable only to someone fleeing coastal California, Boston, New York, or Washington, D.C. It surpasses our threshold of $500,000 for a median professional middle-class house. But we include Boulder anyway because, well, we like it.

This college town is a short drive and a world away from Denver. No big city lights here, just lots of parks (3,800 acres of 'em) and patchouli. About a quarter of Boulder's residents are university students. Most attend the University of Colorado, but for the really far-out there's Naropa Institute, where poet Allen Ginsberg helped found the Jack Kerouac School of Disembodied Poetics. Got that? It's easy to see why Robin Williams's character, Mork from planet Ork (from the 1970s sitcom *Mork and Mindy*), chose Boulder over all other American cities.

Boulder boasts another center of higher learning: the National Center for Atmospheric Research, home to the world's fastest supercomputers. Okay, now we're serious.

Boulder is far more than a place to study, however. Families, young professionals, and tree huggers of every type love it for the laid-back lifestyle it promotes. Webs of bike paths and the surrounding greenbelt allow locals to enjoy the area's forests and fields without ever strapping on a seat belt.

As you would expect, Boulder is not particularly business friendly. This is good news for neighboring Longmont, home to much of Colorado's high-tech industry. Work in Longmont, crash in Boulder. Downtown has loads of artists' co-ops and vegan eateries. Just don't be surprised if your dreadlocked waitress pads over in bare feet.

CHARLOTTESVILLE, VIRGINIA

Metro Population: 160,000
House Price: $395,000

Who said you can't be smart *and* beautiful?

Home to top-rated University of Virginia (ranked as third-best public university by *U.S. News & World Report* in 2003), Charlottesville has the brains, all right. Leafy streets are brimming over with professors, students, and research types. The town's smarts helped it place seventeenth on *Forbes* magazine's 2003 "Best Small Places for Business and Careers." We can only guess that too many lawyers in town kept Charlottesville out of the top ten.

And Charlottesville sure is pretty. Sitting at the foothills of the Blue Ridge Mountains, it is full of emerald lawns and bursting magnolias. Bikers float along the region's rolling hills and picnic in the shade of Shenandoah National Park.

Outside magazine rated Charlottesville eighth on its "Coolest Place to Work, Play, Study, Party, and Live" list in 2003, citing its good music scene, restaurants, Jeffersonian influences, and chichi wineries.

Charlottesville is packed with UVA leftovers. Thousands of residents earn a living at GE-Fanuc, Liberty Fabrics, Sperry, and State Farm Insurance. Writers, consultants, and traders plug in to major cities, the nearest one being Washington, D.C., which is 110 miles away. Proximity to D.C. is why Charlottesville home prices are at the high end of our "reasonable" range.

People old enough to be UVA students' grandparents also find Charlottesville's quality of life irresistible. AARP has named it one of the best towns to retire in.

IOWA CITY, IOWA

Metro Population: 74,000
House Price: $248,000

If Iowa City were a student, it would be class valedictorian.

This heartland university town consistently earns top scores on countless lists: *Forbes*'s "Best Small Places for Business and Careers"; *USA Today*'s "Best Educated Cities"; *Utne Reader*'s "Most Enlightened Towns"; *Men's Journal*'s list of sexy, healthy, and safe places to live; AARP's best college towns in which to retire; the Milken Institute's best small metro economy; Bert Sperling's least stressful; and Expansion Management's top metros for companies to relocate or expand.

Whew!

And the town's pride, the University of Iowa, scored tops on Kaplan's best value for your tuition dollar (2004), noting its outstanding medical program. *Outside* magazine rated it among the top of its list of schools where you can hit the books *and* the backcountry.

Part of Iowa City's strength is that its students stay put after graduation. The line between residents and students is, well, warm and fuzzy. Many students rent farmhouses in the rolling hills and locals feel perfectly comfortable ambling along the Iowa River in the heart of campus.

Iowa City has a cozy turn-of-the-century feel, yet it offers a roster of holistic health practitioners, ethnic eateries, used-book stores, and some of the best pubs in America. Local radio programs broadcast poetry readings from the town's Prairie Lights bookstore and the Joffrey Ballet makes a summer home here.

Now that's an A+.

LAWRENCE, KANSAS

Metro Population: 100,000
House Price: $218,000

With its steep hills, candy-colored Victorian houses, and stately churches, Lawrence looks more New England than Great Plains. One of the country's most charming downtowns, main-drag Massachusetts Street is a shaded haven of restaurants, galleries, and boutiques.

But it's not baby back ribs that propelled Lawrence to fourth place on *Forbes* magazine's "Best Cities" list. The real juice is the University of Kansas's Center for Research, which specializes in life science technology. The respected research facility has attracted hordes of federal research dollars since the mid-1990s. The technical and intellectual synergy among the combined campuses has generated dozens of start-up companies.

For golf fanatics, there are few better places to live. *Golf Digest* dubs Lawrence "One of the Best Little Golf Towns in America."

Old-timers gripe that suburbs and strip malls are gobbling up the outskirts of town. True, the influx of scientists and tech execs has ignited some sprawl, but new homeowners couldn't be happier. Prices this reasonable have nowhere to go but up.

MADISON, WISCONSIN

Metro Population: 427,000
House Price: $268,000

Who doesn't love Madison? Residents celebrate a litany of "lows": cost of living, crime, and unemployment rates (around 3 percent). And you can afford to buy a home in this safety zone.

This city of 207,000 (inside a metro area of 427,000) consistently lands at the top of an impressive variety of "Best Cities" lists for women, creativity, entrepreneurial business growth, raising kids, outdoor sports, and more.

The University of Wisconsin, with forty-one thousand students, scores near the top in many research fields, including biotech.

Don't be surprised if you hear Italian or Japanese chitchat in one of the local coffeehouses. International college students mix with an already diverse population, making it easy to forget you're in the Midwest. University of Wisconsin students aren't the only students getting a great education in Madison. The city's public schools are among the nation's best. The percentage of high school graduates is very high, and low pupil-to-teacher ratios mean your kids actually learn something before grabbing that diploma.

Catch a play or concert at the Madison Repertory Theater, Madison Opera, or Madison Symphony. Bike or Rollerblade (in-line skate) among the two hundred parks within city limits. The air here is remarkably clean . . . though frosty in the winter.

MISSOULA, MONTANA

Metro Population: 72,000
House Price: $253,000

Tool belts and trigonometry are on equal footing in this blue-collar-meets-ivory-tower town.

Sawmill workers and University of Montana professors are next-door neighbors here, sharing the town's affordable housing and good health care. Violent crime is low and future job growth looks sunny. Missoula rated eleventh in *Forbes* magazine's "Best Small Places to Live" index (2003).

The cultural capital of Montana, Missoula has a long-standing reputation as the state's most progressive city. The mix of people here is as refreshing as the Clark Fork River. Intellectuals, East Coast transplants, international students, and Russian and Tibetan immigrants join the locals to make Missoula their home. Hippies and hipsters guzzle hot java together in cozy coffee-houses, especially during the winter. Missoula is far north and averages 183 days with temperatures below freezing. But as a ben-eficiary of Chinook winds, Missoula winters are mild compared to those in the Dakotas, Minnesota, or New England. Snowshoe and cross-country ski nuts love it since there are millions of acres of wilderness surrounding the town.

Discovering other ways to have fun is easy in the town's many restaurants, galleries, and museums. Movie buffs can get their foreign-film fix at the Crystal Theater. Singles can use the ubiq-uitous fireplaces for face-to-face chats with promising dates.

STATE COLLEGE, PENNSYLVANIA

Metro Population: 136,000
House Price: $215,000

No wonder they call it the Heart of Happy Valley.

Home to Pennsylvania State University, State College rated the third *least* stressful small metro area in America on Bert Sperling's "Best Places" list. Criteria: unemployment, crime, commute time, suicide, and divorce.

If you're single, you're psyched. The majority of State College's forty thousand denizens are unmarried folks between eighteen and thirty-four. Downtown, the colonial shops, restau-rants, and pubs are soaked with singles. Pull up a bar stool to watch Penn State's Nittany Lions football team. Don't worry about walking home alone. Streets here are among the safest in the nation. Safe but not dull. Sperling rated it number one of "America's Best Cities for Dating" in 2003.

Money magazine reports the median home price is about $118,900, roughly 10 percent below the national average. Be skeptical of that number, however. It reflects a lot of run-down, off-campus student rentals. We calculated a higher price of $215,000 for a 2,500-square-foot house with modern amenities. That's still cheap! And the job market's future growth looks good.

Forbes rated Pennsylvania State University's hometown thirteenth on its "Best Small Places for Business and Careers" index. Pittsburgh, the nearest big city, is a two-hour drive.

Fifteen More (Reasonably Priced) IQ Campuses to Consider

Ames, Iowa

Amherst, Massachusetts

Bozeman, Montana

Champaign-Urbana, Illinois

Columbus, Ohio

Davis, California

Eugene, Oregon

Fargo, North Dakota

Hanover, New Hampshire

Huntsville, Alabama

Ithaca, New York

Knoxville, Tennessee

Logan, Utah

Pocatello, Idaho

Terre Haute, Indiana

STEROID CITIES

Steroid Cities are those fast-growth metro areas, mainly located in America's South and West, where the sun shines, the air-conditioners hum, and the two languages you'll need to master in addition to English are capitalism and Spanish. One of our favorite Steroid Cities is Santa Rosa, California, located ninety minutes by car north of San Francisco. On either side of Santa Rosa (2000 metro population: 459,000) sits a substantial pocket of tech industry and the better part of America's wine industry. No surprise on grapes; the land and the weather around Santa Rosa are as close to Tuscany as you'll get in the Western Hemisphere. Santa Rosa is a home buyer's bargain store; the houses here cost half as much as those in San Francisco. Therein lies a problem! Half the price of the average San Francisco house is still a whopping $659,000—too much for most professional middle-class Americans seeking price relief. Alas, we couldn't include Santa Rosa in this list. One more note on house prices. Steroid Cities tend to have a lot of cheap housing to accommodate their rapid growth in service-industry jobs. So we added 30 percent to the Coldwell Banker figures to come up with a more realistic price for a 2,500-square-foot house with nice amenities and located in a top school district.

AUSTIN, TEXAS

Metro Population: 1.2 million
House Price: $312,000

Austin has it all.

Anchored by the state capitol, the University of Texas, and nearly one hundred tech companies, led by $40 billion giant Dell, Austin is one smart city. It boasts the best weather in Texas— sunny and dry. Hills and lakes break up the monotony that plagues rival Dallas. Discovered as Hip Town, USA, in the late 1990s, some say this mecca for musicians and artists beats Seattle.

Hike and bike on more than fifty trails; you might bump into longtime resident Lance Armstrong. On sunny days—aka most days—take in the natural limestone pool at Barton Springs and the exotic gardens of Zilker Park. University of Texas students swear Austin's like spring break all year; no wonder so many stick around after graduation, such as famous alum Michael Dell.

Executive-style houses in the Enfield district are reasonably priced, though not cheap. But if that's too much, don't despair. U.T.'s sixty thousand students guarantees a supply of really cheap digs. Live like a grad student and you'll have enough left over to treat your friends to unlimited mesquite barbecue and Celis beer.

BIRMINGHAM, ALABAMA

Metro Population: 921,000
House Price: $275,000

Birmingham hasn't lost its southern soul. Taste it in country-fried steak and butter beans. Hear it in the local folks' drawl, y'all.

It's southern, but it's anything but sleepy. (More Alabama slammer than mint julep.) Six Forbes 500 top companies have headquarters in Birmingham, including Amsouth Bancorp, Saks (yes Saks!), and the financially troubled HealthSouth. Honda bases its largest manufacturing plant in the Western Hemisphere in Birmingham. Experts predict job growth at 5.8 percent for the rest of the decade.

Birmingham's diverse and innovative residents earned the city a top-ten spot on Richard Florida's creativity index for smaller cities. They're also down to earth. "The audience at the symphony concert will discuss college football games coming up the next day," explains Birmingham's Convention and Visitor's Bureau Web site.

Money magazine rated Birmingham one of the best places to live in the United States. House prices are affordable but appreciating quickly. The American Chamber of Commerce Researchers Association reported the average 2,400-square-foot home costs about $203,000 (February 2003). We'll go with a higher price of $275,000 for the best school districts.

When you're not fixing up your new digs, brush up on history at the Birmingham Civil Rights Institute or the Birmingham Museum of Art. Visionland theme park, the city zoo, and the Barber Motorsports Park are kids' favorites.

COLORADO SPRINGS, COLORADO

Metro Population: 517,000
House Price: $274,000

Colorado Springs inspired the famous song "America the Beautiful," written originally as a poem in 1895. The author, Katharine Lee Bates, described the mountains surrounding Pikes Peak, just outside of Colorado Springs, as "purple mountain majesties."

"It was then and there, as I was looking out over the sealike expanse of fertile country spreading so far under those ample skies, that the opening lines of the hymn floated into my mind," Bates wrote.

Americans have long known that Colorado Springs was beautiful, but only recently have they begun to flock to that expanse of swath land in such large numbers. Colorado Springs's metro population shot up 30 percent, to 516,900, between 1990 and 2000.

The town's natural beauty and business friendliness have attracted many new companies. Progressive, whose many divisions comprise the country's third-largest auto insurance group, built three buildings for a thirty-acre campus in Colorado Springs at the end of 2003, adding more than eight hundred new jobs, doubling its number of local employees. The evangelical Christian organization, Focus on the Family, makes its home here.

But there is a secular bohemian life in Colorado Springs, too. Richard Florida rated Colorado Springs number six among smaller metros for creativity.

Grab your walking stick and head to the mountains or throw around a Frisbee in one of the town's many parks. Colorado Springs offers plenty of cheap housing, though prices rise sharply the closer you get to the best neighborhoods around the historic Broadmoor Hotel, located at the base of Pikes Peak.

LAS VEGAS, NEVADA

Metro Population: 1.6 million
House Price: $310,000

Visit Vegas for the Bellagio, Wayne Newton, and never-ending blackjack games. Move to Vegas for cheap housing, low taxes, and warm weather.

More Americans are choosing Las Vegas as their new hometown than any other. The population soared 83.3 percent, to 1.56 million, between 1990 and 2000, making it the nation's fasting growing city, according to the U.S. census.

You'll have no problem finding a job among one-armed bandits and roulette wheels; gambling is still the city's top earner. Card dealers can earn up to $80,000 a year. Valets at large hotels can top six figures. If you want to open a business, you will find local government almost desperate to please. And commercial real estate prices are lower than a showgirl's neckline.

Families tend to favor North Las Vegas, which is building new schools, stores, and restaurants to meet the demand. As housing costs slowly climb, so does smog and traffic.

Tired of the hoo-ha? Tranquility lies just a few miles west of the strip in the Red Rock Canyon National Conservation Area. Climb and cycle among the 2,000-foot-high towers of red, yellow, and black sandstone.

McALLEN, TEXAS

Metro Population: 569,000
House Price: $248,000

In McAllen, you get two towns for the price of one. McAllen trades workers, consumers, and goods with Reynosa, its Mexican sister city four miles south.

Cross the Rio Grande via the International Bridge and grab some fresh tamales and handmade pottery for nickels. Not that life in McAllen is pricey. In 2003 the Chamber of Commerce ranked McAllen as the third-lowest U.S. city in cost of living.

You can find decent housing for a lot cheaper than the figure we cited above. Again, we calculated in modern amenities and a top school district. Downside: Crime is above average.

If you run a manufacturing company, this is your Eden. McAllen produces everything from liquid sweetener to cardboard boxes. General Motors, Whirlpool, and Black & Decker will tell you that good (i.e., low-cost) help is not hard to find in McAllen. That's because unemployment is high.

This paradise is a tropical one, steamy year-round. Birdwatchers flock to the Rio Grande Valley, which sits beneath intercontinental flyways. You'll discover plant and wildlife species such as the ocelot and jaguarundi found nowhere else in the United States.

When you need to fly away from the area, the fourth fastest growing in the United States, the new McAllen-Miller International Airport can send you to Dallas and Houston for connecting flights.

NAPLES, FLORIDA

Metro Population: 251,000
House Price: $498,000

Nestled on ten miles of sun-drenched beaches along the Gulf of Mexico, Naples is a resort and retiree nirvana. Crimson sunsets mesmerize you after lazy afternoons reading romance novels under twenty-foot palms.

If you're amused by the spectacle of argyle-clad seniors clubbing a small white ball around manicured greens, check out Naples's thirty-five golf courses. The town has the highest ratio of golf courses to golfers in the United States and its courses are reputed to be quite challenging. Downtown, amble past pink-hued buildings and boutiques on your way to the nearby Everglades Park or Caribbean Gardens.

Affluent retirees who once crowded into Miami and Fort Lauderdale increasingly opt for this tropical alternative. Naples's population has grown from 152,000 to 251,000, or

65.3 percent, from 1990 to 2000. Housing prices are very expensive along beaches but drop rapidly inland.

Find a job helping others get to Naples. Tourism is the top industry here, along with agriculture.

PROVO, UTAH

Metro Population: 369,000
House Price: $329,000

Single and Mormon? Provo, home to Brigham Young University, is your paradise.

Pretty much everyone else seems to love it, too. Provo and its sister community, Orem, comprise one of the fastest-growing regions in the United States, swelling nearly 40 percent, to 369,000, between 1990 and 2000.

Money magazine ranked this Wasatch Range town one of the twenty-best places to live in the United States, and numerous other groups give Provo top scores for entrepreneurship and small business survival. Taxes are relatively low and the cost of doing business is reasonable.

BYU's thirty thousand students have a lot to do with Provo's appeal. The country's largest private university funnels a bright, young workforce to the area's landscaped office parks. Many are bilingual thanks to the church's practice of sending young people as missionaries around the world.

The supply of fine arts and sports talent is unending. Catch an opera or a college basketball game in the cavernous BYU Marriott Center or take an hour's drive to catch the Utah Jazz in Salt Lake City.

Grab dinner downtown amidst turn-of-the-century buildings and tree-lined streets. Provo has also made it a point to have plenty of parks within easy walking distance from neighborhoods to encourage a family-friendly environment.

Divorce, unemployment, and crime here are so low that demographer Bert Sperling's 2004 index rates Provo as one of the least-stressful cities in the country.

RENO, NEVADA

Metro Population: 340,000
House Price: $470,000

From slot machines to microscopes.

Reno is hedging its bets. With its second-rate gaming industry squeezed between glitzy Las Vegas at one end and Indian casinos at the other, Reno's leaders know that the smart money is moving away from gambling and toward high tech.

That means tapping into the resources of the University of Nevada. The university is jazzing up its nanoscience and engineering programs to attract scientists, engineers, and, most important, research grants—precursors to future wealth and real estate appreciation.

And in the meantime, the university is more than happy to share the Fleischmann Planetarium's simulations of the night sky and assorted astronomical phenomena with local residents. Kids can also catch a gee-whiz movie there on the wraparound screen.

Most of Reno's attractions are much more down to earth, including the Truckee River, which flows right through downtown. Gambling remains the town's top earner (though its economy is increasingly diversified into agriculture and industry). But when you tire of losing money in one of Reno's lackluster casinos—which will be immediately if you live here—you can fish or stroll down Riverwalk, a pedestrian path along the river. For real outdoor fun, the Nevada shore of Lake Tahoe is about twenty miles southwest of town.

TUCSON, ARIZONA

Metro Population: 844,000
House Price: $325,000

Among towering saguaro cacti and wind-sculpted cliffs, you'll find one of the most beautiful rapid-growth cities in the country.

Set in the Sonoran Desert valley, Tucson is all sunshine and fresh, clean air. Its population grew 20 percent, to 486,000, during the last decade, according to the U.S. Census. The population of the surrounding Pima County jumped 27 percent in the same time period, to 844,000 residents. Flocks of job-seeking young families promise to drive expansion in the coming decades.

And where are the jobs? In Tucson's "Optics Valley," a fast-growing center for science and industry in aerospace, software development, bio-industry, environmental technology, and telecommunications. The recent growth is changing Tucson, which a 2003 Microsoft survey ranked near the top of its "Digital Cities" list.

Enjoy Tucson's vibrant legacy of Mexican and traditional Indian cultures in the form of exquisitely handcrafted turquoise jewelry or a mouthful of tamales. Two-step your way into a country and western juke joint, or roar with the crowd at a University of Arizona Wildcats basketball game. Golf is also a Tucson favorite.

Health care costs, unemployment figures, and housing prices are all low. But as with all Steroid Cities, don't be suckered by the low median house prices. Figure on a hefty premium to live in a nice neighborhood in a good school district. Still, $325,000 is not bad for what you get.

YUMA, ARIZONA

Metro Population: 160,000
House Price: $308,000

Snowbirds flew south for the winter . . . and stayed for good.

No longer a mere pit stop off Interstate 10 between Phoenix and San Diego, Yuma is one of the fastest growing towns in America. Over the past ten years, the population of the Yuma area ballooned nearly 50 percent, to 160,000 residents.

Yuma's warm winters, Colorado River beauty, and thirteen golf courses attract ninety thousand snowbirds each winter, many of them in Winnebagos. Each spring, roughly 10 percent decide to stay, and this seems to suit townsfolk just fine.

The town is preserving its natural setting, restoring its downtown buildings, and expanding historic sites. The West Wetlands in the Yuma Crossing National Heritage Area, a former toxic dumping ground, is now home to bike paths, jogging and hiking trails, wetlands, and bird-watching areas.

Agriculture is the city's top industry, followed by tourism and the military. Military folk stationed in Yuma like its friendly, affordable communities so much, many move back when they return to civilian life.

The city's best-known tourist stop is the Yuma Territorial Prison. In use between 1876 and 1909, it housed many of the state's most notorious convicts. Less than ten miles west of Yuma is Baja California; the community greets tourists and winter visitors with colorful dances, outdoor restaurants, and low prices.

Fifteen More (Reasonably Priced) Steroid Cities to Consider

Charlotte, North Carolina
Flagstaff, Arizona
Fort Collins, Colorado
Fort Worth, Texas
Fresno, California
Gainesville, Florida

Greeley, Colorado
Greenville, North Carolina
Jackson, Tennessee
Laredo, Texas
Myrtle Beach, South Carolina
Orlando, Florida
Phoenix, Arizona
Wilmington, North Carolina
Winston-Salem, North Carolina

BOHEMIAN BARGAINS

Bohemian Bargains are core cities in the 150,000 to 750,000 population range with a lively downtown and a reasonable cost of living. We picked them on the basis of their being honest-to-God cities, with real downtowns, more than postmodern sprawls. We didn't include Atlanta, because its downtown has always disappointed us, even though we love the greater metro area, the tony Buckhead district especially. Still, if you like Atlanta for its sheer energy (and its hot dating scene), don't listen to us. Go for it. Sacramento is a sprawl, too, but it contains lively inner-city pockets that will appeal to a San Franciscan or Los Angeleno and it is very cheap by California standards. Bohemian Bargains will appeal particularly to the young and the single.

BALTIMORE, MARYLAND

City Population: 651,000
Metro Population: 2.6 million
House Price: $369,000

Baltimore got its groove back, baby. Pride sparkles in the bold designs of the skyscrapers and museums that surround the Inner Harbor, boast city leaders. You can see it in the smiles of Little Italy's restaurant hosts and in buffed-up neighborhoods such as Fells Point.

The Inner Harbor, now a major tourist attraction, includes a waterfront promenade, museums, tour boats, historic ships, and the innovative National Aquarium.

Those "in the know" call Southwest Baltimore SoWeBo, which is a neighborhood modeled after New York City's SoHo. Artists, musicians, and other assorted bohemians have moved into the area around Hollins Market in the last decade to revive the district. SoWeBo is colorful during the day, but be careful at night. Most of the area is still impoverished and can be dangerous then.

Baltimore boasts the second-highest concentration of professional and technical workers in the United States. The city is a price bargain compared to nearby Washington, D.C. Future job growth looks promising.

CLEVELAND, OHIO

City Population: 478,000
Metro Population: 2.3 million
House Price: $255,000

Cleveland has cleaned up since its polluted Cuyahoga River famously caught fire in 1969. The city is clean, green, and surprisingly sophisticated. The creative offerings here rival many larger cities. The symphony, the Museum of Art, and the theater scene are all phenomenal. On chilly weekends, shake it up with your kids indoors at the Rock and Roll Hall of Fame and Museum or the Great Lakes Science Center. This is a family-friendly place with lots of reasonably priced housing, good schools, decent commutes, and plenty of outdoor fun on Lake Erie.

Cleveland's small business community is clubby and growing. Case Western Reserve University, Cleveland Clinic, and the University of Akron are driving tech-based economic development.

But ask your cardiologist for a permission slip before moving here. The long winters and beef stew plump up many residents, and smokers are everywhere.

DENVER, COLORADO

City Population: 572,000
Metro Population: 2.4 million
House Price: $361,000

Denver delivers.

Don't let a potential pay cut prevent you from moving to the Mile-High City. The Rockies are calling! Camp, ski, and hike in the region's thirty-five ski areas and fifteen million acres of national parks.

You'll be able to afford it. The job market is growing and a $75,000 income here buys you a lifestyle that would cost you $200,000 a year in San Francisco.

Downtown is more cosmopolitan than you might expect. Check out the Denver Center for Performing Arts, the Denver Museum of Nature and Science, or Larimer Square, where restored Victorians house art galleries, cafés, and boutiques.

Picnic at the Red Rock amphitheater in the summertime, where you'll meet your new neighbors and soak up live music. Artists, naturalists, and students love Denver, many vegetarians among them. But according to Forbes.com, most locals would sooner eat barbecued buffalo, a local favorite, than tofu and sprouts.

Sports fans get their game on in Denver, with an assortment of pro and college teams playing year-round. Where you find sports fans, you usually find beer. In Denver, brewing beer is its own art form. Besides the huge breweries of Coors and Anheuser-Busch, the Denver area is filled with microbreweries and brew pubs, all within walking distance of one another downtown.

Denver International Airport, a thirty-minute drive from downtown, is the seventh-busiest airport in the country and the tenth busiest in the world. It will take you anywhere.

MILWAUKEE, WISCONSIN

City Population: 597,000
Metro Population: 1.5 million
House Price: $332,000

Who can resist a city famed for beer and bratwurst? Job growth here may not be as fast as other cities, but that's not keeping away young professionals. The place is just too darn much fun. *Forbes* listed it twelfth among the country's best place for singles, highlighting the city's corner bars, summer festivals, and midwestern friendliness. The new Milwaukee Art Museum and the Brewers' ballpark give Milwaukee singles plenty of flirting ground.

If Gen Xers or boomers are closer to your age group, check your date's ID card. He or she just may be a Marquette University student.

Yuppies, students, and just about everyone here seem to enjoy the city's fifteen thousand acres of parks with their baseball diamonds, tennis courts, and eighty-nine miles of bikeways. Winters are frigid, so get sun while you can: Lake Michigan beaches are just a few miles away.

Milwaukee has landed near the top of several best-places-to-live lists in recent years thanks to its low rates of crime, unemployment, and home prices. Most public school districts are good, consistent with the Upper Midwest's emphasis on public education. But in the poorest districts, where schools are bad, private vouchers are available—Milwaukee's commonsense solution to the age-old problem of school inequity.

PITTSBURGH, PENNSYLVANIA

City Population: 335,000
Metro Population: 2.4 million
House Price: $288,000

Pittsburgh is a far cry from the polluted factory town it used to be. Since the last steel mills closed in the late 1980s, proud Pittsburghers scrubbed the Smoky City clean and cultivated a strong tech industry.

Pittsburgh retains a chilly, serious feel but its natural beauty bursts forth. Three rivers and the Allegheny Mountains hug the city and give it a playfully hilly landscape. At night, lights twinkle from the city's fifteen bridges.

National magazines rate Pittsburgh among the best cities for doing business, raising a family, even riding a bike. The city gets high marks for friendliness; learning and culture, legacies of great magnates like Carnegie and Mellon; and quirky neighborhoods. These days Pittsburghers put their innovative energies into technology, but they've been inventors for generations: Big Macs, banana splits, bingo, and the first radio broadcast were born here. Downside: crime and dicey race relations.

Though the local business community tries hard to attract new young professionals, the unattached may want to look elsewhere. *Forbes* says the "paltry" nighttime offerings make Pittsburgh a pit for singles.

PORTLAND, OREGON

City Population: 529,000
Metro Population (includes Vancouver, Washington):
  1.9 million
House Price: $312,000

Get off a plane in Portland and feel your blood pressure begin to drop. Oregon's largest city is laaaaaid back. According to *Lonley Planet,* "Investment bankers wear Birkenstocks, coffee shops double as board rooms, and everybody but everybody is outdoors on the weekend."

Portlanders love their city for its relaxed pace and natural offerings: the city sits at the nexus of two great rivers, surrounded by immense forests and hushed volcanoes. They are just as proud of their downtown art galleries, eateries, and brew pubs as they are of their wilderness.

Endless inner-city parks make Portland look more golf course than urban grid. If you do manage to get stressed, bubble away tight muscles in the town's ubiquitous hot tubs. It's no wonder Portland is among the fastest-growing cities in the United States.

Politically conservative folk and go-go businesspeople should avoid this metropolis of 1.9 million. Most residents are strictly liberal and favor slow growth.

Portland International Airport is less than ten miles from downtown.

RALEIGH, NORTH CAROLINA

City Population: 276,000
Metro Population (includes Durham and Chapel Hill):
    1.2 million
House Price: $268,000

Who said love triangles have to end badly? Raleigh/Durham/Chapel Hill—known as the Triangle—have enjoyed a civic love-fest for years. The trio consistently helps one another to the top of several "Best Places to Live" lists, which none might reach alone.

Some of the country's best minds have moved to the Triangle, for its concentration of universities, medical centers, and research facilities. Many of these workers, delighted with the area's Blue Ridge Mountain beauty and relaxed pace of life, have chosen to stay, enhancing local businesses or starting their own. Employers of note include tech firms such as SAS Institute and Red Hat and major divisions of Nortel, IBM, and MCI WorldCom.

Bohemians want a piece of the Triangle as much as doctors and techies. Legions of writers, artists, and musicians electrify the creative scene and keep it buzzing. Some of them are recent UNC and Duke students who liked the region so much they made it their new hometown. The Triangle has one of the highest ratios of singles in the United States, according to *Forbes*, which rated Raleigh-Durham the ninth-best city in the United States for singles in 2003.

And if the nightlife is somewhat sleepy, there's always a ball game to catch. Duke and the University of North Carolina, Chapel Hill, usually sport nationally ranked teams in basketball. If you like baseball, check out the AAA Durham Bulls at the Athletic Park, a minor league jewel designed by the same architects who thought up Baltimore's Camden Yards.

Raleigh-Durham International Airport is a short hop.

SACRAMENTO, CALIFORNIA

City Population: 426,000
Metro Population: 1.6 million
House Price: $349,000

Wonks and bureaucrats have long flocked to this capital city to set policy and pull a paycheck. These days, paparazzi, Terminator fans, and movie agents are moving in to drool over California's new governor, Arnold Schwarzenegger.

Government has new cachet and the state capitol building itself has been restored. However, the public sector is no longer the top employer here. Business is. (Only a generation ago, half of local workers were public employees. Today that's down to 30 percent.) *Entrepreneur* magazine counted Sacramento among its top twenty entrepreneurial cities. No surprise. Greater Sacramento has been invigorated by Silicon Valley refugees, who have poured in by the truckload into a swath from Sacramento's trendy Old Town to Sierra foothill towns such as Auburn.

Housing is infinitely more affordable here than in the San Francisco Bay Area, which is about ninety minutes away by car.

Also ninety minutes away by car is Lake Tahoe and some of America's best skiing, boating, and rafting.

ST. LOUIS, MISSOURI

City Population: 348,000
Metro Population: 2.6 million
House Price: $247,000

You don't have to be a beer-bellied sports fan to appreciate St. Louis's charms, but it helps. Budweiser's home city boasts St. Louis Cardinals baseball and Rams football. If guzzling brew and shouting from the stands at Busch Memorial Stadium isn't your idea of fun, worry not. You have plenty of other venues to choose from.

Restaurants, theaters, and boutiques keep the nonfan occupied. The symphony is internationally recognized and the jazz scene is jumping. Anheuser-Busch is the city's largest employer and Monsanto, the agricultural giant, also keeps its headquarters here. Washington University is rising in the national rankings—ninth-best overall university in the 2003 rankings by *U.S. News & World Report.* "Wash U" hosts one of the world's most advanced plant sciences research centers at the futuristic Danforth Center. The downside is, if you didn't attend Wash U, it might take you longer to crack the downtown business elite.

Housing is pretty darn cheap. Based on other quality-of-life factors—environment, crime, education—Rand McNally rated St. Louis in the top 10 percent of the country's 343 metro areas. Hospitals and nursing facilities are so good, the Milken Institute ranked it thirteenth in the nation for health care.

The city's towering steel Gateway Arch honors the generations of pioneers that arrived before. Visitors often make it their first stop, before visiting the restored Union Station, first-rate museums, and numerous attractions geared toward children.

ST. PAUL, MINNESOTA

City Population: 269,000
Metro Population (includes Minneapolis): 2.7 million
House Price: $397,000

No sibling rivalry here. St. Paul and its better-known twin, Minneapolis, are both celebrating their ascent to the top of national lists. The Twin Cities are among the best places to raise a family *or* be single, get a great education, find a job, own a small business, *and* cultivate your inner Picasso. Demographer Bert Sperling listed the area among the least stressful in the country based on low rates of unemployment, crime, commute time, and other factors.

Author David Brooks, in his book *Bobos in Paradise*, counted the Twin Cities among the country's premier places where people of either bohemian or bourgeois habits could feel comfortable. A cappuccino and a Volvo are never far away.

These twins aren't identical: St. Paul, the state capital, is smaller and has an older, East Coast feel. For nocturnal action, take a taxi to Rice Park, the center of St. Paul's nightlife. Be sure to check out the adjacent Ordway Music Theater. If you're craving more variety, shimmy over to Minneapolis, a ten-minute drive away, where the bars and clubs put ripples in the Mississippi River.

The Twin Cities manage to be wholesome and hip at the same time. Though residents are typically hardworking, sports-loving outdoorsy types, Twin City celebs including Prince, Garrison Keillor, the filmmaking Coen brothers, and former Minnesota governor Jesse "the Body" Ventura have pumped up their cool rating. Yah, you betcha.

Still not cool enough? Slide down to the St. Paul Winter Carnival, where you can ice fish, build ice castles, or peg your friend with a festive snowball.

The Minneapolis-St. Paul International Airport is fifteen miles southeast of Minneapolis and about the same distance southwest of St. Paul.

Minnesota Temperature Conversion Chart*

60° F.: Southern Californians shiver uncontrollably. Minnesotans sunbathe.

50° F.: New Yorkers try to turn on the heat. Minnesotans plant gardens.

40° F.: Italian and English cars won't start. Minnesotans drive with the windows down.

32° F.: Distilled water freezes. Crane Lake's water gets thicker.

20° F.: Floridians don coats, thermal underwear, gloves, wool hats. Minnesotans throw on a flannel shirt.

15° F.: New York landlords finally turn up the heat. Minnesotans have the last cookout before it gets cold.

0° F.: All the people in Miami die. Minnesotans close the windows.

–10° F.: Californians fly away to Mexico. The Girl Scouts in Minnesota are selling cookies door-to-door.

–25° F.: Hollywood disintegrates. Minnesotans get out their winter parkas.

–40° F.: Washington, D.C., runs out of hot air. Minnesotans let the dogs sleep indoors.

–100° F.: Santa Claus abandons the North Pole. Minnesotans get frustrated because they can't start their cars.

–460° F.: All atomic motion stops (absolute zero on the Kelvin scale). Minnesotans start saying, "Cold 'nuff for ya?"

–500° F.: Hell freezes over. The Vikings win the Super Bowl.

*Web posting; author unknown

Fifteen More Bohemian Bargains to Consider

Buffalo, New York
Cincinnati, Ohio
Grand Rapids, Michigan
Hartford, Connecticut
Indianapolis, Indiana
Kansas City, Missouri
Louisville, Kentucky
Memphis, Tennessee
Miami, Florida
Nashville, Tennessee
New Orleans, Louisiana
Providence, Rhode Island
Rochester, New York
Tampa, Florida
Wichita, Kansas

TELECOMMUTING HEAVENS

Let's say you perform white-collar work of a kind that doesn't require you to meet with customers or coworkers regularly. Maybe you write software or design promotional brochures. Maybe you manage assets or consult. Millions of Americans hold such portable jobs in the age of cable modems and Google. So let's further suppose that by choice or by the boot of your (former) employer, you suddenly have the option of working anywhere. Where would you go? (No, you can't pick Aspen, Jackson Hole, Martha's Vineyard, Lake Tahoe, or Maui. They're *way* too expensive!) Personally, I would head out to where I could do my best thinking, yet not become so isolated I would go crazy. I would want reliable high-band Internet connections, nice weather of the western sunny and dry type, infinite hiking trails, a small airport close by with a mechanic named Ace or Wolfgang who knew every inch and hum of my airplane, spicy Mexican food and ice-cold beer with lime wedges, something like a graduate school for Swedish masseuses where I might lend my body in the cause of scientific advancement, and a church where I could repent. Anyway, that's my idea of telecommuting heaven. What's yours?

ALBUQUERQUE, NEW MEXICO

City Population: 449,000
House Price: $255,000

Slooow down there, pardner. Albuquerque is no longer just a stopover on the way to trendy, pricey Santa Fe (fifty-five miles northeast of town).

Native, Hispanic, and Anglo-Americans comprise the bulk of the city's 449,000 residents, and Albuquerque's character was sculpted by these three cultures. Leave your car behind and inhale the town's unique southwestern charm and history. Pick up a hand-thrown clay bowl in a shop on Central Avenue, the town's main drag, or sip coffee on the University of New Mexico's pleasant campus.

Besides unique local art, architecture, and food, the city also offers inexpensive housing. Living here generally costs half as much as living in Santa Fe. Travelers use cheaper Albuquerque as a convenient base for exploring nearby deserts, mountains, and Indian sites. You won't find the tourist schlock (or the tourist prices) of nearby Taos.

Take a hike along the beautiful seven-mile La Luz Trail to the top of the Sandia Mountains. The trail passes through high desert and pine forest, where you'll see spectacular views over Albuquerque, the West Mesa, and the mountain ranges beyond. You may even spot a coyote. Skiing and excellent trout fishing are also nearby.

Albuquerque International Airport, New Mexico's premier gateway, is just five miles south of downtown.

BEND, OREGON

City Population: 52,000
House Price: $381,000

Miami, Honolulu, and Los Angeles have nothing on Bend, Oregon. The sun shines three hundred days a year here.

Bend is tucked between the Cascade Range and central Oregon's high desert, which makes for pleasant weather year-round. The mountains buffer storms and provide a four-season outdoor playground for golfing, biking, climbing, and more. Mount Bachelor Ski Resort offers outstanding skiing ten months a year. Nearby Sun River is a golfer's paradise.

Bend's economy is healthy and looks to stay that way. Bend began to diversify its economy in the early 1980s after a sharp recession sawed away at this former lumber town's prosperity.

Tourism, health care, and retail are three of Bend's top industries. St. Charles Medical Center, a large regional institution, employs 1,500 residents and recently completed a new trauma center and upgraded the intensive-care unit and a family birthing center. Oregonians travel from surrounding counties to shop at Bend's huge outlet mall featuring Eddie Bauer, Carter's, Dansk, and other stores.

The city recently finished $3 million worth of urban renewal projects in the downtown business district. A former run-down alley is now a pedestrian plaza. Streets are clean, buildings are restored, and rusting plumbing is new again.

The food is surprisingly innovative for a town that's a four-hour drive from Portland, the nearest large city. Don't miss Cafe Rosemary, Marz Planetary Bistro, and Bend's oldest restaurant, the Pine Tavern.

BRANSON, MISSOURI

City Population: 7,000
House Price: $212,000

Discover a secret getaway RV travelers and retirees have known about for years. Well, it can't be too much of a secret, because 7 million tourists visit Branson each year.

Three big mountain-fed lakes—Table Rock, Taneycomo, and Bull Shoals—offer Branson some of the country's best fishing and wilderness fun. If you prefer playing with fish to eating them, scuba dive, Jet Ski, or sail on the sparkling waters. Millions of acres of pristine Ozark mountain forests surround the lakes. Camping, climbing, and cycling opportunities here are endless.

Byways magazine named Branson the top motor home destination of the entire decade. Travel author Arthur Frommer listed Branson as one of the "10 Great Summer Drives" for 2003. *Bassmaster* magazine ranked Branson as one of the nine top retirement fishing hot spots in the country (March 2003).

If the views and fresh trout dinners don't keep you smiling, the entertainment will. Dolly Parton, the Hughes brothers, Larry Gatlin, and scores of other singers and comedians pass through town to perform for residents.

More fun is on the way. The town says it will open Branson Landing on the Taneycomo waterfront in 2005, featuring 500,000 square feet of retail space for shopping, dining, and entertainment. Branson already serves as the job, service, and shopping center for a two-county area with fifty thousand year-round residents. Branson is a regional kernel that promises to pop well into the next decades.

BURLINGTON, VERMONT

City Population: 39,000
House Price: $348,000

If you're a fan of Rush Limbaugh or Fox News's Sean Hannity, stay away!

Burlington is a lefty paradise, a magnet for university students, nuptial-seeking gay couples, and upper-class bobos, a term coined by David Brooks.

Bobos favor $4 lattes, Volvos, Sierra Club memberships, and private schools for their children, all the while talking the prole talk. You'll find aspiring bobos among University of Vermont students in the countless bars and restaurants lining downtown Burlington's cobblestone streets. If you need to borrow a cup of sugar—assuming it hasn't been banned by the time this book comes out—your neighbor's door may already be open. Crime in this town of thirty-nine thousand is so rare, some residents ditch the locks.

Pack your parka. Lake Champlain winds howl through Burlington streets much of the year. Winters are white and the skiing is as good as it gets on the U.S. East Coast at mountain resorts such as Sugarbush and Killington.

Though Ben and Jerry birthed their company here, Burlington is no friend to new business. If you follow city politics, you won't be surprised. Burlington is the rare U.S. town to elect a socialist mayor—Bernie Sanders, 1981–1989. (Sanders is now an independent, representing Vermont in the House of Representatives.) Burlington International Airport has daily commercial service from most major northeastern airports.

DURANGO, COLORADO

City Population: 14,000
House Price: $273,000

No matter how modern your life may be, your imagination will float back in time in Durango. Home to Mesa Verde National Park, the area's ancient cliff dwellings and pit houses reveal ancestral pueblo life dating back to the 500s. There are more than four thousand known archeological sites in the park, six hundred of which are cliff dwellings built on mesa tops and canyon coves.

Desk jockeys, ditch your computer and hike the rigorous San

Juan Mountains trails. Natural hot springs await your tired feet. In the winter, slice through the slopes at one of the many nearby ski resorts.

Or don't leave Durango at all. The downtown area of Durango has almost as many restaurants per capita as San Francisco, the restaurant capital of the western United States. Vegetarians, worry not. You'll find a wide selection of veggie-friendly locales serving up southwestern tofu galore.

After a tough day of telecommuting, spend your dough at one of Durango's saloons or (two) minimal-stakes casinos.

Durango is located in southwestern Colorado at an elevation of 6,512 feet.

The Durango–La Plata County airport has daily flights to Denver, Albuquerque, Houston, and Phoenix.

HILTON HEAD, SOUTH CAROLINA

Island Population: 34,000
House Price: $312,000

Want to live on a balmy subtropical island without leaving the East Coast? Hilton Head Island, with its twelve miles of broad Atlantic beach, may be your answer. Squeeze in a round of golf at one of the manicured courses before heading back to your home office. Wander among thick forests of palmettos, magnolias, and towering pines to clear your mind for that crucial tele-conference.

Hilton Head is the largest barrier island off the Atlantic coast between Long Island and the Bahamas. Forty miles north of Savannah, its unspoiled sea marshes, creeks, and lagoons draw tens of thousands of tourists each year.

During summer vacation, Hilton Head's island population of thirty-four thousand can surge to fifty thousand. Tourists inject more than a billion and a half dollars into the economy each year. The millions they pay in sales taxes build new bike paths, keep the beaches spotless, and enrich local cultural offerings. More than half the jobs on the island are tourism-related.

Real estate is the other major industry in Hilton Head, employing roughly five hundred agents on the island.

Savannah/Hilton Head International Airport provides direct flights to major cities around the country.

HOT SPRINGS, ARKANSAS

City Population: 36,000
House Price: $232,000

She's pretty, hot, smart, and talented. Oh, and she rocks! Hot Springs is the kind of town everyone wants to check out.

Pretty: Hot Springs sits in the Diamond Lake Region of the scenic Ouachita Mountains. Lake Hamilton and Lake Catherine border the city and provide 328 miles of shoreline. Lake Ouachita, just thirty minutes from downtown Hot Springs, has forty thousand acres of crystal clear water and nearly seven hundred miles of unspoiled shoreline. There's no shortage of fishing, hunting, and horseback riding here.

Hot: The first federally protected land in the nation's history, Hot Springs National Park features 147° F. thermal waters. End your day at the spa with a Swedish massage or facial.

Smart: Hot Springs is home to the Arkansas School of Math and Science, a state high school with three hundred of the state's best junior and senior high students. The school is also a site for teacher training.

Talented: Acclaimed as one of the nation's fastest-growing art centers, Hot Springs has been included in John Villani's *The 100 Best Small Art Towns in America*. The *New York Times*, *Art World News*, *Travel & Leisure*, and others have given the town high marks.

Hot Springs' Documentary Film Festival attracts approximately twenty thousand people to Hot Springs each year to view classic, experimental, American, and international documentaries.

MOAB, UTAH

City Population: 5,000
House Price: $364,000

Strap on your helmet and jump on your mountain bike. It doesn't get any better than this.

Pedal and hop among the most varied, pristine terrain in the country. In Moab, mountain valleys butt up against forests of spruce, fir, and aspen. The red-rock cliffs surround town and spill into the parched desert. Trails thread through the entire region up to the La Sal Mountains, eighteen miles to the east, which reach elevations of nearly 13,000 feet.

Tourism swells this town of five thousand during the spring and fall when adventure travelers use it as a launch point for jeeps, airplanes, and white-water rafts.

Get in shape before relocating to Moab because life here revolves around recreation: Golf, cross-country skiing, and camping are also popular. When you're feeling less energetic, kick back in one of Moab's microbreweries or invite friends to the rodeo.

The closest commercial airport is in Grand Junction, Colorado, two hours away by car. Salt Lake City International Airport, four hours away by car, is the closest international airport. (Private jets can land at Canyonlands Field, twenty minutes from Moab.)

SANDPOINT, IDAHO

City Population: 6,835
Metro Population: 32,000
House Price: $287,000

If you spent your childhood tinkering with toy trains, this town will captivate you.

Sandpoint is one of the West's greatest railroading towns, originally a transit point for timber. The Burlington Northern,

Montana Rail Link, and Spokane International rail systems all meet here to create "the Funnel," a bustling rail crossroads with more than forty trains a day passing through. Rail buffs come from around the world to see it.

Sandpoint also attracts artists who add to the town's remarkably diverse community.

National groups recognize Sandpoint's visual and performing arts offerings as outstanding for a town its size.

The area's natural beauty inspires artists and laypeople alike. Mountains, lush valleys, and crystal-clear Lake Pend Oreille, the largest lake in Idaho, dominate the vistas. Throw a line in the water or hit a few balls at the Hidden Lakes or Elks golf courses. In the winter, you can shush down the slopes at the Schweitzer Ski Basin, a large employer in the region. Retailer Coldwater Creek and specialty food maker Litehouse also employ a large number of locals here.

Sandpoint has its very own winery, Pend d'Oreille Winery, which sells award-winning wines from the world-class vineyards of the Northwest. Sip a crisp Pinot Noir at the winery's new downtown location or take a tour with some friends.

Sandpoint is friendly to small businesses, which can take advantage of a business incubator at the Bonner Business Center.

SEDONA, ARIZONA

City Population: 10,000
House Price: $499,000

High prices nearly knocked Sedona from our list. Then again, where else can you clean your aura, hike among the country's most bewitching canyons, and conduct an international conference call in the same afternoon?

Spiritualists say Sedona is the spot where the earth's restorative energy is closest to the surface. Healers are so popular here that the Chamber of Commerce Web site lists "New

Age" next to "Manufacturing" and "Retail" in its industries section. Meditation centers, holistic spas, and Reiki practitioners abound.

Melt into the sheer beauty of Sedona's red rock formations. Everyone else does. Surrounding town, tawny cliffs tower above the raw desert floor as wind hums through box canyons. Sunsets make the ancient mesas and knolls appear to glow from within.

It's no wonder that Hollywood has filmed more than a hundred movies and TV shows here.

Your next-door neighbor is as likely to be a retired sales executive as a sculptor. Sedona attracts snowbirds and artists alike. If you need to see new faces, stroll down to the local sushi joint or pizzeria, where tourists mix with the locals. Among them are savvy art collectors who come to score deals on local pottery and southwestern paintings.

When you want to touch earth, Phoenix is two hours away by car.

Fifteen More (Reasonably Priced) Telecommuting Heavens to Consider

Anacortes, Washington
Angel Fire, New Mexico
Astoria, Oregon
Biloxi, Mississippi
Brainerd, Minnesota
Clemson, South Carolina
Freeport, Maine
Gatlinburg, Tennessee
Mariposa, California
Michigan City, Indiana
Savannah, Georgia
Sisters, Oregon
Stockbridge, Massachusetts
White Sulphur Springs, West Virginia
Whitefish, Montana

Acknowledgments

This book, being a personal journey and investigation into twenty-first-century American geography and life change, lists one author. Its completion required the help of several colleagues and friends. At the top of the list is James Daly, who joined me in pulling together the broad scope of this project. Jim and I have known each other for ten years; we worked together just after I started *Forbes ASAP.* Jim later wrote for *Wired* and then started *Business 2.0* magazine, taking it from nothing to 380,000 subscribers before it was sold to Time Warner. Entrepreneur, writer, editor extraordinaire, and a onetime pilot himself, Jim helped me through the most difficult job of all. That was to convert me from an eight-hundred-word magazine columnist to a book writer, tantamount to going from one-hundred-meter dashes to marathons. If you detect the author's legs going wobbly at times in this book, the fault is mine, not Jim's. In Part 3, I relied on the research and hard work of Adrienne Sanders.

I am ever grateful to four brothers named Forbes, who own the magazine that has employed me since 1992: Steve, Kip, Bob, and Tim are rare gentlemen and the finest bosses anybody could have. Special thanks goes to Bob Forbes's son, Miguel, who suggested I write a book someday. Of course, I wouldn't be working at *Forbes* and have the confidence to share my opinions with 4.5 million readers every two weeks were it not for George Gilder, my mentor and friend. Another good pal within this cabal of capitalist rowdies is Andy Kessler, who now and then reviews my work, both my *Forbes* columns and this book, and always offers sage advice. Andy is a former Wall Street analyst and hedge-fund manager who has written a book himself, *Wall Street Meat,* and has another on the way, *Running Money.* These are hilarious first-person accounts of investment banking and venture capitalism.

On the flying front, this book would not be possible without instructors David Schoebel, who got me through my private pilot certificate, and Glen Davis, with whom I completed my instrument certification. As instructors and men, both are princes. (Glen also is married to Merrill Vaughn, who edits my "Digital Rules" column at *Forbes,* as well as the columns of Steve Forbes and Caspar Weinberger.) I'd like to thank Paul Bowen for dangling his body and camera outside the cargo door of a Bonanza A36 airplane in order to take photos of me piloting the Skyhawk. You can see more of Paul's photos at www.life2where.com.

Others from the flying world who have shaped my thoughts are Tom Haines, the editor of *AOPA Pilot* magazine, Lane Wallace of *Flying* magazine, and John and Martha King, who sell training videos through their King Schools catalog and Web site and are the world's best ambassadors of small-plane aviation.

My editor at Crown Business, John Mahaney, pushed me through several drafts, at least two more than I had banked on. John never gives up, which is why he is a rising star in the Random House constellation. His assistant, Shana Drehs, was a delight to work with throughout this project. I would like to thank agent Wes Neff of the Leigh Bureau for making a match with Crown Business. Thanks also to Anne Pace and Tony D'Amelio of the Washington Speaker's Bureau and Monie Begley, the vice president of communications at *Forbes,* for getting the word out on *Life 2.0*—and with whom I can count on to enjoy spasmodic laughing jags at a moment's notice. If this book turns out to be a marketplace success, kudos to Nancy Keuch Rosa and Vincent Caprio.

Lastly, I could not have written this book without the organizational help of administrative assistant Gheeva Chung, and the love, affection, and (especially) tolerance of my wife, Marji.

Index

About the Author

Rich Karlgaard is the publisher of *Forbes* magazine. In his "Digital Rules" column, Rich writes about technology, entrepreneurship, regional economic development, and the future of business and work. He also lectures on these subjects and is a regular participant on the Fox News Channel's *Forbes on Fox*.

He was raised in Bismarck, North Dakota, by a homemaker and a high school athletic director, and attended public schools, where he gave more thought to sports than classes. He graduated from Stanford University with a B.A. in political science. Before joining *Forbes*, Rich cofounded the 2,500 member Churchill Club, for which he shared a Northern California Entrepreneur of the Year award, given by Ernst & Young. Rich has also started two magazines, and he sits on several boards.

Rich is married, with two children.

When he is not working or spending time with his family, Rich likes to fly his airplane around the country and meet the people who make America unique and great.

Rich would love to hear from readers who have found the where of their happiness—or are still searching. Contact him at his Web site, www.life2where.com.